KB087083

적중 100

영어 기출 문제집

중 3

비상 | 김진완

Best Collection

구성과 특징

교과서의 주요 학습 내용을 중심으로 학습 영역별 특성에 맞춰 단계별로 다양한 학습 기회를 제공하여
단원별 학습능력 평가는 물론 중간 및 기말고사 시험 등에 완벽하게 대비할 수 있도록 내용을 구성

Words & Expressions

Step1　　Key Words 단원별 핵심 단어 설명 및 풀이
　　　　　Key Expression 단원별 핵심 숙어 및 관용어 설명
　　　　　Word Power 반대 또는 비슷한 뜻 단어 배우기
　　　　　English Dictionary 영어로 배우는 영어 단어

Step2　　실력평가 단원별 수시평가 대비 주관식, 객관식 문제풀이

Step3　　서술형 대비 학업성취도 및 수행능력평가 대비 서술형 문제풀이

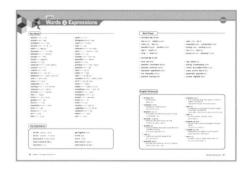

Conversation

Step1　　핵심 의사소통 소통에 필요한 주요 표현 방법 요약
　　　　　핵심 Check 기본적인 표현 방법 및 활용능력 확인

Step2　　대화문 익히기 교과서 대화문 심층 분석 및 확인

Step3　　교과서 확인학습 빈칸 채우기를 통한 문장 완성 능력 확인

Step4　　기본평가 시험대비 기초 학습 능력 평가

Step5　　실력평가 단원별 수시평가 대비 주관식, 객관식 문제풀이

Step6　　서술형 대비 학업성취도 및 수행능력평가 대비 서술형 문제풀이

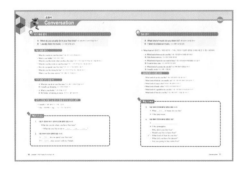

Grammar

Step1　　주요 문법 단원별 주요 문법 사항과 예문을 알기 쉽게 설명
　　　　　핵심 Check 기본 문법사항에 대한 이해 여부 확인

Step2　　기본평가 시험대비 기초 학습 능력 평가

Step3　　실력평가 단원별 수시평가 대비 주관식, 객관식 문제풀이

Step4　　서술형 대비 학업성취도 및 수행능력평가 대비 서술형 문제풀이

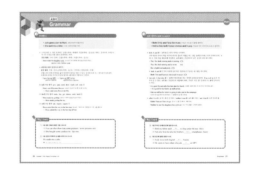

Reading

Step1　　구문 분석 단원별로 제시된 문장에 대한 구문별 분석과 내용 설명
　　　　　확인문제 문장에 대한 기본적인 이해와 인지능력 확인

Step2　　확인학습A 빈칸 채우기를 통한 문장 완성 능력 확인

Step3　　확인학습B 제시된 우리말을 영어로 완성하여 작문 능력 키우기

Step4　　실력평가 단원별 수시평가 대비 주관식, 객관식 문제풀이

Step5　　서술형 대비 학업성취도 및 수행능력평가 대비 서술형 문제풀이
　　　　　교과서 구석구석 교과서에 나오는 기타 문장까지 완벽 학습

Composition

|영역별 핵심문제|
단어 및 어휘, 대화문, 문법, 독해 등 각 영역별 기출문제의 출제 유형을 분석하여 실전에 대비하고 연습할 수 있도록 문제를 배열

|단원별 예상문제|
기출문제를 분석한 후 새로운 시험 출제 경향을 더하여 새롭게 출제될 수 있는 문제를 포함하여 시험에 완벽하게 대비할 수 있도록 준비

|서술형 실전 및 창의사고력 문제|
학교 시험에서 점차 늘어나는 서술형 시험에 집중 대비하고 고득점을 취득하는데 만전을 기하기 위한 학습 코너

|단원별 모의고사|
영역별, 단계별 학습을 모두 마친 후 실전 연습을 위한 모의고사

교과서 파헤치기

- **단어Test1~3** 영어 단어 우리말 쓰기, 우리말을 영어 단어로 쓰기, 영영풀이에 해당하는 단어와 우리말 쓰기
- **대화문Test1~2** 대화문 빈칸 완성 및 전체 대화문 쓰기
- **본문Test1~5** 빈칸 완성, 우리말 쓰기, 문장 배열연습, 영어 작문하기 복습 등 단계별 반복 학습을 통해 교과서 지문에 대한 완벽한 습득
- **구석구석지문Test1~2** 지문 빈칸 완성 및 전문 영어로 쓰기

Lesson 7

Spend Wisely

🎙 의사소통 기능

- 어떤 것에 만족하거나 불만이 있는지 묻기
  A: How do you like this dress?
  B: The design is cool and interesting.
- 후회하는 일 말하기
  A: What's wrong with your laptop?
  B: It makes too much noise and gets overheated.
  I should have read more reviews.

🎙 언어 형식

- 접속사 as
  As more and more people get on the bandwagon, others are more likely to get on it.

- 수의 일치
  Half of the boys on his soccer team **wear** those shoes.

교과서
Words & Expressions

Key Words

- **aboard** [əbɔ́:rd] 부 ~에 탑승하고, ~에 타서
- **above** [əbʌ́v] 전 ~ 위에
- **affect** [əfékt] 동 ~에 영향을 주다
- **allowance** [əláuəns] 명 용돈
- **although** [ɔ:lðóu] 접 비록 ~이지만
- **anchor** [ǽŋkər] 명 닻 동 닻을 내리다
- **behavior** [bihéivjər] 명 행동, 행위
- **billion** [bíljən] 명 10억
- **combine** [kəmbáin] 동 결합하다
- **compare** [kəmpɛ́ər] 동 비교하다
- **compete** [kəmpí:t] 동 경쟁하다
- **complete** [kəmplí:t] 동 완성하다
- **concept** [kánsept] 명 개념
- **consume** [kənsú:m] 동 소비하다, 소모하다
- **convenient** [kənví:njənt] 형 편리한, 간편한
- **deal** [di:l] 명 거래
- **difference** [dífərəns] 명 차이, 차이점
- **disappear** [disəpíər] 동 사라지다
- **discount** [dískaunt] 명 할인 동 할인하다
- **effect** [ifékt] 명 효과
- **encourage** [inkə́:ridʒ] 동 부추기다, 조장하다
- **endanger** [indéindʒər] 동 위험에 빠뜨리다
- **even though** 비록 ~이지만
- **fix** [fiks] 동 고정하다
- **furniture** [fə́:rnitʃər] 명 가구

- **immediately** [imí:diətli] 부 즉시, 바로
- **influence** [ínfluəns] 동 ~에 영향을 주다
- **lack** [læk] 명 부족, 결핍
- **laptop** [lǽptɑp] 명 휴대용 노트북 컴퓨터
- **last** [læst] 동 오래가다, (기능이) 지속되다
- **match** [mætʃ] 동 어울리다
- **mention** [ménʃən] 동 언급하다, 말하다
- **miss** [mis] 동 놓치다
- **overheated** [ouvərhítid] 형 지나치게 뜨거운, 과열된
- **parade** [pəréid] 명 행렬, 퍼레이드
- **purchase** [pə́:rtʃəs] 동 구매하다, 구입하다
- **quality** [kwáləti] 명 질, 품질, 특성, 자질
- **quarter** [kwɔ́:rtər] 명 4분의 1
- **raise** [reiz] 동 기르다, 키우다
- **refund** [rifʌ́nd] 명 환불
- **release** [rilí:s] 동 출시하다, 발매하다
- **replace** [ripléis] 동 바꾸다, 교체하다
- **spending** [spéndiŋ] 명 지출
- **striped** [straipt] 형 줄무늬가 있는
- **suit** [su:t] 동 어울리다
- **tight** [tait] 형 꽉 조이는, 딱 붙는
- **unplanned** [ənplǽnd] 형 미리 계획하지 않은
- **wagon** [wǽgən] 명 사륜 마차, 짐마차
- **waste** [weist] 동 낭비하다, 소모하다

Key Expressions

- **as such** 그러한 결과로
- **at a glance** 한눈에, 즉시
- **a pair of** ~ 한 짝의 ~
- **be likely to** ~할 가능성이 있다, ~하기 쉽다
- **end up –ing** 결국 ~하게 되다
- **for a moment** 잠깐
- **go well with** ~와 잘 어울리다
- **go window shopping** 진열된 상품을 구경하고 다니다
- **in comparison** 비교해 보면
- **in this way** 이런 방식으로

- **just because** 단지 ~라는 이유로
- **keep track of** ~을 기록하다
- **lead to** ~로 이어지다
- **more and more** 점점 더 많은
- **more than half** 반 이상의
- **on display** 진열된, 전시된
- **soon after** 직후
- **spend A on 동사ing** A를 ~하는 데 쓰다
- **the next time 주어+동사** 다음번에 ~할 때에
- **when it comes to** ~에 관해서, ~에 대해 말하자면

Word Power

※ 서로 비슷한 뜻을 가진 어휘

- ☐ **affect** ~에 영향을 주다 – **influence** ~에 영향을 주다
- ☐ **effect** 결과, 효과 – **result** 결과, 성과
- ☐ **lack** 부족, 결핍 – **shortage** 결핍, 부족
- ☐ **purchase** 구매하다, 구입하다 – **buy** 사다
- ☐ **replace** 바꾸다, 교체하다 – **substitute** 대신하다

- ☐ **complete** 완성하다 – **perfect** 완벽하게 하다
- ☐ **immediately** 즉시, 바로 – **at once** 즉시
- ☐ **mention** 언급하다, 말하다 – **refer to** 언급하다
- ☐ **quality** 질, 품질 – **characteristic** 특질, 특징
- ☐ **suit** 어울리다 – **match** 어울리다

※ 서로 반대의 뜻을 가진 어휘

- ☐ **above** ~ 위에 ↔ **under** ~ 아래에
- ☐ **difference** 차이(점) ↔ **similarity** 유사(성)
- ☐ **encourage** 부추기다, 조장하다 ↔ **discourage** 낙담시키다
- ☐ **purchase** 구매하다, 구입하다 ↔ **sell** 팔다
- ☐ **unplanned** 미리 계획하지 않은 ↔ **planned** 미리 계획된

- ☐ **convenient** 편리한, 간편한 ↔ **inconvenient** 불편한, 곤란한
- ☐ **disappear** 사라지다 ↔ **appear** 나타나다
- ☐ **endanger** 위험에 빠뜨리다 ↔ **save** 구하다
- ☐ **tight** 꽉 조이는, 딱 붙는 ↔ **loose** 헐거운, 느슨한
- ☐ **waste** 낭비하다, 소모하다 ↔ **save** 절약하다

※ 접두사 en-: en-+특정 어근: 동사로 만들어 '~하게 하다', '어떤 상태가 되게 하다', '안에'라는 의미를 더함.

- ☐ **en-** + **able** → **enable** 가능케 하다
- ☐ **en-** + **courage** → **encourage** 조장하다, 권유하다
- ☐ **en-** + **hance** → **enhance** 향상시키다, 높이다
- ☐ **en-** + **rich** → **enrich** 풍부하게 하다

- ☐ **en-** + **close** → **enclose** 에워싸다, 둘러싸다
- ☐ **en-** + **force** → **enforce** 집행하다, 강요하다
- ☐ **en-** + **large** → **enlarge** 확대하다, 확장하다
- ☐ **en-** + **danger** → **endanger** 위험에 빠뜨리다

※ 접두사 com-: com-+특정 어근: '함께'라는 의미를 더함.

- ☐ **com-** + **bine** → **combine** 결합하다
- ☐ **com-** + **pare** → **compare** 비교하다
- ☐ **com-** + **pile** → **compile** 편찬하다
- ☐ **com-** + **pound** → **compound** 합성의

- ☐ **com-** + **pany** → **company** 회사, 동료
- ☐ **com-** + **pete** → **compete** 경쟁하다
- ☐ **com-** + **pose** → **compose** 구성하다
- ☐ **com-** + **promise** → **compromise** 타협하다

English Dictionary

- ☐ **affect** ~에 영향을 주다
  - → to have an influence on someone or something, or to cause a change in someone or something
  - 어떤 사람이나 사물에 영향을 미치다, 혹은 어떤 사람이나 사물에 변화를 야기하다

- ☐ **combine** 결합하다
  - → to join together to make a single thing or group
  - 하나의 물건 혹은 하나의 집단으로 만들기 위해 합치다

- ☐ **concept** 개념
  - → a principle or idea
  - 어떤 원리나 생각

- ☐ **consume** 소비하다, 소모하다
  - → to use fuel, energy, or time, especially in large amounts or to eat or drink, especially a lot of something
  - 연료, 에너지, 혹은 시간을 특히 많은 양으로 쓰다, 또는 특히 어떤 것을 많이 먹고 마시다

- ☐ **convenient** 편리한, 간편한
  - → suitable for your purposes and needs and causing the least difficulty
  - 목적이나 필요에 맞고 어려움을 최소한으로 야기하는

- ☐ **encourage** 부추기다, 조장하다
  - → to support an activity or make it more likely
  - 어떤 활동을 지원하거나 더 쉽게 만들다

- ☐ **endanger** 위험에 빠뜨리다
  - → to put someone or something at risk or in danger of being harmed, damaged, or destroyed
  - 어떤 사람이나 사물을 해를 입고 망가지고 파괴되는 위험에 처하게 하다

- ☐ **lack** 부족, 결핍
  - → a condition of not having any or enough of something, especially something necessary or wanted
  - 특히 필요하거나 원하는 어떤 것이 조금도 없거나 충분하지 않은 상태

- ☐ **suit** 어울리다
  - → to be right for a particular person, situation, or occasion
  - 어떤 특정한 사람이나 상황, 또는 경우에 알맞다

- ☐ **tight** 꽉 조이는, 딱 붙는
  - → rather small and fit closely to your body
  - 다소 작거나 몸에 밀착되게 맞는

01 접두사 en-을 붙여 동사를 만들 때, en이 '~하게 하다'의 의미를 가지지 <u>않는</u> 단어를 고르시오.

① enlarge   ② enclose   ③ enable
④ enforce   ⑤ enrich

02 다음 밑줄 친 부분과 의미가 가장 가까운 것을 고르시오.

> We have to <u>change</u> this carpet soon.

① replace   ② repair   ③ remove
④ impact   ⑤ preserve

서답형

03 다음 주어진 단어를 이용하여 우리말에 맞도록 빈칸에 알맞은 말을 쓰시오.

> 축구에 관해서라면, Mark가 최고의 선수이다.
> ➡ _____ soccer, Mark is the best player. (when, come)

04 다음 영영풀이에 해당하는 단어로 알맞은 것은?

> to use fuel, energy, or time, especially in large amounts or to eat or drink, especially a lot of something

① contain   ② require
③ maintain   ④ assume
⑤ consume

05 다음 짝지어진 단어의 관계가 〈보기〉와 같은 것끼리 짝지어진 것을 고르시오.

> ┤ 보기 ├
> quality – characteristic

> ⓐ tight – loose
> ⓑ endanger – save
> ⓒ effect – result
> ⓓ replace – substitute
> ⓔ encourage – discourage

① ⓐ, ⓑ   ② ⓐ, ⓔ   ③ ⓑ, ⓒ
④ ⓒ, ⓓ   ⑤ ⓓ, ⓔ

06 다음 밑줄 친 부분의 의미로 알맞지 <u>않은</u> 것은?

① His words had a soothing <u>effect</u>. (효과)
② It is difficult to define the <u>concept</u> of beauty. (개념)
③ Your opinion will <u>affect</u> many people. (영향을 주다)
④ I receive an <u>allowance</u> from my parents. (허락)
⑤ The bus was nearly empty as she stepped <u>aboard</u>. (~에 타서)

07 다음 빈칸에 알맞은 단어를 고르시오.

> The shirt is beautiful. _____, it is cheap.

① Thus   ② Although
③ Furthermore   ④ Therefore
⑤ Likewise

01 다음 빈칸에 공통으로 들어갈 접두사를 쓰시오.

> • I made the two plans for _____parison.
> • We finally reached a _____promise.
> • Three judges _____pose the committee.

02 다음 주어진 우리말에 맞게 빈칸을 채우시오.

(1) 그 학생들 중 3분의 1이 그들의 지출을 기록한다.
   ➡ One third of the students record their
   _____. (one word)

(2) 다음번에 우리가 만날 때, 나는 더 건강해질 것
   이다.
   ➡ The _____ we meet, I will be
   healthier. (two words)

(3) 날씨가 좋지 않았음에도 불구하고 우리는 하이
   킹을 갔다.
   ➡ We went hiking _____ the
   weather was not good. (two words)

(4) 너는 보통 진열된 상품을 구경하고 다니는 것을
   좋아하니?
   ➡ Do you usually like to _____
   _____? (three words)

03 다음 빈칸에 공통으로 들어갈 말을 쓰시오.

> • The painting is currently _____
> display in New York.
> • Tickets are _____ sale from the
> booking office.

04 다음 빈칸에 들어갈 전치사를 〈보기〉에서 골라 쓰시오.

> ┤ 보기 ├
> at   for   in   with   as

(1) I think this blouse goes well _____
   the skirt you are wearing.
(2) _____ comparison to her problems,
   mine seems small.
(3) You should hold your breath _____ a
   moment.
(4) I noticed what had happened _____ a
   glace.
(5) _____ such, he was a man with
   persistence.

05 다음 빈칸에 알맞은 말을 〈보기〉에서 골라 쓰시오. (한 단어는
한 번만 사용할 것, 형태 변화 가능.)

> ┤ 보기 ├
> combine   compare   endanger   mention

(1) Did I _____ that I will move to
   Canada next month?
(2) You should _____ prices before
   you buy things.
(3) He wants to _____ his job with
   pleasure.
(4) The fire _____ animals in the
   forest.

Conversation

① 어떤 것에 만족하거나 불만이 있는지 묻기

> **A:** Can I try on that cap with stars over there? 저기 별들이 그려진 모자를 써 볼 수 있나요?
> **B:** Sure. How do you like it? 그럼요. 어떠세요?
> **A:** The design is nice, but I don't think the color suits me. Do you have it in black? 디자인은 좋은데, 색이 제게 안 어울리는 것 같아요. 이거 검은색으로 있나요?

■ 어떤 것에 만족하거나 불만이 있는지 물어보는 표현으로 'How do you like it?(마음에 드니?)'을 쓸 수 있다. 이외에도 'Are you satisfied with ~?(~에 만족하십니까?)', 'How is ~?(~는 어떠십니까?)', 'Are you enjoying ~?(~이 마음에 드십니까?)' 등이 있다.

어떤 것에 만족하거나 불만이 있는지 묻기

- How do you like ~?
- Are you satisfied[happy] with ~?
- How is ~?
- Are you enjoying ~?
- Do you like ~?

■ 'How do you like ~?'는 상대방의 의견 혹은 만족 여부를 물을 때 사용한다. 이미 지난 일에 대한 만족 여부를 물을 때는 'How did you like ~?'를 쓸 수 있다. 'Do you like ~?'는 상대방의 구체적인 의견보다는 단순히 만족 여부에 초점을 둘 때 사용한다.

■ 'How do you like ~?'는 상대방의 만족이나 불만족을 묻는 표현이고, 'What do you like?'은 '무엇을 좋아하니?'라는 의미로 상대방이 좋아하는 것을 묻는 표현이다.

핵심 Check

1. 다음 대화의 빈칸에 들어갈 말로 가장 적절한 것은?

> **A:** Hi, I'm looking for a backpack for hiking.
> **B:** These two are popular among hikers. _____
> **A:** The green one is lighter than the blue one. I'll take the lighter one.

① How were the backpacks?
② How do you like them?
③ Did you enjoy the backpacks?
④ What do you like?
⑤ What is your favorite?

2 후회하는 일 말하기

A: What's wrong with your laptop? 노트북에 무슨 문제가 있어?

B: It makes too much noises and gets overheated. I should have read more reviews. 소음이 너무 심하고 과열이 돼. 난 후기를 더 많이 읽어 봤어야 했어.

■ 'I should have p.p. ~.'는 어떤 일을 했어야 했다고, 또는 하지 말았어야 했다고 후회할 때 사용한다. 예를 들어, 공부를 열심히 하지 않은 것을 후회하며 더 열심히 공부했어야 했다고 말할 때는 'I should have studied harder!'라고 말할 수 있다.

■ 과거 사실에 대해 후회나 유감을 나타낼 때 '~했어야 했다'는 의미로 'should have p.p. ~'를 쓴다. 이 때 조동사 should 뒤에는 과거의 일을 의미하므로 동사원형 대신 'have+p.p.'를 써야 한다. 이외에도 'I regret -ing ~.', 'I wish I had p.p. ~.', 'If I could, I would+동사원형 ~.' 등으로 쓸 수 있다.

■ 'should have p.p.'는 '~했어야 했는데 (못했다)'라는 후회의 의미이고, 'could have p.p.'는 '~할 뻔 했다'라는 가능성의 의미이고, 'must have p.p.'는 '~이었음이 틀림없다'라는 추측의 의미를 갖는다.

후회하는 일 말하기

• I should have checked the size before buying it.
= I regret not checking the size before buying it.
= I wish I had checked the size before buying it.
= If I could, I would check the size before buying it.

핵심 Check

2. 괄호 안에 주어진 단어를 이용하여 밑줄 친 우리말을 영작하시오.

> **A:** Are you okay? You look tired today.
> **B:** Yeah, I missed the school bus again. <u>내가 더 일찍 일어났어야 했는데.</u> (get up earlier)

➡  _____

Listen & Talk 1 A-2

M: Good morning. Welcome to Kelly's Sporting Goods Store.

W: Hi, I'm ❶looking for a backpack for hiking.

M: These two are ❷popular among hikers. ❸How do you like them?

W: The green one is ❹lighter than the blue one. I'll take the lighter one.

M: Great choice.

M: 안녕하세요. Kelly의 스포츠 용품 가게에 오신 것을 환영합니다.

W: 안녕하세요, 저는 하이킹할 때 쓸 배낭을 찾고 있어요.

M: 이 두 개가 하이킹하시는 분들 사이에서 인기가 있어요. 어떠세요?

W: 초록색 배낭이 파란색 배낭보다 더 가볍네요. 더 가벼운 걸로 할게요.

M: 탁월한 선택입니다.

❶ look for: ~을 찾다
❷ popular: 인기 있는 among: ~ 중에, ~ 사이에
❸ 'How do you like ~?'는 어떤 사물이나 사건 등에 관해 상대방의 만족이나 불만족을 묻고자 할 때 사용한다.
❹ lighter는 light(가벼운)의 비교급이다.

Check(√) True or False

(1) The woman will buy the green backpack. T ☐ F ☐

(2) The woman wants to buy a backpack for books. T ☐ F ☐

Listen & Talk 2 A-1

M: Oh, this coat is ❶too uncomfortable.

W: Why? ❷What's wrong with it?

M: It's too ❸tight.

W: Didn't you ❹try it on before buying it?

M: No. It was my size, so I just bought it. I ❺should have tried it on.

M: 오, 이 코트는 너무 불편해.

W: 왜? 무슨 문제가 있니?

M: 너무 꽉 껴.

W: 사기 전에 입어 보지 않았어?

M: 아니. 내 사이즈여서 그냥 사 버렸어. 난 그것을 입어 봤어야 했어.

❶ too: 너무 uncomfortable: 불편한
❷ 'What's wrong with you?'는 '무슨 문제가 있니?'라는 의미로 불만족의 원인이나 걱정을 물을 때 사용하는 표현이다.
❸ tight: 꽉 조이는, 딱 붙는
❹ try on: (옷 등을 시험 삼아) 입어 보다
❺ 'I should have p.p. ~.'는 어떤 일을 했어야 했다고, 했다고 후회할 때 사용한다.

Check(√) True or False

(3) The man tried on the coat before he bought it. T ☐ F ☐

(4) The coat is comfortable but tight. T ☐ F ☐

Listen & Talk 2 A-2

W: Hey, Eric. Camilla and I ❶are going to watch a movie. Do you want to join us?

M: I'd love to, but I can't. ❷I've spent all of my ❸allowance for this week.

W: Didn't you just get ❹it a few days ago? How did you spend it all?

M: I'm not sure. I ❺should have kept track of my ❻spending.

W: 안녕, Eric. Camilla랑 나는 영화를 보러 갈 거야. 우리랑 같이 갈래?
M: 그러고 싶지만, 안 돼. 이번 주 용돈을 전부 써 버렸거든.
W: 너 고작 며칠 전에 받지 않았어? 어떻게 다 써 버렸어?
M: 잘 모르겠어. 내 지출을 기록했어야 했어.

❶ be going to 동사원형: ∼할 것이다
❷ have spent는 현재완료형으로 여기에서는 '완료' 용법으로 사용하였다.
❸ allowance: 용돈
❹ it은 allowance를 가리킨다.
❺ 과거 사실에 대해 후회나 유감을 나타낼 때 '∼했어야 했다'는 의미로 'should have p.p. ∼'를 쓴다. '주어 should have p.p. ∼'와 같은 의미로 '주어+regret not+동명사 ∼.', '주어+wish+주어+had p.p. ∼.', 'If+주어+could, 주어+would+동사원형 ∼.' 등이 있다. keep track of: ∼을 기록하다
❻ spending: 지출

Check(√) True or False

(5) Eric received an allowance a few days ago.   T ☐ F ☐

(6) Camilla and Eric are going to watch a movie.   T ☐ F ☐

Wrap Up 1

M: Good morning. May I help you?

W: ❶I'd like to buy a T-shirt for my sister. She's eleven years old.

M: ❷How do you like this red one? This character is ❸quite popular among children.

W: Well, she doesn't like animation characters that much. Can I see the blue one?

M: You mean this blue striped T-shirt? Its design is simple and cool.

W: Yes, ❹I think my sister will like it. I'll take it.

M: 안녕하세요. 도와 드릴까요?
W: 저는 여동생에게 티셔츠를 사 주고 싶어요. 그 애는 11살이에요.
M: 이 빨간색 티셔츠는 어떠세요? 이 캐릭터는 아이들 사이에서 꽤 인기가 있어요.
W: 글쎄요, 그 애는 만화 캐릭터를 그다지 좋아하지 않아요. 파란색 티셔츠 좀 볼 수 있을까요?
M: 파란색 줄무늬 티셔츠 말씀이시죠? 그건 디자인이 단순하고 멋있어요.
W: 네, 제 여동생이 좋아할 것 같아요. 그걸로 할게요.

❶ would like to 동사원형: ∼하고 싶다(= want to 동사원형)
❷ 'How do you like ∼?'는 '∼는 어떠니?'라는 뜻으로 어떤 것에 대한 의견을 물을 때 쓰인다. 비슷한 표현인 'Are you satisfied[happy] with ∼?'는 직접적으로 만족이나 불만족 여부를 물을 때 쓸 수 있다.
❸ quite는 부사로 '꽤, 상당히'의 의미이다.
❹ think의 목적어는 that my sister will like it이다. 접속사 that은 생략했다

Check(√) True or False

(7) The woman wants to buy a T-shirt with animation characters for her sister.   T ☐ F ☐

(8) What the woman will choose is the blue striped T-shirt.   T ☐ F ☐

Listen & Talk 1 A-1

M: Hi, can I help you with anything?

W: Yes, can I ❶try on that cap with stars ❷ over there?

M: Sure. ❸How do you like it?

W: The design is nice, but I don't think the color ❹suits me. Do you have it in black?

M: Yes. I'll get one from the back. *(pause)* Here it is.

W: Great. I'll take it.

❶ try on: (옷 등을 시험 삼아) 입어 보다
❷ over there: 저기에, 저쪽에
❸ 'How do you like ~?'는 '~는 어때?'라는 의미로 상대방에게 어떤 것에 대한 만족 또는 불만족을 묻는 표현이다.
❹ suit: 어울리다

Listen & Talk 1 B

W: Hi, Luke. Is that a new speaker?

M: Yes, I ❶bought it a few weeks ago.

W: It looks cool. ❷How do you like it?

M: It's ❸convenient. I can take it anywhere and listen to music. The sound ❹quality is good, too.

W: Great. How long does the battery ❺last?

M: About 2 hours. The battery doesn't last long.

W: That's too bad.

M: Yeah, but I'm ❻pretty happy with it, anyway.

❶ bought는 buy(사다)의 과거형이다.
❷ 'How do you like ~?'는 '너는 ~이 어떠니?'라는 뜻으로 어떤 것에 대한 만족이나 불만족을 묻는 표현이다. 바꿔 쓸 수 있는 표현으로 'Are you satisfied [happy] with ~?', 'How is ~?', 'Are you enjoying ~?', 'Do you like ~?' 등이 있다.
❸ convenient: 편리한, 간편한 ❹ quality: 질, 품질
❺ last: 오래가다, (기능이) 지속되다 ❻ pretty: 아주, 매우

Listen & Talk 2 B

M: Did you get a new phone, Jamie? It's just like mine.

W: Yeah, I got it last weekend ❶on sale.

M: It was on sale? But it ❷has just been ❸ released, hasn't it?

W: Right, but the store on Green Street is having ❹a year-end sale.

M: Oh, I bought mine ❺at full price!

W: Really? That's too bad. They're selling them at a 40 percent discount.

M: I ❻should have checked the sales before buying mine.

❶ on sale: 할인 중인
❷ 현재완료형인 have+p.p.와 부사 just를 사용하면 '방금 ~하다'로 해석된다. (완료 용법)
❸ release: 출시하다, 발매하다 ❹ a year-end sale: 연말 세일
❺ at full price: 정가에, 제값에
❻ 'should have p.p. ~'는 '~했어야 했는데 (사실은 하지 않았다)'의 뜻으로 과거 사실에 대한 유감을 나타내는 표현이다. '주어+regret not+동명사 ~.', '주어+wish+주어+had p.p ~.', 'If+주어+could, 주어+would+동사원 형 ~.' 등으로 바꿔 쓸 수 있다.

Communication Step A

M: Hi, Riley. ❶I heard that you bought a laptop online. ❷How do you like it?

W: Oh, ❸I'm not happy with it.

M: Why? What's wrong?

W: It makes too much noise and ❹gets overheated. ❺I should have read more reviews.

M: Oh, then you should ❻ask for your money back.

W: The online store won't ❼give me back my money because I've used it for a week.

M: ❽How about calling the online shop and explaining your problem?

W: Yeah, I think I should ❾do that.

❶ 어떤 내용을 들어서 알고 있음을 표현할 때 'I heard that+주어+동사'의 형태로 말할 수 있다.
❷ 'How do you like ~?'는 어떤 물건이나 사건 등에 관해 상대방의 만족이나 불만족을 묻고자 할 때 사용한다.
❸ 어떤 것에 대해 만족이나 불평을 표현할 때 '나는 ~이 만족스럽다/그다 지 만족스럽지 않다'라는 의미의 'I'm (not) really[so] happy[satisfied] with ~.'로 말할 수 있다. 만족스럽지 않은 경우에 'I want to complain about ~.'으로도 바꿔 말할 수 있다.
❹ makes와 gets는 문장의 동사로, 접속사 and로 연결되어 있다. get 다음에 형용사가 오면, '(~의 상태가) 되다, (~하기에) 이르다'의 의미이다.
❺ 'I should have p.p. ~.'는 어떤 일을 했어야 했다고 후회할 때 사용한다.
❻ ask for: 요청하다 ❼ give back: 돌려주다
❽ 'How about ~?'은 '~하는 게 어때?'라는 뜻으로 상대방에게 권유할 때 사용하는 표현이고, about은 전치사이기 때문에 뒤에 명사나 동명사가 올 수 있다. explaining은 calling과 접속사 and로 연결되어 있다.
❾ do that은 'call the online shop and explain my problem'을 의미한다.

● 다음 우리말과 일치하도록 빈칸에 알맞은 말을 쓰시오.

Listen & Talk 1 A

1. M: Hi, can I _____ you with anything?

   W: Yes, can I _____ _____ that cap with stars over there?

   M: Sure. _____ _____ _____ _____ it?

   W: The design is nice, _____ I don't think the color _____ me.
   Do you _____ it in black?

   M: Yes. I'll get _____ from the back. *(pause)* Here it is.

   W: Great. I'll take it.

2. M: Good morning. Welcome _____ Kelly's Sporting Goods Store.

   W: Hi, _____ _____ _____ a backpack for hiking.

   M: These two are _____ _____ hikers. _____ _____
   _____ _____ them?

   W: The _____ _____ _____ _____ _____ the blue
   _____. I'll take the lighter one.

   M: Great choice.

Listen & Talk 1 B

W: Hi, Luke. Is that a new speaker?

M: Yes, I _____ it a few weeks _____.

W: It _____ cool. _____ _____ _____ _____ it?

M: It's _____. I can take it _____ and listen to music. The sound
_____ is good, too.

W: Great. _____ _____ does the battery _____?

M: About 2 hours. The battery _____ _____ long.

W: That's _____ _____.

M: Yeah, but I'm _____ _____ with it, anyway.

해석

1. M: 안녕하세요, 무엇을 도와 드릴까요?
   W: 네, 저기 별들이 그려진 모자를 써 볼 수 있나요?
   M: 그럼요. 어떠세요?
   W: 디자인은 좋은데, 색이 제게 안 어울리는 것 같아요. 이거 검은색으로 있나요?
   M: 네. 제가 안쪽에서 가져다 드릴게요. (잠시 후) 여기 있어요.
   W: 좋아요. 그걸로 할게요.

2. M: 안녕하세요. Kelly의 스포츠 용품 가게에 오신 것을 환영합니다.
   W: 안녕하세요, 저는 하이킹할 때 쓸 배낭을 찾고 있어요.
   M: 이 두 개가 하이킹하시는 분들 사이에서 인기가 있어요. 어떠세요?
   W: 초록색 배낭이 파란색 배낭보다 더 가볍네요. 더 가벼운 걸로 할게요.
   M: 탁월한 선택입니다.

W: 안녕, Luke. 그거 새 스피커니?
M: 응, 몇 주 전에 샀어.
W: 멋져 보인다. 그거 어때?
M: 편리해. 나는 그것을 어디든지 가져가서 음악을 들을 수 있어. 음질도 좋아.
W: 좋다. 배터리가 얼마나 오래가니?
M: 2시간 정도야. 배터리가 그렇게 오래 가지 않아.
W: 그거 안타깝구나.
M: 응, 하지만 어쨌든 나는 꽤 만족해.

Listen & Talk 2 A

1. M: Oh, this coat is _____ _____.

   W: Why? _____ _____ _____ _____?

   M: It's too _____.

   W: Didn't _____ _____ _____ _____ _____ _____ it?

   M: No. It was my size, _____ I just bought it. I _____ _____ _____ it _____.

2. W: Hey, Eric. Camilla and I _____ _____ _____ _____ a movie. Do you want to join us?

   M: I'd love to, but I can't. _____ _____ all of my _____ for this week.

   W: Didn't you just _____ _____ a few days ago? How did you spend it all?

   M: I'm not sure. I _____ _____ _____ _____ _____ _____ _____.

1. M: 오, 이 코트는 너무 불편해.
   W: 왜? 무슨 문제가 있니?
   M: 너무 꽉 껴.
   W: 사기 전에 입어 보지 않았어?
   M: 아니. 내 사이즈여서 그냥 사 버렸어. 난 그것을 입어 봤어야 했어.

2. W: 안녕, Eric. Camilla랑 나는 영화를 보러 갈 거야. 우리랑 같이 갈래?
   M: 그러고 싶지만, 안 돼. 이번 주 용돈을 전부 써 버렸거든.
   W: 너 고작 며칠 전에 받지 않았어? 어떻게 다 써 버렸어?
   M: 잘 모르겠어. 내 지출을 기록했어야 했어.

Listen & Talk 2 B

M: Did you get a new phone, Jamie? It's just like mine.

W: Yeah, I got it last weekend _____ _____.

M: It was _____ _____? But it _____ _____ _____ _____, hasn't it?

W: Right, but the store on Green Street _____ _____ a year-end sale.

M: Oh, I bought mine _____ _____ _____!

W: Really? That's too bad. They're selling them _____ a 40 percent _____.

M: I _____ _____ _____ _____ _____ _____ buying mine.

M: 새 전화기를 샀니, Jamie? 내 것과 똑같다.
W: 응, 나는 이것을 지난주 할인할 때 샀어.
M: 그거 할인 중이었어? 하지만 그것은 막 출시되었잖아, 그렇지 않아?
W: 맞아, 하지만 Green가에 있는 가게에서 연말 할인 판매를 하더라.
M: 오, 나는 내 것을 정가를 주고 샀는데!
W: 정말? 그것 참 안됐다. 40퍼센트 할인하여 팔고 있어.
M: 내 것을 사기 전에 할인 판매를 확인했어야 했어.

Communication Step A

M: Hi, Riley. I _____ _____ _____ _____ a laptop online. How do you like it?

W: Oh, I'm _____ _____ with _____.

M: _____? _____ wrong?

W: It makes too much noise and _____ _____. I should _____ _____ more reviews.

M: Oh, then you should ask _____ your money back.

W: The online store _____ _____ _____ _____ my money because _____ _____ it for a week.

M: How about _____ the online shop and _____ your problem?

W: Yeah, I think I should _____ that.

Wrap Up

1. M: Good morning. May I help you?

   W: _____ _____ _____ buy a T-shirt for my sister. She's eleven years old.

   M: _____ _____ _____ _____ _____ _____ _____? This character is quite popular among children.

   W: Well, she doesn't like animation characters _____ much. Can I see the blue _____?

   M: You mean this blue _____ T-shirt? _____ design is simple and cool.

   W: Yes, I think my sister will like it. I'll _____ it.

2. W: Jake, here's a package for you.

   M: It's my helmet. I bought it at an _____ _____ _____ a few days ago.

   W: Oh, open it and _____ _____ _____ _____ it.

   M: Okay. *(pause)* Oh, this outer part _____ _____ _____ _____. The seller _____ _____ it's perfectly fine though.

   W: Didn't you check the pictures of the helmet _____ you bought it?

   M: No, _____ _____ _____ the seller. I _____ _____ _____ _____ _____.

   W: You _____ _____ the seller and _____ _____ _____ _____.

M: 안녕, Riley. 네가 온라인으로 노트북을 샀다고 들었어. 그거 어때?

W: 아, 나는 별로 마음에 들지 않아.

M: 왜? 무슨 문제가 있어?

W: 소음이 너무 심하고 과열이 돼. 난 후기를 더 많이 읽어 봤어야 했어.

M: 오, 그럼 환불을 요청해 봐.

W: 내가 그것을 일주일 동안 사용했기 때문에 온라인 가게는 환불을 해 주지 않을 거야.

M: 온라인 가게에 전화해서 문제를 설명하는 건 어때?

W: 응, 그렇게 해야 할 것 같아.

1. M: 안녕하세요. 도와 드릴까요?

   W: 저는 여동생에게 티셔츠를 사 주고 싶어요. 그 애는 11살이에요.

   M: 이 빨간색 티셔츠는 어떠세요? 이 캐릭터는 아이들 사이에서 꽤 인기가 있어요.

   W: 글쎄요, 그 애는 만화 캐릭터를 그다지 좋아하지 않아요. 파란색 티셔츠 좀 볼 수 있을까요?

   M: 파란색 줄무늬 티셔츠 말씀이시죠? 그건 디자인이 단순하고 멋있어요.

   W: 네, 제 여동생이 좋아할 것 같아요. 그걸로 할게요.

2. W: Jake, 여기 네 소포가 있어.

   M: 그거 내 헬멧이야. 며칠 전에 온라인 중고 가게에서 샀어.

   W: 오, 열어서 보여 줘.

   M: 그래. (잠시 후) 아, 이 바깥 부분이 조금 깨졌어. 하지만 판매자는 이것이 완벽하게 괜찮다고 말했어.

   W: 사기 전에 헬멧 사진을 확인해 보지 않았니?

   M: 아니, 나는 그냥 판매자를 믿었어. 조금 더 확인을 했어야 했어.

   W: 너는 판매자에게 전화해서 환불을 요청해야 해.

01 다음 대화의 빈칸에 알맞은 것을 고르시오.

> M: Hi, can I help you with anything?
>
> W: Yes, can I try on that cap with stars over there?
>
> M: Sure. _____
>
> W: The design is nice, but I don't think the color suits me. Do you have it in black?
>
> M: Yes. I'll get one from the back. *(pause)* Here it is.
>
> W: Great. I'll take it.

① What do you think of this black hat?

② How do you like it?

③ What do you like?

④ Which cap do you like better, the one with stars or black one?

⑤ Please tell me where to buy it.

[02~03] 다음 대화를 읽고 물음에 답하시오.

> M: _____
>
> W: _____
>
> M: _____
>
> W: _____
>
> M: No. It was my size, so I just bought it. I ⓐ_____.

02 위 대화의 빈칸에 들어갈 말을 〈보기〉에서 골라 순서대로 바르게 배열한 것은?

> ┤ 보기 ├
>
> (A) Didn't you try it on before buying it?
>
> (B) It's too tight.
>
> (C) Oh, this coat is too uncomfortable.
>
> (D) Why? What's wrong with it?

① (B) – (A) – (C) – (D)   ② (B) – (C) – (A) – (D)

③ (C) – (A) – (B) – (D)   ④ (C) – (B) – (A) – (D)

⑤ (C) – (D) – (B) – (A)

03 위 대화의 빈칸 ⓐ에 알맞은 것을 고르시오.

① should have tried it on   ② should not have tried it on

③ cannot have tried it on   ④ must have tried it on

⑤ may have tried it on

01 다음 대화의 빈칸에 들어갈 알맞은 것을 <u>모두</u> 고르면?

> **A:** _____
> **B:** I love them. They are very comfortable.

① What do you like in your new pants?
② How do you like your new pants?
③ Are you concerned about your new pants?
④ Are you enjoying your new pants?
⑤ Are you satisfied with your new pants?

[02~03] 다음 대화를 읽고 물음에 답하시오.

> **M:** Oh, this coat is too uncomfortable.
> **W:** Why? (A)_____
> **M:** It's too tight.
> **W:** (B)_____
> **M:** No. It was my size, so I just bought it. 난 그것을 입어 봤어야 했어.

02 위 대화의 빈칸 (A)와 (B)에 들어갈 말을 〈보기〉에서 골라 기호를 쓰시오.

> ┤ 보기 ├
> ⓐ What do you think of this coat?
> ⓑ Didn't you try it on before buying it?
> ⓒ How about trying it on?
> ⓓ Can I help you with anything?
> ⓔ What's wrong with it?
> ⓕ Can I see the loose one?

➡ (A) _____ (B) _____

03 밑줄 친 우리말에 맞게 주어진 단어를 알맞게 배열하시오.

➡ _____ (it, have, on, should, tried, I)

04 다음 빈칸에 가장 알맞은 말을 고르시오.

> **A:** I heard that you bought some iced tea online. How do you like it?
> **B:** Oh, I'm not happy with it.
> **A:** Why? What's wrong?
> **B:** There is too much sugar in it.
> _____

① I should not have read more reviews.
② I should bring more food with less sugar.
③ I should have checked the nutrition facts first.
④ I should buy it at online used store a few days ago.
⑤ I should have kept track of my spending.

05 다음 중 짝지어진 대화가 <u>어색한</u> 것은?

① A: I bought a new cell phone last week.
   B: How do you like it?
   A: I like it a lot. It's very light.
② A: Are you happy with your new books?
   B: Yes, I am. They are interesting.
③ A: How did you like it?
   B: I liked it a lot. It was delicious.
④ A: How do you like the weather there?
   B: I love it. It's sunny and warm.
⑤ A: I watched a new movie last Sunday.
   B: It looks really interesting. How did you like it?
   A: No, I'm not. It's boring.

[06~07] 다음 대화를 읽고 물음에 답하시오.

M: Did you get a new phone, Jamie? It's just like mine. (①)

W: Yeah, I got it last weekend on sale.

M: It was on sale? (②) But it (A)_____, hasn't it?

W: Right, but the store on Green Street is having a year-end sale. (③)

M: Oh, I bought mine at full price!

W: Really? (④) They're selling them at a 40 percent discount.

M: I (B)_____ the sales before buying mine. (⑤)

06 위 대화의 ①~⑤ 중 주어진 문장이 들어갈 곳은?

That's too bad.

① ② ③ ④ ⑤

07 다음 빈칸 (A)와 (B)에 들어갈 말로 알맞게 짝지어진 것은?

(A) (B)

① has just released – should check

② has just released – should not have checked

③ has just been released – should check

④ has just been released – should have checked

⑤ has just been released – should not have checked

[08~09] 다음 대화를 읽고 물음에 답하시오.

W: Hi, Luke. Is that a new speaker?

M: Yes, I bought it a few weeks ago.

W: It looks cool. (A)_____

M: It's convenient. I can take it anywhere and listen to music. The sound quality is good, too.

W: Great. How long does the battery last?

M: About 2 hours. The battery doesn't last long.

W: That's too bad.

M: Yeah, but I'm pretty happy with it, anyway.

08 위 대화의 빈칸 (A)에 알맞은 말을 고르시오.

① When did you buy it?

② How long can you use it?

③ How do you like it?

④ What's wrong with it?

⑤ How do you get it?

09 위 대화를 읽고 답할 수 없는 질문을 고르시오.

① How is the sound quality of the new speaker?

② What will Luke use the new speaker for?

③ When did Luke buy the new speaker?

④ Are Luke satisfied with the new speaker?

⑤ How long does the battery last?

Conversation 서술형 시험대비

01 그림을 보고, should have와 주어진 단어를 이용해 빈칸을 채우시오.

Alison

> A: What's the problem?
> B: Alison _____.
> (warm, wear, jacket)

[02~04] 다음 대화를 읽고 물음에 답하시오.

> M: Hi, Riley. I heard that you bought a laptop online. (A)_____
> W: Oh, I'm not happy with it.
> M: Why? What's wrong?
> W: It makes too much noise and gets overheated. (a)난 후기를 더 많이 읽어 봤어야 했어.
> M: Oh, then you should ask for your money back.
> W: The online store won't give me back my money because I've used it for a week.
> M: How about calling the online shop and (B)_____ (explain) your problem?
> W: Yeah, I think I should do that.

02 대화의 흐름상 빈칸 (A)에 들어갈 말을 주어진 단어를 이용해 문장을 완성하시오.

➡ _____ (like, it)

03 빈칸 (B)에 괄호 안의 단어를 문맥에 맞게 고쳐 채우시오.

➡ _____

04 밑줄 친 우리말 (a)를 주어진 단어를 이용해 영작하시오.

➡ _____
(reviews, read, more)

[05~06] 다음 대화를 읽고 물음에 답하시오.

> M: Did you get a new phone, Jamie? It's just like mine.
> W: Yeah, I got it last weekend (A)_____ sale.
> M: It was (A)_____ sale? But it has just been released, hasn't it?
> W: Right, but the store on Green Street is having a year-end sale.
> M: Oh, I bought mine (B)_____ full price!
> W: Really? That's too bad. They're selling them at a 40 percent discount.
> M: (C)_____ (buying, sales, checked, mine, before, should, I, have, the)

05 빈칸 (A)와 (B)에 알맞은 전치사를 쓰시오.

➡ (A) _____ (B) _____

06 빈칸 (C)를 괄호 안에 주어진 단어를 알맞게 배열하여 채우시오.

➡ _____
_____

Grammar

① 접속사 as

> • **As** more and more people get on the bandwagon, others are more likely to get on it. 더 많은 사람들이 밴드왜건에 올라탈수록 다른 사람들이 더욱 그것에 올라타려고 한다.

■ 접속사 as는 보통 'as+주어+동사 ~, 주어+동사 ….'의 형태로 사용하며, 종속절을 문장의 주절에 연결하는 종속접속사로서 부사절을 이끈다.

　• **As** I entered the room, they applauded. 내가 방안에 들어서자 그들은 박수를 쳤다.

■ 접속사 **as**의 역할

　(1) 비례, 추이: ~함에 따라서, ~에 비례하여

　• **As** it grew darker, it became colder. 어두워짐에 따라 더욱 추워졌다.

　(2) 시간: ~할 때, ~하는 동안, ~하면서

　• He came up **as** she was speaking. 그녀가 이야기하고 있을 때 그가 왔다.

　(3) 이유: ~해서, ~이므로, ~ 때문에

　• **As** I am ill, I will not go. 몸이 아파서 나는 안 가겠다.

　(4) 방식(양태): ~하듯이, ~하는 것처럼, ~ 같이, ~하는 대로, ~와 마찬가지로

　• **As** food nourishes our body, so books nourish our mind. 음식이 몸의 영양이 되는 것처럼 책은 마음의 영양이 된다.

　(5) 비교: ~와 같이, ~와 같은 정도로, ~만큼

　• She can walk as quickly **as** I can. 그녀는 나만큼 빨리 걸을 수 있다.

　(6) 양보: 비록 ~할지라도, ~이지만, ~이긴 하나

　• Rich **as** she is, she is not happy. 그녀는 부자이긴 하지만 행복하지는 않다.

■ 전치사 **as**: ~ 같이, ~로서(자격)

전치사 as 뒤에는 명사나 명사구가 오지만 접속사 as 뒤에는 '주어+동사'가 오는 것에 유의한다.

　• It can be used **as** a knife. (전치사) 그건 나이프 대용으로 쓸 수가 있다.

　• We didn't go, **as** it rained hard. (접속사) 비가 몹시 쏟아져서 우리는 가지 않았다.

핵심 Check

1. 다음 빈칸에 공통으로 들어갈 알맞은 단어를 고르시오. (대 · 소문자 구분 안 함)

> • _____ she grew older, she became weaker.
> • Do _____ I tell you.

① that　② what　③ since　④ as　⑤ for

② 수의 일치

> • **Half of the boys** on his soccer team **wear** those shoes. 그의 축구팀에 있는 소년들의 반이 그 축구화를 신는다.

■ '부분을 나타내는 명사+of' 다음에 명사가 올 때 동사의 수를 명사의 수에 일치시킨다.
   ※ 부분을 나타내는 말+단수 명사: 단수 동사
      부분을 나타내는 말+복수 명사: 복수 동사
   • **Some of the music was** weird. 그 음악의 일부는 기묘했다.
   • **Some of the studies show** positive results. 그 연구들 중 일부는 긍정적인 결과를 보여준다.

■ 부분을 나타내는 명사에는 most, all, some, half, percent, rest, part, 분수(one-third, two-thirds) 등이 있다.
   • **Most of the rooms face** the sea. 그 방들의 대부분은 바다를 향하고 있다.

   cf. 1. many of/(a) few of/a number of+복수 명사+복수 동사
          much of/(a) little of/+단수 명사, the number of+단수(복수) 명사+단수 동사

   • **Many of the pictures show** violence. 많은 장면들이 폭력을 보여줍니다.
   • **Much of the region is** lowland. 그 지역은 많은 부분이 저지대이다.

   cf. 2. one of+복수 명사+단수 동사

   • **One** of the screws **is** loose. 그 나사들 중 하나가 헐겁다.

   cf. 3. none of+단수 명사+단수 동사
          none of+복수 명사+단수 동사[복수 동사]

   • **None** of these computers **works[work]**. 이 컴퓨터들이 하나도 작동이 안 된다.

   cf. 4. every, each, -thing, -one, -body, 시간, 거리, 금액, 무게, 학문 이름+단수 명사+단수 동사

   • **Every** move **was** painful. 몸을 움직일 때마다 아팠다.

   ※ 시제의 일치
      주어와 종속절의 시제를 일치시켜야 한다.
      주절의 동사가 현재시제인 경우 종속절에는 모든 시제를 쓸 수 있지만, 주절의 동사가 과거시제인 경우 종속절의 시제는 과거나 과거완료가 온다.
      주절의 시제가 과거일지라도 종속절이 불변의 진리, 격언, 현재의 습관, 과학적 사실 등을 나타내면 현재시제를 쓴다.
   • She **said** that knowledge **is** power.(진리) 그녀는 지식은 힘이라고 말했다.

핵심 Check

2. 괄호 안에 주어진 어휘를 빈칸에 현재형으로 알맞게 쓰시오.
   (1) The rest of the paper _____ on the table. (be)
   (2) Quite a few of the members _____ present. (be)
   (3) More than one third of wage earners _____ concerned about reduced wages. (be)

01 다음 각 문장의 빈칸에 as를 넣을 때 <u>어색한</u> 것은?

① Leave the papers _____ they are.

② My mother was crying _____ I waved her goodbye.

③ _____ he aged, his memory got worse.

④ The trouble is _____ we are short of money.

⑤ Her voice lowered _____ she spoke.

02 다음 빈칸에 알맞은 것을 고르시오.

Half of the money _____ mine.

① being   ② to be   ③ was

④ were   ⑤ are

03 다음 문장의 빈칸에 가장 알맞은 말은?

_____ he grows older, Ted gets more popular.

① As   ② Because   ③ What

④ Whether   ⑤ That

04 다음 빈칸에 들어갈 수 있는 말이 <u>다른</u> 하나는?

① The orchestra was tuning up _____ we entered the hall.

② _____ she gave no sign, I was sure she had seen me.

③ The new rules could mean the end of football _____ we know it.

④ _____ we get older, our bodies become less efficient at burning up calories.

⑤ I like him _____ he is honest.

05 다음 우리말을 괄호 안에 주어진 어휘를 이용하여 영작하시오.

시간이 지날수록 나는 너를 사랑한다. (as, go by, 7 단어)

➡ _____

01 다음 밑줄 친 as 중 나머지 넷과 쓰임이 다른 하나는?

① As the prices of the tickets increase, people are less likely to go to concerts.

② As I was tired, I fell asleep early.

③ You don't need to be unconfident, as you are perfect the way you are.

④ We are, as you know, a leading company in the industry of benchmarking.

⑤ He is widely acknowledged as the best player in the world.

02 다음 밑줄 친 as 중 나머지 넷과 그 뜻이 다른 하나는?

① As you grow older, you will become wiser.

② The game was called off as it rained cats and dogs.

③ As she practiced the piano, she enjoyed it more and more.

④ As the movie progresses, the tension builds.

⑤ As she got older, offers of modelling work began to dry up.

03 다음 두 문장을 한 문장으로 바꾸어 쓸 때 알맞게 표현한 것을 고르시오.

• The graph shows.
• People are spending more and more money on food.

① Although the graph shows, people are spending more and more money on food.

② If the graph shows, people are spending more and more money on food.

③ As the graph shows, people are spending more and more money on food.

④ Since the graph shows, people are spending more and more money on food.

⑤ After the graph shows, people are spending more and more money on food.

04 다음 빈칸에 공통으로 들어갈 알맞은 말을 고르시오.

(1) All of my songs _____ written by myself.
(2) A quarter of all the people surveyed _____ don't-knows.
(3) Only half of the rooms _____ occupied at that time.

① to be   ② being   ③ be

④ was   ⑤ were

05 다음 중 어법상 어색한 것은?

① Most of the students listen to music while studying.

② Some of the pie is missing.

③ Thirty percent of the country is plains.

④ About one third of all the students in our school wears glasses.

⑤ One of the most important things in a partner is a sense of humor.

서답형

06 다음 문장에서 어법상 어색한 단어 한 개를 찾아서 고치시오.

> One fourth of the students likes to go on a picnic, but the others don't.

➡ _____

중요

07 다음 빈칸에 공통으로 들어갈 알맞은 말을 고르시오. (대 · 소문자 무시)

> (1) _____ you spend more time giving thanks, you will be happier.
> (2) More people want to buy them _____ the price of apples falls.
> (3) They were all dressed _____ clowns.

① because   ② as   ③ while
④ when   ⑤ what

[08~09] 다음 우리말을 어법상 알맞게 영작한 것을 고르시오.

08

> 햄버거를 더 많이 먹음에 따라, 우리는 더 많은 소를 키워야 한다.

① As we eat more hamburgers, we need to raise more cows.
② Because we eat more hamburgers, we need to raise more cows.
③ Even though we eat more hamburgers, we need to raise more cows.
④ Since we eat more hamburgers, we need to raise more cows.
⑤ If we eat more hamburgers, we need to raise many cows.

09

> 그 문제를 축소하기 위해 많은 조치가 취해졌다.

① The number of measures was taken to reduce the problem.
② The number of measures were taken to reduce the problem.
③ A number of measures was taken to reduce the problem.
④ A number of measures were taken to reduce the problem.
⑤ A great deal of measures were taken to reduce the problem.

중요

10 다음 밑줄 친 as가 어법상 문장 속에서 바르게 쓰인 것을 고르시오.

① As every product sells well, being tested before being sold.
② Do you think as these latest changes will do any good?
③ Ann got a lot of experience as she traveled a lot.
④ Now she's caught up in a love triangle and doesn't know as to do.
⑤ In addition, as they were unable to mobilize the resources they needed.

11 다음 빈칸에 들어갈 말이 나머지와 다른 하나는?

① Half of the money _____ mine.
② Seventy percent of the participants _____ Asian.
③ Some of the teachers _____ criticized for poor performance.
④ The old part of the cities _____ destroyed during the war.
⑤ Most of the houses _____ built of stone.

12 다음 주어진 문장의 밑줄 친 as와 가장 가까운 뜻의 as가 쓰인 것을 고르시오.

> <u>As</u> more and more people get on the bandwagon, others are more likely to get on or follow it.

① Famous <u>as</u> she is, she is still quite modest.
② <u>As</u> it was raining heavily, we couldn't go out.
③ <u>As</u> she was advised, she practiced speaking constantly.
④ The audience fell silent <u>as</u> the curtain rose.
⑤ Picasso became more and more famous <u>as</u> he painted with more freedom.

13 다음 두 문장을 한 문장으로 연결할 때 가장 적절한 것은?

> • Nick tried many Korean dishes while he was in Seoul.
> • Nick tried *samgyupsal*.

① Nick tried many Korean dishes while he was in Seoul *samgyupsal* was one of the dishes.
② Nick tried *samgyupsal* that he tried Korean dishes while he was in Seoul.
③ Nick tried many Korean dishes while he was in Seoul that *samgyupsal* was.
④ One of the Korean dishes Nick tried in Seoul was *samgyupsal*.
⑤ One of the dishes which Nick tried were *samgyupsal*.

14 다음 중 밑줄 친 as의 쓰임이 적절하지 않은 것을 고르시오.

① <u>As</u> you exercise harder, your heart rate will increase.
② A monkey is a monkey <u>as</u> he wears a gold ring.
③ <u>As</u> time went by, we became more confident and happy to meet them.
④ You'll experience more things <u>as</u> you grow up.
⑤ <u>As</u> you read more, you will be able to read faster.

15 다음 우리말을 바르게 영작한 것을 고르시오.

> 그녀는 그녀의 남편이 매일 아침 커피 한 잔을 마신다고 말했다.

① She said that her husband drinks a cup of coffee every morning.
② She says that her husband drinks a cup of coffee every morning.
③ She said that her husband has drunk a cup of coffee every morning.
④ She said that her husband had drunk a cup of coffee every morning.
⑤ She says that her husband drank a cup of coffee every morning.

16 우리말과 일치하도록 괄호 안에 주어진 어휘를 바르게 배열하시오.

> 비록 이상해 보일지 모르지만, 그것들은 실제 사람들이 일상생활에서 마주하고 있는 공포다.
> → (it, as, seem, strange, may), they are actually real fears that people confront every day.

➡ _____

01 다음 우리말과 일치하도록 괄호 안에 주어진 어구를 바르게 배열하여 영작하시오.

(1) 로마에 가면 로마인 방식대로 해라. (Rome, the Romans, you, are, do, do, as, when, in)

➡ _____

(2) 그 노래가 더 유명해질수록, 그는 더 많은 사람들에게 알려졌다. (he, people, the song, known, was, became, popular, more, more, as, to)

➡ _____
_____

(3) 그 물의 절반 가량이 미국에서 동물을 키우기 위해 사용된다. (half, animals, the water, about, is, raise, used, the U.S., to, in, of)

➡ _____
_____

(4) 전체 인구의 약 14퍼센트는 교육의 부족으로 읽는 법을 알지 못한다. (all people, 14 percent, education, lack, know, don't, read, due, how, about, to, to, of, of)

➡ _____
_____

02 다음 문장에서 어법상 어색한 것을 바르게 고쳐 다시 쓰시오.

(1) I caught him just though he was leaving the building.

➡ _____

(2) As brave he was, he could not help weeping at the sight.

➡ _____
_____

(3) Each blind student were paired with a sighted student.

➡ _____
_____

(4) Jeff buys soccer shoes because more than half of the boys on his team wears them.

➡ _____
_____

(5) Most of the allowance are spent on clothes and one fourth of the allowance are spent on snacks.

➡ _____
_____

03 다음 문장을 as를 이용하여 같은 뜻의 문장으로 바꿔 쓰시오.

(1) The more love you give, the more love you will receive.

➡ _____
_____

(2) The harder you exercise, the healthier you become.

➡ _____
_____

04 그림을 보고, 주어진 어휘를 이용하여 빈칸을 알맞게 채우시오.

Only one of them at the party _____ on the sofa. (sit)

05 그림을 보고, 주어진 어휘를 이용하여 빈칸을 알맞게 채우시오.

_____ at night, you will get fatter. (eat more)

06 괄호 안에 주어진 동사를 어법에 맞게 빈칸에 쓰시오.

(1) Most of the boys _____ to eat hamburgers. (like)

(2) All of the stars seen in the sky _____ part of our Milky Way Galaxy. (be)

(3) None of the audience really _____ me. (know)

(4) The teacher told us that the Moon _____ around the earth once in 30 days. (go)

(5) The number of students _____ day by day. (decrease)

(6) I knew that World War II _____ in 1945. (end)

07 주어진 두 문장을 〈보기〉처럼 하나의 문장으로 쓰시오.

┤ 보기 ├
• Julie gave Edan some money.
• Edan bought a new backpack with only half of the money.
→ Only half of the money that Julie gave to Edan was used to buy a new backpack by him.

(1) • Sophie wrote many books.
  • Steve read about two thirds of them.
  ➡ _____
  _____

(2) • Mom made the food.
  • Mike threw away some of the food.
  ➡ _____
  _____

(3) • Dominic has a few hobbies.
  • Basketball is his hobby.
  ➡ _____

Why We Buy What We Buy

Have you ever wondered why you've bought things that you don't
<small>간접의문문(의문사+주어+동사)</small> <small>목적격 관계대명사</small>
even want or need? Let's consider what affects us when it comes to
<small>간접의문문(의문사(주어)+동사+목적어)</small>
buying things.
<small>동명사(to의 목적어)</small>

Why do I want to buy what my friends bought?

Jeff goes to the shopping center and sees a pair of soccer shoes on
display. He recognizes the shoes at a glance because more than half of
<small>이유를 이끄는 접속사(~ 때문에)</small>
the boys on his soccer team wear them. Although he already has many
<small>half of+명사: 명사에 수의 일치 (the boys에 수의 일치를 하여 복수동사 wear)</small> <small>양보의 부사절을 이끄는 접속사</small>
pairs of soccer shoes, he ends up buying another new pair.

We can use the "bandwagon effect" to explain Jeff's behavior. A
<small>to부정사의 부사적 용법 중 목적(~하기 위해서)</small>
bandwagon is a wagon in a parade that encourages people to jump
<small>encourage+목적어+to부정사</small>
aboard and enjoy the music. As more and more people get on the
<small>접속사(~함에 따라)</small>
bandwagon, others are more likely to get on or follow it. In this way,
people tend to buy something just because other people have bought it.
<small>단지 ~이기 때문에</small>

**Why do I buy a pair of pants and a bag after I have bought a new
coat?**

Lisa buys a coat that she really loves. Immediately, she realizes that
<small>목적격 관계대명사(+불완전한 절)</small> <small>명사절 접속사(+완전한 절)</small>
her pants do not match her new coat. So, she buys new pants that go
perfectly with her new coat. But she sees that none of her bags match
<small>none of+명사: 명사에 수의 일치</small>
her new clothes. So, she buys a new bag. Most of her money is spent
<small>Most of+명사: 명사에 수의 일치(단수동사 is)</small>
on buying the new items to complete her new look.
<small>= in order to complete</small>

affect: ~에 영향을 주다
when it comes to: ~에 관해서,
~에 대해 말하자면
effect: 효과
behavior: 행동, 행위
wagon: 사륜마차, 짐마차
parade: 행렬, 퍼레이드
encourage: 부추기다
aboard: 탑승하고
on display: 진열된, 전시된
at a glance: 한눈에, 즉시
be likely to: ~하기 쉽다
immediately: 즉시
match: 어울리다

 확인문제

● 다음 문장이 본문의 내용과 일치하면 T, 일치하지 <u>않으면</u> F를 쓰시오.

1 Jeff sees a pair of soccer shoes on display in the shopping center. ☐

2 As more and more people get on the bandwagon, others are more likely to avoid it. ☐

What made Lisa search for new items immediately after buying
a new coat? The "Diderot effect" may explain it. Denis Diderot, a
French writer, received a new gown as a gift. Soon after receiving
the gift, he noticed that all of his furniture did not go well with his
new gown. So, he ended up replacing most of it. The Diderot effect,
therefore, is the concept that purchasing a new item often leads to
more unplanned purchases.

Why do I buy things just because they are on sale?
Nathan goes window shopping and sees a pair of headphones. He
checks the price and finds out that they are $200. He thinks that the
headphones are too expensive. The sales person approaches him and
says, "You can get a 20 percent discount on those headphones." Even
though the discounted price is still not very low, Nathan decides to
buy the headphones.

The situation described above is an example of the "anchoring
effect."

The price mentioned first affects our opinion of prices mentioned
afterwards. For example, if we start with $200, then $160 will seem
cheap in comparison. Furthermore, as the difference of the two prices
becomes bigger, the effect will be more powerful. As such, the price
mentioned first acts as an "anchor" that fixes our thoughts about the
price of an item.
Just like Jeff and his friends, we tend to buy things without seriously
considering why we are buying them. As these effects have shown,
many things influence our purchases. The next time you decide to buy
something, think for a moment about why you are buying it.

furniture: 가구
replace: 바꾸다
concept: 개념
purchase: 구입, 구매
go well with: ~와 잘 어울리다
lead to: ~로 이어지다
discount: 할인; 할인하다
mention: 언급하다, 말하다
furthermore: 더욱이
anchor: 닻; 닻을 내리다
fix: 고정하다
go window shopping: 진열된 상품을 구경하며 다니다
in comparison: 비교해 보면
influence: ~에 영향을 주다
for a moment: 잠깐

 확인문제

● 다음 문장이 본문의 내용과 일치하면 T, 일치하지 않으면 F를 쓰시오.

1 Most of Lisa's money is spent on repairing the new items. ☐

2 A French writer, Denis Diderot, received a new gown as a gift. ☐

3 Nathan decides to buy the headphones because the discounted price is low. ☐

● 우리말을 참고하여 빈칸에 알맞은 말을 쓰시오.

1 Have you ever wondered _____ _____ _____ _____ _____ you don't even want or need?

2 Let's consider _____ _____ _____ when it comes to _____ things.

3 Why do I want to buy _____ _____ _____?

4 Jeff _____ to the shopping center and _____ _____ _____ _____ soccer shoes _____ _____.

5 He _____ the shoes at a glance _____ more than _____ _____ _____ _____ on his soccer team _____ them.

6 _____ he already has _____ _____ _____ soccer shoes, he _____ _____ _____ another new pair.

7 We can use the "_____ _____" _____ _____ Jeff's behavior.

8 A bandwagon is a wagon in a parade _____ _____ people _____ _____ and enjoy the music.

9 As _____ _____ _____ _____ _____ get on the bandwagon, _____ _____ more _____ _____ _____ _____ _____ or follow it.

10 In this way, people tend _____ _____ something _____ _____ other people _____ _____.

11 Why do I _____ _____ _____ _____ pants and a bag _____ I _____ _____ a new coat?

12 Lisa buys a coat _____ she really loves. Immediately, she _____ _____ her pants do not _____ her new coat.

13 So, she buys new pants _____ _____ perfectly _____ her new coat.

14 But she sees _____ _____ _____ her new clothes.

15 So, she _____ a new bag. _____ _____ _____ _____ _____ spent _____ buying the new items _____ _____ her new look.

16 What _____ Lisa _____ _____ new items immediately _____ _____ a new coat?

1 여러분은 원하거나 필요로 하지도 않는 것들을 자신이 왜 구입했는지 궁금해 한 적이 있는가?

2 물건들을 구입하는 것에 관하여 무엇이 우리에게 영향을 주는지 생각해 보자.

3 나는 왜 친구들이 산 것을 사고 싶은 걸까?

4 Jeff는 쇼핑센터에 가서 진열되어 있는 축구화 한 켤레를 보게 된다.

5 그의 축구팀에 있는 소년들의 반 이상이 그 축구화를 신기 때문에 그는 그 신발을 한눈에 알아챈다.

6 이미 그에게는 축구화가 많이 있지만 결국 그는 또 다른 새 축구화를 사 버리고 만다.

7 우리는 Jeff의 행동을 설명하기 위해 '밴드왜건 효과'를 이용할 수 있다.

8 밴드왜건(악대차)은 사람들이 올라타서 음악을 즐기게끔 부추기는 퍼레이드에 있는 사륜마차이다.

9 더 많은 사람들이 밴드왜건에 올라탈수록 다른 사람들이 더욱 그것에 올라타거나 그것을 따라가려 한다.

10 이런 식으로, 사람들은 단지 다른 사람들이 어떤 것을 샀다는 이유로 그것을 구매하는 경향이 있다.

11 나는 왜 새 코트를 구입한 후에 바지와 가방을 사는 걸까?

12 Lisa는 정말 마음에 드는 코트를 산다. 그녀는 그녀의 바지가 새 코트와 어울리지 않는다는 것을 즉시 알아차린다.

13 그래서 그녀는 새 코트와 완벽하게 어울리는 새 바지를 구입한다.

14 하지만 그녀는 자신의 가방 중 어느 것도 새로운 옷들과 어울리지 않는다는 것을 알게 된다.

15 그래서 그녀는 새 가방을 산다. 그녀의 돈 대부분이 그녀의 새로운 모습을 완성하기 위하여 새로운 물품을 사는 데 쓰인다.

16 무엇이 Lisa로 하여금 새 코트를 산 후 즉시 새로운 물품을 찾게 했을까?

17 The "Diderot effect" may ________ ________. Denis Diderot, a French writer, ________ a new gown ________ a gift.

18 Soon ________ ________ the gift, he ________ ________ all of his ________ did not ________ ________ with his new gown. So, he ended up ________ ________ ________ ________.

19 The Diderot effect, ________, is the concept ________ ________ ________ ________ ________ often ________ ________ more ________ purchases.

20 Why do I buy things just because ________ ________ ________ ________?

21 Nathan ________ ________ ________ and ________ a pair of headphones.

22 He ________ the price and ________ ________ ________ they are $200. He thinks ________ the headphones are ________ ________.

23 The sales person ________ ________ and says, "You can get a 20 percent ________ ________ those headphones."

24 ________ ________ the discounted price ________ ________ not very ________, Nathan decides ________ ________ the headphones.

25 The situation ________ ________ is an example of the "________ ________."

26 The price ________ first ________ our ________ ________ ________ mentioned afterwards.

27 ________ ________, if we start with $200, then $160 will ________ ________ ________ ________.

28 ________, as the difference of the two prices ________ ________, the effect will ________ ________ ________.

29 ________ ________, the price ________ ________ acts as an "________" that ________ ________ ________ about the price of an item.

30 ________ ________ Jeff and his friends, we tend ________ ________ things without seriously ________ ________ ________ ________ ________ them.

31 ________ these effects ________ ________, many things ________ our purchases.

32 ________ ________ ________ you decide to buy something, ________ for a moment ________ ________ ________ ________ ________ it.

17 '디드로 효과'가 그것을 설명해 줄지도 모른다. 프랑스 작가인 Denis Diderot는 선물로 새 가운을 받았다.

18 그 선물을 받은 후에 곧 그는 그의 모든 가구가 새로운 가운과 어울리지 않는다는 것을 알아챘다. 그래서 그는 결국 대부분의 가구를 바꾸고 말았다.

19 그러므로 디드로 효과는 새로운 물품을 구입하는 것이 흔히 계획에 없던 더 많은 구매로 이어진다는 개념이다.

20 나는 왜 단지 할인 중이라는 이유로 물건을 구입하는 걸까?

21 Nathan은 진열된 상품을 구경하러 가서 헤드폰을 하나 본다.

22 그는 가격을 확인하고 그것이 200달러임을 알게 된다. 그는 그 헤드폰이 너무 비싸다고 생각한다.

23 점원이 그에게 다가와 "이 헤드폰에 20퍼센트 할인을 받을 수 있어요."라고 말한다.

24 비록 할인된 가격이 여전히 별로 저렴하지는 않지만 Nathan은 그 헤드폰을 사기로 결심한다.

25 위에 기술된 상황은 '앵커링 효과'의 한 예이다.

26 처음에 언급된 가격이 이후에 언급되는 가격에 대한 우리의 의견에 영향을 미친다.

27 예를 들어, 만약 우리가 200달러로 시작한다면, 비교해 볼 때 160달러는 저렴해 보일 것이다.

28 그뿐만 아니라, 두 가격의 차이가 커질수록 그 효과는 더욱 강력해질 것이다.

29 이와 같이 처음에 언급된 가격이 물건의 가격에 대한 우리의 생각을 고정하는 '닻'으로서 작동한다.

30 Jeff와 그의 친구들처럼, 우리는 우리가 왜 물건들을 사는지 진지하게 고려하지 않고 그것들을 구입하는 경향이 있다.

31 이러한 효과들이 보여 주듯이, 많은 것들이 우리의 구매에 영향을 미친다.

32 다음번에 여러분이 어떤 것을 구매하려고 결정할 때에는, 자신이 그것을 왜 사려는지 잠시 동안 생각해 보아라.

● 우리말을 참고하여 본문을 영작하시오.

1 여러분은 원하거나 필요로 하지도 않는 것들을 자신이 왜 구입했는지 궁금해 한 적이 있는가?
➡ _____

2 물건들을 구입하는 것에 관하여 무엇이 우리에게 영향을 주는지 생각해 보자.
➡ _____

3 나는 왜 친구들이 산 것을 사고 싶은 걸까?
➡ _____

4 Jeff는 쇼핑센터에 가서 진열되어 있는 축구화 한 켤레를 보게 된다.
➡ _____

5 그의 축구팀에 있는 소년들의 반 이상이 그 축구화를 신기 때문에 그는 그 신발을 한눈에 알아챈다.
➡ _____
_____

6 이미 그에게는 축구화가 많이 있지만 결국 그는 또 다른 새 축구화를 사 버리고 만다.
➡ _____

7 우리는 Jeff의 행동을 설명하기 위해 '밴드왜건 효과'를 이용할 수 있다.
➡ _____

8 밴드왜건(악대차)은 사람들이 올라타서 음악을 즐기게끔 부추기는 퍼레이드에 있는 사륜마차이다.
➡ _____
_____

9 더 많은 사람들이 밴드왜건에 올라탈수록 다른 사람들이 더욱 그것에 올라타거나 그것을 따라가려 한다.
➡ _____

10 이런 식으로, 사람들은 단지 다른 사람들이 어떤 것을 샀다는 이유로 그것을 구매하는 경향이 있다.
➡ _____

11 나는 왜 새 코트를 구입한 후에 바지와 가방을 사는 걸까?
➡ _____

12 Lisa는 정말 마음에 드는 코트를 산다. 그녀는 그녀의 바지가 새 코트와 어울리지 않는다는 것을 즉시 알아차린다.
➡ _____
_____

13 그래서 그녀는 새 코트와 완벽하게 어울리는 새 바지를 구입한다.
➡ _____

14 하지만 그녀는 자신의 가방 중 어느 것도 새로운 옷들과 어울리지 않는다는 것을 알게 된다.
➡ _____

15 그래서 그녀는 새 가방을 산다. 그녀의 돈 대부분이 그녀의 새로운 모습을 완성하기 위하여 새로운 물품을 사는 데 쓰인다.
➡ _____

16 무엇이 Lisa로 하여금 새 코트를 산 후 즉시 새로운 물품을 찾게 했을까?
➡ _____

17 '디드로 효과'가 그것을 설명해 줄지도 모른다. 프랑스 작가인 Denis Diderot는 선물로 새 가운을 받았다.
➡ _____

18 그 선물을 받은 후에 곧 그는 그의 모든 가구가 새로운 가운과 어울리지 않는다는 것을 알아챘다. 그래서 그는 결국 대부분의 가구를 바꾸고 말았다.
➡ _____
_____

19 그러므로 디드로 효과는 새로운 물품을 구입하는 것이 흔히 계획에 없던 더 많은 구매로 이어진다는 개념이다.
➡ _____
_____

20 나는 왜 단지 할인 중이라는 이유로 물건을 구입하는 걸까?
➡ _____

21 Nathan은 진열된 상품을 구경하러 가서 헤드폰을 하나 본다.
➡ _____

22 그는 가격을 확인하고 그것이 200달러임을 알게 된다. 그는 그 헤드폰이 너무 비싸다고 생각한다.
➡ _____

23 점원이 그에게 다가와 "이 헤드폰에 20퍼센트 할인을 받을 수 있어요."라고 말한다.
➡ _____

24 비록 할인된 가격이 여전히 별로 저렴하지는 않지만 Nathan은 그 헤드폰을 사기로 결심한다.
➡ _____

25 위에 기술된 상황은 '앵커링 효과'의 한 예이다.
➡ _____

26 처음에 언급된 가격이 이후에 언급되는 가격에 대한 우리의 의견에 영향을 미친다.
➡ _____

27 예를 들어, 만약 우리가 200달러로 시작한다면, 비교해 볼 때 160달러는 저렴해 보일 것이다.
➡ _____

28 그뿐만 아니라, 두 가격의 차이가 커질수록 그 효과는 더욱 강력해질 것이다.
➡ _____
_____

29 이와 같이 처음에 언급된 가격이 물건의 가격에 대한 우리의 생각을 고정하는 '닻'으로서 작동한다.
➡ _____
_____

30 Jeff와 그의 친구들처럼, 우리는 우리가 왜 물건들을 사는지 진지하게 고려하지 않고 그것들을 구입하는 경향이 있다.
➡ _____
_____

31 이러한 효과들이 보여 주듯이, 많은 것들이 우리의 구매에 영향을 미친다.
➡ _____

32 다음번에 여러분이 어떤 것을 구매하려고 결정할 때에는, 자신이 그것을 왜 사려는지 잠시 동안 생각해 보아라.
➡ _____

[01~04] 다음 글을 읽고 물음에 답하시오.

Have you ever wondered why you've bought things that you don't even want or need? Let's consider what affects us when it comes to buying things.

Why do I want to buy (A)_____?

Jeff goes to the shopping center and sees a pair of soccer shoes on display. He recognizes the shoes at a glance because more than half of the boys on his soccer team wear them. Although he already has many pairs of soccer shoes, he ends up buying another new pair.

We can use the "bandwagon effect" to explain Jeff's behavior. A bandwagon is a wagon in a parade that encourages people to jump aboard and enjoy the music. As more and more people get on the bandwagon, others are more likely to get on or follow it. In this way, people tend to buy something just because other people have bought it.

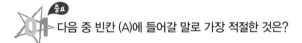

01 다음 중 빈칸 (A)에 들어갈 말로 가장 적절한 것은?

① luxurious things
② what my friends bought
③ what my friends want me to buy
④ things that is not good for me
⑤ what I need most

02 Where does Jeff go? Answer in English with a full sentence.

➡ _____

03 다음과 같이 풀이되는 말을 위 글에서 찾아 쓰시오.

> the things that a person or an animal does

➡ _____

04 다음 중 위 글을 읽고 답할 수 있는 것은?

① What did Jeff want to buy at the shopping center?
② How many pairs of soccer shoes does Jeff have?
③ When Jeff sees the shoes on display, what does he do?
④ How many members are there on Jeff's soccer team?
⑤ When did people start to use a bandwagon?

[05~08] 다음 글을 읽고 물음에 답하시오.

Why do I buy a pair of pants and a bag after I have bought a new coat?

Lisa buys a coat that she really loves. Immediately, she realizes that her pants do not match her new coat. So, she buys new pants that go perfectly with her new coat. (①) But she sees that none of her bags match her new clothes. (②) So, she buys a new bag. Most of her money is spent on buying the new items to complete her new look. (③)

What made Lisa search for new items immediately after buying a new coat? (④) Denis Diderot, a French writer, received a new gown as a gift. Soon after receiving the gift, he noticed that all of his furniture did not go well with his new gown. (⑤) So, he ended up replacing most of it. The Diderot effect, therefore, is the concept that purchasing a new item often leads to more unplanned purchases.

05 (①)~(⑤) 중 주어진 문장이 들어가기에 적절한 곳은?

> The "Diderot effect" may explain it.

①   ②   ③   ④   ⑤

06 Choose two things that Lisa didn't buy.

① a hat   ② a coat   ③ pants

④ shoes   ⑤ a bag

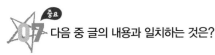

07 다음 중 글의 내용과 일치하는 것은?

① Lisa bought two pairs of pants.

② Denis Didreot is one of Lisa's friends.

③ Denis gave someone a new gown as a gift.

④ Lisa spent money on what she planned to buy.

⑤ What Lisa wanted was to complete her new look.

서답형
08 What did Lisa do after buying her new clothes? Answer in English.

➡ _____

[09~13] 다음 글을 읽고 물음에 답하시오.

Why do I buy things just because they are ①on sale?

Nathan goes window shopping and sees a pair of headphones. He checks the price and finds out that they are $200. He thinks that the headphones are ②too expensive. The sales person approaches him and says, "You can get a 20 percent discount on those headphones." Even though the discounted price is still not very ③low, Nathan decides to buy the headphones.

The situation described above is an example of the "anchoring effect." The price mentioned first affects our opinion of prices mentioned ④before. (A)_____, if we start with $200, then $160 will seem cheap in comparison. Furthermore, as the difference of the two prices becomes ⑤bigger, the effect will be more powerful. As such, the price mentioned first acts as an "anchor" that fixes our thoughts about the price of an item.

09 밑줄 친 ①~⑤ 중 글의 흐름상 어색한 것은?

①   ②   ③   ④   ⑤

10 빈칸 (A)에 들어갈 말로 가장 적절한 것은?

① Nevertheless   ② Therefore

③ For example   ④ However

⑤ On the other hand

11 What is the passage mainly talking about?

① What makes people buy things they don't need?

② The reason we buy something only because it is on sale.

③ The reason some products are constantly on sale while others are not.

④ Who determines a price of a product on sale?

⑤ What kind of products attract people most?

서답형
12 According to the passage, what is the price of the headphones which fixes Nathan's thought about the price of them? Answer in English.

➡ _____

서답형
13 What does the sales person say when he approaches Nathan? Answer in English.

➡ _____

_____

[14~18] 다음 글을 읽고 물음에 답하시오.

Have you ever wondered why you've bought things ①that you don't even want or need? Let's consider what affects us when it comes to ②buy things.

Why do I want to buy ③what my friends bought?

(A) Although he already has many pairs of soccer shoes, he ends up buying another new pair.

(B) As more and more people get on the bandwagon, others are more likely to get on or follow it. In this way, people tend to buy something just because ④other people have bought it.

(C) Jeff goes to the shopping center and sees a pair of soccer shoes on display. He recognizes the shoes at a glance because more than half of the boys on his soccer team wear them.

(D) We can use the "bandwagon effect" ⑤ to explain Jeff's behavior. A bandwagon is a wagon in a parade that encourages people to jump aboard and enjoy the music.

14 자연스러운 글이 되도록 (A)~(D)를 바르게 나열한 것은?

① (B)–(A)–(C)–(D) ② (B)–(D)–(A)–(C)
③ (C)–(A)–(D)–(B) ④ (C)–(B)–(A)–(D)
⑤ (D)–(A)–(B)–(C)

15 밑줄 친 ①~⑤ 중 어법상 바르지 않은 것은?

①   ②   ③   ④   ⑤

16 What does Jeff see at the shopping center? Answer in English.

➡ _____

17 위 글의 제목으로 가장 적절한 것은?

① What Makes You Survive?
② What Makes You Feel Happy?
③ Things That Money Can't Buy
④ What Makes Us Spend Money?
⑤ Ways To Be a Good Consumer: Follow Your Friends

서답형
18 What can we use to explain Jeff's behavior?

➡ _____

[19~22] 다음 글을 읽고 물음에 답하시오.

Why do I buy a pair of pants and a bag (A)_____?

Lisa buys a coat that she really loves. Immediately, she realizes that her pants do not match her new coat. So, she buys new pants that go perfectly with her new coat. But she sees that none of her bags match her new clothes. So, she buys a new bag. Most of her money is spent (B)_____ buying the new items to complete her new look.

What made Lisa search for new items immediately after buying a new coat? The "Diderot effect" may explain it. Denis Diderot, a French writer, received a new gown as a gift. Soon after receiving the gift, he noticed that all of his furniture did not go well with his new gown. So, he ended up replacing most of (C)it. The Diderot effect, therefore, is the concept (D)that purchasing a new item often leads to more unplanned purchases.

서답형
19 주어진 단어를 활용하여 빈칸 (A)에 들어갈 말을 완성하시오.

(after / have bought)

➡ _____

20 빈칸 (B)에 들어갈 말과 같은 말이 들어가는 것은?

① The refrigerator broke _____.

② What does the T.C. stand _____?

③ Jina was brought _____ by her sister.

④ Don't put _____ what you have to do today.

⑤ What does the insect mainly live _____?

21 밑줄 친 (C)가 가리키는 것을 위 글에서 찾아 쓰시오.

➡ _____

22 밑줄 친 (D)와 쓰임이 다른 것은?

① The fact that she betrayed us is true.

② They thought that you lied to them.

③ The name that he mentioned is yours.

④ It is true that the earth is round.

⑤ The news that he won first prize is true.

[23~25] 다음 글을 읽고 물음에 답하시오.

Why do I buy things just ①because they are on sale?

Nathan goes window shopping and sees a pair of headphones. He checks the price and finds out ②that they are $200. He thinks that the headphones are too expensive. The sales person ③approaches to him and says, "You can get a 20 percent discount on those headphones." Even though the discounted price is still not very low, Nathan decides ④to buy the headphones.

The situation described above is an example of the "anchoring effect." The price mentioned first affects our opinion of prices mentioned afterwards. For example, if we start with $200, then $160 will seem cheap in comparison. Furthermore, as the difference of the two prices ⑤becomes bigger, the effect will be more powerful. As such, the price mentioned first acts as an "anchor" that fixes our thoughts about the price of an item.

Just like Jeff and his friends, we tend to buy things without seriously considering why we are buying them. As (a)these effects have shown, many things influence our purchases. The next time you decide to buy something, think for a moment about (A)_____.

23 밑줄 친 ①~⑤ 중 어법상 바르지 않은 것은?

① ② ③ ④ ⑤

24 빈칸 (A)에 들어갈 말로 가장 적절한 것은?

① who made you spend money

② why you are buying it

③ when you started to think

④ what influences your life style

⑤ how you spend money wisely

25 What have the underlined (a)these effects shown?

➡ _____

_____

[01~05] 다음 글을 읽고 물음에 답하시오.

Have you ever wondered why you've bought things that you don't even want or need? Let's consider (A)물건을 구매하는 것에 관하여 무엇이 우리에게 영향을 주는지.

Why do I want to buy what my friends bought?

Jeff goes to the shopping center and sees a pair of soccer shoes on display. He recognizes the shoes at a glance because more than half of the boys on his soccer team ⓐwear them. Although he already has many pairs of soccer shoes, he ends up buying another new pair.

We can use the "bandwagon effect" to explain Jeff's behavior. A bandwagon is a wagon in a parade that encourages people to jump aboard and enjoy the music. As more and more people get on the bandwagon, others are more likely to get on or follow ⓑit. In this way, people tend to buy something just because other people have bought it.

01 주어진 단어를 활용하여 밑줄 친 우리말 (A)를 영어로 쓰시오.

(affect / when / come)

➡ _____

02 밑줄 친 ⓐ를 어법에 맞게 쓰시오.

➡ _____

03 밑줄 친 ⓑ가 가리키는 것을 위 글에서 찾아 쓰시오.

➡ _____

04 What is likely to happen when more and more people get on the bandwagon? Answer in English.

➡ _____
_____

05 According to the "bandwagon effect," why do people tend to buy something?

➡ _____

[06~09] 다음 글을 읽고 물음에 답하시오.

Why do I buy a pair of pants and a bag after I have bought a new coat?

Lisa buys a coat that she really loves. Immediately, she realizes that her pants do not match her new coat. So, she buys new pants that go perfectly with her new coat. But she sees that none of her bags match her new clothes. So, she buys a new bag. Most of her money is spent on buying the new items to complete her new look.

What made Lisa search for new items immediately after buying a new coat? The "Diderot effect" may explain it. Denis Diderot, a French writer, received a new gown as a gift. Soon after receiving the gift, he noticed that all of his furniture did not go well with his new gown. So, he ended up replacing most of it. The Diderot effect, therefore, is the concept that purchasing a new item often leads to more unplanned purchases.

06 What does Lisa buy at first?

➡ _____

07 What does Lisa realize after buying a new coat? Answer in English.

➡ _____

_____

08 Write the reason why Diderot replaced most of his furniture after receiving a new gown as a gift. Use the phrase 'It was because.'

➡ _____

_____

09 다음 중 위 글의 내용과 일치하지 <u>않는</u> 곳을 한 군데 찾아 바르게 고쳐 쓰시오.

> Lisa buys a series of new items because, according to the "Diderot effect," one new item leads to a series of planned purchases.

➡ _____

[10~13] 다음 글을 읽고 물음에 답하시오.

Why do I buy things just because they are on sale?

Nathan goes window shopping and sees a pair of headphones. He checks the price and finds out that they are $200. He thinks that the headphones are too expensive. The sales person approaches him and says, "You can get a 20 percent discount on those headphones." Even though the discounted price is still not very low, Nathan decides to buy the headphones.

The situation described above is an example of the "anchoring effect." The price mentioned first affects our opinion of prices mentioned afterwards. For example, if we start with $200, then $160 will seem cheap in comparison.

Furthermore, as the difference of the two prices becomes bigger, the effect will be more powerful. As such, the price mentioned first acts as an "anchor" that fixes our thoughts about the price of an item.

Just like Jeff and his friends, we tend to buy things without seriously considering why we are buying them. As these effects have shown, many things influence our purchases. The next time you decide to buy something, think for a moment about why you are buying it.

10 What does Nathan see when he goes window shopping? Answer in English.

➡ _____

11 What does Nathan find out when he checks the price of the headphone?

➡ _____

12 다음과 같이 풀이되는 말을 위 글에서 찾아 쓰시오.

> a heavy object that is dropped into the water to prevent a boat from moving

➡ _____

13 What does the writer suggest we should do the next time we decide to buy something? Answer in English.

➡ _____

_____

Language in Use

- It is difficult to compare the results in detail.
  특정 어근 앞에 com-을 붙이면 '함께'라는 의미를 더한다. com+pare(가지런히 놓다) → compare(비교하다)
- We encourage children to think for themselves.

구문해설 · in detail: 상세히 · for oneself: 스스로

해석

- 결과를 상세히 비교하는 것은 어렵다.
- 우리는 아이들이 스스로 생각하도록 장려한다.

Grammar in Real Life B Look and Write

1. About half of the water is used to raise animals in the U.S.
   부분을 나타내는 말은 뒤에 오는 명사의 수에 따라 그 수가 결정된다.(the water/is)
2. One third of the world's food is wasted —1.3 billion tons every year.
   the world's food에 맞춰 is
3. In Somalia, only ten percent of the children go to school.
   the children에 맞춰 go
4. About fourteen percent of all people don't know how to read due to lack of
   약   all people에 맞춰 don't know   의문사+to부정사(= how they should read)
   education.

구문해설 · raise: 키우다 · waste: 낭비하다 · billion: 10억 · due to: ~ 때문에 · lack: 부족, 결핍
· education: 교육

1. 물의 절반 가량이 미국에서 동물을 키우기 위해 사용된다.
2. 세계 식량의 삼분의 일, 즉 매년 13억 톤이 낭비된다.
3. 소말리아에서는 단지 10퍼센트의 아이들이 학교에 다닌다.
4. 전체 인구의 약 14퍼센트는 교육의 부족으로 읽는 법을 알지 못한다.

Think & Write C

I did a survey about allowance. First, I asked 10 students how often they get
                                                간접의문문(의문사+주어+동사) ask의 직접목적어
an allowance. Twenty percent of the students get an allowance every week and
                                the students에 수의 일치
seventy percent of the students get an allowance every month. Second, I asked

them what they spend most of their allowance on. Most of the allowance is
     asked와 on의 목적어 역할을 함.   the allowance에 수의 일치
spent on clothes and one fourth of the allowance is spent on snacks.
                      4분의 1(분자는 기수, 분모는 서수)
Lastly, I asked them whether they think that they should get a higher
                      ask의 직접목적어(명사절 접속사: ~인지 아닌지)
allowance. Ninety percent of the students think that they should get a higher

allowance.

구문해설 · survey: 설문 조사 · allowance: 용돈 · spend+시간/돈+on ~: ~에 시간이나 돈을 쓰다
· whether: ~인지 아닌지

저는 용돈에 관하여 설문 조사를 했습니다. 우선, 저는 10명의 학생들에게 그들이 얼마나 자주 용돈을 받는지 물었습니다. 20퍼센트의 학생들은 매주 용돈을 받고, 70퍼센트의 학생들은 매달 용돈을 받습니다. 두 번째로, 저는 학생들에게 어디에 용돈의 대부분을 쓰는지 물었습니다. 대부분의 용돈은 옷에 쓰이고, 용돈의 4분의 1은 간식에 쓰입니다. 마지막으로, 저는 학생들에게 그들이 더 많은 용돈을 받아야 한다고 생각하는지 물었습니다. 학생들의 90퍼센트는 그들이 더 많은 용돈을 받아야 한다고 생각합니다.

Words & Expressions

01 다음 밑줄 친 부분과 의미가 가장 가까운 것을 고르시오.

> Young people tend to be greatly affected by their peer group.

① invented   ② controlled
③ improved   ④ generated
⑤ influenced

02 다음 빈칸에 들어갈 알맞은 말을 고르시오.

> That jacket _____ your skirt perfectly.

① matches   ② consumes   ③ lasts
④ replaces   ⑤ adapts

03 다음 괄호 안의 단어를 문맥에 맞게 고쳐 문장을 완성하시오.

> The new teacher _____ students to think creatively. (courage)

04 다음 빈칸에 공통으로 들어갈 말을 쓰시오.

> • _____ and more people are using the Internet.
> • The roads were closed for _____ than half an hour.

Conversation

[05~06] 다음 대화를 읽고 물음에 답하시오.

> W: Hey, Eric. Camilla and I are going to watch a movie. (①) Do you want to join us?
> M: I'd love to, but I can't. (②) I've spent all of my allowance for this week. (③)
> W: Didn't you just get it a few days ago? (④)
> M: I'm not sure. (⑤) (A)내 지출을 기록했어야 했어. (keep, spending, track)

05 ①~⑤ 중 주어진 문장이 들어갈 곳은?

> How did you spend it all?

①   ②   ③   ④   ⑤

06 밑줄 친 (A)의 우리말과 일치하도록 주어진 단어를 이용하여 영작하시오.

➡ _____

[07~08] 다음 대화를 읽고 물음에 답하시오.

> A: I heard (A)_____ you bought some iced tea online. (a)How do you like it?
> B: Oh, I'm (B)_____ with it.
> A: Why? What's wrong?
> B: There is too much sugar in it. I (C)_____ the nutrition facts first.

07 다음 빈칸 (A)~(C)에 들어갈 말이 알맞게 짝지어진 것은?

① what – not happy – should check
② what – satisfied – should have checked
③ that – satisfied – should check
④ that – satisfied – should have checked
⑤ that – not happy – should have checked

08 밑줄 친 (a)와 바꿔 쓸 수 없는 것을 고르시오.

① Are you satisfied with it?
② Are you enjoying it?
③ Do you like it?
④ Why do you like it?
⑤ Are you happy with it?

[09~10] 다음 대화를 읽고 물음에 답하시오.

M: Good morning. May I help you?
W: I'd like to buy a T-shirt for my sister. She's eleven years old. (①)
M: How do you (A)_____ this red one? (②) This character is quite popular among children. (③)
W: Well, she doesn't (B)_____ animation characters that much. (④)
M: You mean this blue striped T-shirt? Its design is simple and cool. (⑤)
W: Yes, I think my sister will like it. I'll take it.

09 ①~⑤ 중 주어진 문장이 들어갈 곳은?

Can I see the blue one?

①   ②   ③   ④   ⑤

10 빈칸 (A)와 (B)에 공통으로 들어갈 말을 쓰시오.

➡ _____

[11~12] 다음 대화를 읽고 물음에 답하시오.

M: Good morning. Welcome to Kelly's Sporting Goods Store.
W: Hi, I'm looking for a backpack for hiking.
M: These two are popular among hikers.
_____

W: The green one is lighter than the blue one. I'll take the lighter one.
M: Great choice.

11 대화의 흐름상 빈칸에 들어갈 말을 주어진 단어를 이용해 문장을 완성하시오.

➡ (1) _____ (how, like)
(2) _____ (satisfied)

12 〈보기〉의 @~@ 중 대화를 읽고 답할 수 있는 것을 모두 고른 것은?

┌─ 보기 ┐
ⓐ Which backpack does the woman take, the green one or the blue one?
ⓑ Which backpack is lighter, the green one or the blue one?
ⓒ What will the woman use a backpack for?
ⓓ Which backpack is more popular, the green one or the blue one?
└─────┘

① ⓐ, ⓑ   ② ⓐ, ⓑ, ⓒ
③ ⓐ, ⓑ, ⓒ, ⓓ   ④ ⓑ, ⓒ
⑤ ⓑ, ⓒ, ⓓ

Grammar

13 다음 중 어법상 옳지 않은 것은?

① As you learn more, you can achieve more.
② As the price goes up, the demand goes down.
③ As you were reborn as an animal, which animal would you be?
④ You have to show your ticket as you go in.
⑤ I couldn't borrow the book from him as James was not at home.

14 다음 중 어법상 옳은 문장을 <u>모두</u> 고르시오.

① One of the highlights were seeing the Taj Mahal.

② 10 percent of the students work to earn money.

③ The number of employees were reduced from 40 to 25.

④ The rest of the money are used to run other government programs.

⑤ Two hours is enough for me to take a walk.

15 다음 밑줄 친 부분이 어법상 옳지 <u>않은</u> 것을 고르시오.

① <u>As she entered the room</u>, she turned the TV on.

② Furthermore, <u>as the difference of the two prices becomes bigger</u>, the effect will be more powerful.

③ <u>As the study shows</u>, those who drink diet sodas tend to get fatter.

④ She earns her living <u>as a freelance journalist</u>.

⑤ Jane met him <u>so as he was leaving the building</u>.

16 다음 문장의 빈칸에 들어갈 말로 알맞은 말은?

> Last weekend, a few of his friends _____ at the party.

① is   ② are   ③ was

④ were   ⑤ has been

17 다음 문장의 밑줄 친 as와 의미상 쓰임이 같은 것을 고르시오.

> <u>As</u> you make more money, you'll want to spend more.

① <u>As</u> the weather gets hotter, more people go to the beach.

② <u>As</u> she was sick, he cared for his wife day and night.

③ <u>As</u> I would not be a slave, so I would not be a master.

④ I wish I could speak English as easily <u>as</u> Korean.

⑤ She was liked by many people <u>as</u> she was honest.

18 다음 문장에서 어법상 어색한 것을 바르게 고쳐 다시 쓰시오.

(1) One third of the students is here.

   ➡ _____

(2) Much of the house were ruined by the heavy rain.

   ➡ _____

(3) Ten percent of the girls wants to learn Spanish.

   ➡ _____

(4) None of the furniture in our house are made of wood.

   ➡ _____

(5) Last night she said that she took a shower every day.

   ➡ _____

_____

19 다음 문장에서 잘못된 것을 내용에 맞게 한 단어만 고치시오.

(1) She never took a taxi, as she could afford to.

➡ _____

(2) I usually sleep with the window open as it's really cold.

➡ _____

(3) Korea is regarded like the Mecca of cosmetic surgery.

➡ _____

20 다음 문장에서 어법상 틀린 부분을 찾아 바르게 고쳐 쓰시오.

Only 20 percent of students in my school enjoys outdoor activities.

➡ _____

Reading

[21~24] 다음 글을 읽고 물음에 답하시오.

Have you ever wondered why you've bought things that you don't even want or need? Let's consider ①what affects us when it comes to buying things.

Why do I want to buy what my friends bought?

Jeff goes to the shopping center and ② sees a pair of soccer shoes ③on display. He recognizes the shoes at a glance because more than half of the boys on his soccer team wear them. Although he already has many pairs of soccer shoes, he ends up (A)_____.

We can use the "bandwagon effect" to explain Jeff's behavior. A bandwagon is a wagon in a parade that encourages people to jump aboard and ④enjoys the music. As more and more people get on the bandwagon, others are more likely to get on or follow it. In this way, people tend to buy something just because other people have bought ⑤it.

21 글의 흐름상 빈칸 (A)에 들어갈 말로 가장 적절한 것은?

① throwing them away
② passing by them in the end
③ buying his friends new soccer shoes
④ focusing on playing games
⑤ buying another new pair

22 ①~⑤ 중 어법상 바르지 않은 것을 찾아 바르게 고쳐 쓰시오.

➡ _____

23 다음 중 글의 내용과 일치하지 않는 곳을 한 군데 찾아 바르게 고쳐 쓰시오.

As people jump on the bandwagon in a parade, people tend to buy things just because no other people have bought them.

➡ _____

24 다음 중 위 글을 읽고 답할 수 있는 것은?

① How often does Jeff go to the shopping center?
② What does Jeff recognize as soon as he sees the shoes?
③ What makes Jeff go to the shopping center?
④ Who invented the term "bandwagon effect" first?
⑤ Who made a bandwagon first in the world?

[25~28] 다음 글을 읽고 물음에 답하시오.

Why do I buy a pair of pants and a bag after I have bought a new coat?

Lisa buys a coat that she really loves. Immediately, she realizes that her pants do not match her new coat. So, she buys new pants that go perfectly with her new coat. But she sees that none of her bags match her new clothes. So, she buys a new bag. Most of her money is spent on buying the new items to complete her new look.

What made Lisa search for new items immediately after buying a new coat? The "Diderot effect" may explain it. Denis Diderot, a French writer, received a new gown as a gift. Soon after receiving the gift, he noticed that all of his furniture did not go well with his new gown. So, he ended up replacing most of it. The Diderot effect, (A)_____, is the concept that purchasing a new item often leads to more unplanned purchases.

25 빈칸 (A)에 들어갈 말로 가장 적절한 것은?

① on the other hand   ② however
③ therefore   ④ for instance
⑤ furthermore

26 What does Lisa buy after buying a new coat?

➡ _____

27 What did Diderot do when he noticed all of his furniture didn't go well with his new gown? Answer in English.

➡ _____

28 Choose one that is TRUE.

① Lisa receives a coat as a gift.
② Lisa keeps buying new items because she needs them.
③ Lisa already had a pair of pants perfectly matching her new coat.
④ What Lisa planned to buy was just a coat.
⑤ Diderot was not satisfied with the new gown, so he replaced it with a new one.

[29~30] 다음 글을 읽고 물음에 답하시오.

I did a survey about allowance. First, I asked 10 students (A)_____. Twenty percent of the students get an allowance every week and seventy percent of the students get an allowance every month. Second, I asked them what they spend most of their allowance on. Most of the allowance is spent on clothes and one fourth of the allowance is spent on snacks. Lastly, I asked them whether they think that they should get a higher allowance. Ninety percent of the students think that they should get a higher allowance.

29 빈칸 (A)에 들어갈 말로 가장 적절한 것은?

① how they usually spend their allowance
② how much allowance they save
③ how often they buy things with their allowance
④ how much allowance they get
⑤ how often they get an allowance

30 On what is most of the allowance spent? Answer in English.

➡ _____

01 출제율 90%

다음 짝지어진 단어의 관계가 같도록 빈칸에 알맞은 단어를 주어진 철자로 시작하여 쓰시오.

(1) immediately : at once = buy : p_____

(2) waste : save = loose : t_____

02 출제율 95%

다음 괄호 안의 단어를 문맥에 맞게 고쳐 빈칸에 쓰시오.

What's the _____ between these two computers? (differ)

03 출제율 100%

빈칸 (A)~(C)에 들어갈 말이 바르게 짝지어진 것을 고르시오.

- We're spending a lot more (A)_____ food than we used to.
- We need a system to (B)_____ track of all our expenses.
- There is no doubt that stress can (C)_____ to physical illness.

(A)	(B)	(C)
① on	have	result
② on	make	lead
③ on	keep	lead
④ in	keep	lead
⑤ in	make	result

04 출제율 90%

다음 영영풀이 해당하는 단어를 주어진 철자로 시작하여 빈칸에 쓰고, 알맞은 것을 골라 문장을 완성하시오.

- a_____ : to have an influence on someone or something, or to cause a change in someone or something
- c_____ : to join together to make a single thing or group
- c_____ : a principle or idea

(1) We need to come up with a new _____ now.

(2) Every choice you make _____ your life.

(3) He wants to _____ his job with pleasure.

05 출제율 95%

다음 대화의 빈칸에 들어갈 말을 〈보기〉에서 골라 순서대로 배열하시오.

W: Hi, Luke. Is that a new speaker?
M: _____
W: _____
M: _____
W: _____
M: About 2 hours. The battery doesn't last long.
W: That's too bad.
M: Yeah, but I'm pretty happy with it, anyway.

(A) Great. How long does the battery last?
(B) It looks cool. How do you like it?
(C) It's convenient. I can take it anywhere and listen to music. The sound quality is good, too.
(D) Yes, I bought it a few weeks ago.

➡ _____

[06~07] 다음 대화를 읽고 물음에 답하시오.

M: Hi. (A)_____

W: Yes, can I try on that cap with stars over there?

M: Sure. (B)_____

W: The design is nice, but I don't think the color suits me. (C)_____

M: Yes. I'll get one from the back. *(pause)* Here it is.

W: Great. I'll take it.

출제율 95%

06 위 대화의 빈칸 (A)~(C)에 들어갈 말을 〈보기〉에서 골라 기호를 쓰시오.

---- 보기 ----

ⓐ Are you enjoying your new cap?

ⓑ How do you like it?

ⓒ What's wrong?

ⓓ Can I help you with anything?

ⓔ Do you have it in black?

ⓕ Didn't you check the picture of it?

ⓖ How about trying on that cap?

➡ (A) _____ (B) _____ (C) _____

출제율 90%

07 위 대화에서 다음 영영풀이에 해당하는 단어를 찾아 쓰시오.

> to be right for a particular person, situation, or occasion

➡ _____

[08~11] 다음 대화를 읽고 물음에 답하시오.

M: Hi, Riley. (①) I heard that you bought a laptop online. How do you like it?

W: Oh, I'm not happy with it.

M: Why? What's wrong?

W: (②) I should have read more reviews.

M: (③) Oh, then you should ask (A)_____ your money back.

W: (④) The online store won't give me back my money (B)_____ I've used it for a week.

M: (⑤) How about calling the online shop and explaining your problem?

W: Yeah, I think I should (a)do that.

출제율 100%

08 ①~⑤ 중 주어진 문장이 들어갈 곳은?

> It makes too much noise and gets overheated.

①   ②   ③   ④   ⑤

출제율 90%

09 빈칸 (A)에 알맞은 전치사를 쓰시오.

➡ _____

출제율 95%

10 빈칸 (B)에 알맞은 말을 고르시오.

① therefore   ② because

③ but   ④ before

⑤ until

출제율 90%

11 밑줄 친 (a)do that이 가리키는 것을 쓰시오.

➡ _____

12 다음 빈칸에 알맞은 말을 고르시오.

> A: Clara, are you okay?
> B: Yeah, I missed the school bus again.
> _____

① I should have gotten up earlier.
② I should have stayed home in bed.
③ I should not have the alarm.
④ I must have told it earlier.
⑤ I must have taken the subway.

13 다음 밑줄 친 as의 쓰임이 다른 하나를 고르시오.

① As he grew up, he got more interested in history.
② As we need more land to raise cows on, we cut more trees to make land.
③ We soon went back as it was getting darker.
④ As a joke to please her, Jake told a story that he made up.
⑤ As he ran faster and faster, his heart pounded loudly.

14 다음 문장에서 어법상 틀린 부분을 찾아 바르게 고쳐 쓰시오.

> The greater part of the expenses was collected from the members.

➡ _____

15 다음 두 문장을 접속사 as를 이용하여 한 문장으로 고치시오.

> • People eat more junk food.
> • They may gain more weight.

➡ _____
_____

16 다음 빈칸에 들어갈 말이 나머지와 다른 하나는?

① Most of the kids _____ wearing caps.
② Some of the pie _____ missing.
③ There _____ several reasons why I can't come.
④ None of the books _____ worth reading.
⑤ A number of new homes _____ being built in this area.

17 다음 문장을 접속사 as를 이용하여 바꿔 쓰시오.

> The more you run, the stronger you become.

➡ _____

[18~21] 다음 글을 읽고 물음에 답하시오.

Why do I buy things just because they are (A) [for sale / on sale]?

Nathan goes window shopping and sees a pair of headphones. He checks the price and finds out that they are $200. He thinks that the headphones are too expensive. The sales person approaches him and says, "You can get a 20 percent discount on those headphones." (B)[Even though / Because] the discounted price is still not very low, Nathan decides to buy the headphones.

The situation described above is an example of the "anchoring effect." The price mentioned first affects our opinion of prices mentioned afterwards. For example, if we start with $200, then $160 will seem cheap in comparison. Furthermore, as the difference of the two prices becomes bigger, the effect will be ⓐ_____. As such, the price mentioned first acts as an "anchor" that (C)[fixes / releases] our thoughts about the price of an item.

Just like Jeff and his friends, we tend to buy things without seriously considering why we are buying them. As these effects have shown, many things influence our purchases. The next time you decide to buy something, think for a moment about why you are buying it.

출제율 100%

18 (A)~(C)에서 글의 흐름상 옳은 것끼리 바르게 짝지어진 것은?

① for sale – Even though – fixes
② for sale – Even though – releases
③ on sale – Even though – fixes
④ on sale – Because – releases
⑤ on sale – Because - fixes

출제율 95%

19 위 글의 내용에 맞게 빈칸에 알맞은 말을 쓰시오.

> The price mentioned first works like an _____. If the price mentioned later is _____ than the first, you will think that the item is cheap.

출제율 100%

20 Choose one that is TRUE.

① Our purchases are influenced by only one thing.
② Nathan finds out on his own that the headphone is on sale.
③ Nathan thinks the price of the headphones is reasonable.
④ The headphone is on Nathan's shopping list.
⑤ Nathan buys the headphone because he is affected by the anchoring effect.

출제율 95%

21 According to the "anchoring effect," what affects our opinion of prices mentioned afterwards? Answer in English.

➡ _____

_____

[22~24] 다음 글을 읽고 물음에 답하시오.

I did a survey about allowance. First, I asked 10 students how often they get an allowance. Twenty percent of the students ①get an allowance every week and seventy percent of the students get an allowance every month. Second, I asked them ②what they spend most of their allowance on. Most of the allowance ③is spent on clothes and one fourth of the allowance is spent ④on snacks. Lastly, I asked them ⑤that they think that they should get a higher allowance. Ninety percent of the students think that they should get a higher allowance.

출제율 95%

22 밑줄 친 ①~⑤ 중 어법상 바르지 않은 것은?

①   ②   ③   ④   ⑤

출제율 90%

23 What do nine students think about their allowance? Answer in English.

➡ _____

출제율 100%

24 위 글을 읽고 답할 수 있는 것은?

① When was the survey conducted?
② How many students were asked for the survey?
③ How often do they buy clothes?
④ How much allowance do they want to get?
⑤ How long does it take them to spend all of their allowance?

01 그림을 보고 괄호 안에 주어진 어휘를 이용하여 과거 사실에 대해 유감을 나타내는 말로 빈칸을 채우시오.

A: What's the problem?
B: Sam and Ted _____
_____. (an umbrella, bring, should)

02 밑줄 친 문장과 비슷한 뜻을 가진 문장을 주어진 단어를 이용하여 쓰시오.

A: How do you like this dress?
B: The design is cool and interesting.

➡ (1) (enjoy) _____
(2) (satisfied) _____
(3) (happy) _____

03 대화의 흐름상 빈칸에 들어갈 말을 주어진 〈조건〉에 맞춰 쓰시오.

┤ 조건 ├
• 6 단어로 후회하는 일 말하기
• 대화에 나와 있는 어휘 이용하기

M: Oh, this coat is too uncomfortable.
W: Why? What's wrong with it?
M: It's too tight.
W: Didn't you try it on before buying it?
M: No. It was my size, so I just bought it.
_____

➡ _____

04 〈보기〉에 주어진 단어를 활용하여 빈칸을 알맞게 채우시오.

┤ 보기 ├
be   die   have   spend

(1) Half of the money _____ for children in need last month.
(2) Economics _____ not the subject which I'm good at.
(3) I knew that Frida Kahlo _____ in 1954.
(4) The number of homeless people _____ increased dramatically.

05 다음 우리말에 맞도록 괄호 안에 주어진 어휘를 알맞게 배열하시오.

(1) 내가 말하고 있을 때, Jason이 내게 다가왔다. (Jason, I, me, speaking, came, was, to, as, up)
➡ _____

(2) 그는 젊지만 아주 현명했다. (he, he, young, wise, was, was, very, as)
➡ _____

(3) 이러한 효과들이 보여 주듯이, 많은 것들이 우리의 구매에 영향을 미친다. (effects, things, influence, purchases, these, many, shown, our, have, as)
➡ _____
_____

(4) 세계 식량의 삼분의 일이 낭비된다. (one, third, of, the world's food, is, wasted)
➡ _____

Have you ever wondered why you've bought things that you don't even want or need? Let's consider what affects us when it comes to buying things.

Why do I want to buy what my friends bought?

Jeff goes to the shopping center and sees a pair of soccer shoes on display. He recognizes the shoes at a glance because more than half of the boys on his soccer team wear them. Although he already has many pairs of soccer shoes, he ends up buying another new pair.

We can use the "bandwagon effect" to explain Jeff's behavior. A bandwagon is a wagon in a parade that encourages people to jump aboard and enjoy the music. As more and more people get on the bandwagon, others are more likely to get on or follow it. In this way, people tend to buy something just because other people have bought it.

06 According to the passage, why does Jeff buy a pair of soccer shoes on display? Answer in English with a full sentence.

➡ _____

_____

07 What kind of wagon is a bandwagon? Answer in English with a full sentence.

➡ _____

_____

Why do I buy a pair of pants and a bag after I have bought a new coat?

Lisa buys a coat that she really loves. Immediately, she realizes that her pants do not match her new coat. So, she buys new pants that go perfectly with her new coat. But she sees that none of her bags match her new clothes. So, she buys a new bag. Most of her money is spent on buying the new items to complete her new look.

What made Lisa search for new items immediately after buying a new coat? The "Diderot effect" may explain it. Denis Diderot, a French writer, received a new gown as a gift. Soon after receiving the gift, he noticed that all of his furniture did not go well with his new gown. So, he ended up replacing most of it. The Diderot effect, therefore, is the concept that purchasing a new item often leads to more unplanned purchases.

08 Why does Lisa spend most of her money on buying new items? Answer in English with a full sentence.

➡ _____

09 What may explain Lisa's spending? Answer in English.

➡ _____

10 What concept is the "Diderot effect?" Answer in English.

➡ _____

01 다음 문장의 빈칸에 알맞은 말을 〈조건〉에 맞춰 쓰시오.

조건

- 후회하는 일 말하기
- should 이용하기

I went to school yesterday, even though I felt sick. Today I feel even worse. I _____
_____.

02 〈보기〉와 같이, 주어진 문장의 빈칸을 채워 본인만의 문장을 쓰시오.

보기

As the night becomes darker, the stars become brighter.

(1) As I understood her better, _____.
(2) As I didn't eat anything, _____.
(3) As I spend more money, _____.
(4) As the boy grows older, _____.

03 10명의 학생을 대상으로 한 설문 조사의 응답을 읽고 그 결과를 설명하는 글을 완성하시오.

Q: How often do you get an allowance?
　□ every week (2명) □ every month (7명)
Q: What do you spend most of your allowance on?
　□ clothes (용돈의 대부분) □ snacks (용돈의 4분의 1)
Q: Do you think you should get a higher allowance?
　□ Yes (9명)   □ No (1명)

I did a survey about allowance. First, I asked 10 students _____.
_____ percent of the students get an allowance _____ and _____
_____. Second, I asked them what they
spend most of their allowance on. Most of the allowance is _____ and
_____ is spent on snacks. Lastly, I asked them _____
_____. _____
_____.

단원별 모의고사

01 다음 빈칸에 공통으로 들어갈 말을 쓰시오.

- Which shoes _____ best with this dress?
- I will _____ window shopping with my friend next weekend.

02 다음 우리말에 맞도록 빈칸에 알맞은 말을 쓰시오. (주어진 단어를 이용하고, 철자가 주어진 경우 주어진 철자로 시작할 것.)

(1) 나는 다음 해에 티켓이 더 비싸질 가능성이 있다고 생각한다. (likely)

➡ I think tickets _____ more expensive next year.

(2) 나는 이 딱 붙는 바지가 편하지 않다.

➡ I am not _____ in these tight pants.

(3) 나는 내가 한 말을 곧 후회했다.

➡ I regretted my words s_____ a_____.

(4) 나는 무슨 일이 일어났었는지 한눈에 알아챘다.

➡ I noticed what had happened _____ _____. (at)

03 다음 빈칸에 알맞은 단어를 〈보기〉에서 골라 쓰시오

┌─── 보기 ┌───
although   because   when
└──────────

(1) _____ it comes to cooking, he is better than me.

(2) Just _____ I don't complain, people think I'm satisfied.

(3) _____ the sun was shining, it wasn't very warm.

04 다음 괄호 안의 단어를 문맥에 맞게 고쳐 빈칸에 쓰시오.

In _____ there are those living in wealth and luxury. (compare)

[05~06] 다음 대화를 읽고 물음에 답하시오.

M: Good morning. ⓐMay I help you?

W: ⓑI'd like to buy a T-shirt for my sister. She's eleven years old.

M: (A)이 빨간색 티셔츠는 어떠세요? This character is quite popular among children.

W: Well, ⓒshe likes animation characters that much. Can I see the blue one?

M: You mean this blue striped T-shirt? ⓓIts design is simple and cool.

W: ⓔYes, I think my sister will like it. I'll take it.

05 밑줄 친 ⓐ~ⓔ 중 흐름상 또는 어법상 어색한 것을 고르시오.

① ⓐ   ② ⓑ   ③ ⓒ   ④ ⓓ   ⑤ ⓔ

06 밑줄 친 (A)의 우리말과 일치하도록 주어진 단어를 이용하여 영작하시오. (like, how)

➡ _____

[07~08] 다음 대화를 읽고 물음에 답하시오.

M: Did you get a new phone, Jamie? It's just like mine.

W: Yeah, I got it last weekend on sale.

M: It was on sale? But it has just been released, hasn't it?

W: Right, but the store on Green Street is having a year-end sale.

M: Oh, I bought mine at full price!

W: Really? That's too bad. They're selling them at a 40 percent discount.

M: (A)I should have checked the sales before buying mine.

07 밑줄 친 (A)의 문장과 바꿔 쓸 수 있는 문장을 주어진 단어를 이용하여 쓰시오.

➡ _____

_____ (regret)

➡ _____

_____ (wish)

08 위 대화의 내용과 일치하지 않는 것을 고르시오.

① 남자는 정가에 전화기를 샀다.
② 여자는 지난 주말에 새 전화기를 샀다.
③ 남자는 할인 판매를 확인했었다.
④ 여자는 남자와 같은 전화기를 샀다.
⑤ 전화기는 출시된 지 얼마 되지 않았다.

[09~10] 다음 대화를 읽고 물음에 답하시오.

M: Hi, Riley. I heard that you bought a laptop online. How do you like it?

W: Oh, I'm not happy with it.

M: Why? What's wrong?

W: It makes too much noise and gets overheated. I (A)_____ have read more reviews.

M: Oh, then you (B)_____ ask for your money back.

W: The online store (C)_____ give me back my money because I've used it for a week.

M: How about calling the online shop and explaining your problem?

W: Yeah, I think I (D)_____ do that.

09 빈칸 (A)~(D)에 들어갈 말을 〈보기〉에서 골라 쓰시오. (중복 사용가능)

┌─ 보기 ─┐
should   shouldn't   will   won't
└─────────┘

➡ (A) _____   (B) _____
(C) _____   (D) _____

10 위 대화의 내용과 일치하지 않는 것을 고르시오.

① Riley가 산 노트북은 소음이 심하고 과열이 된다.
② Riley는 새로 산 노트북이 문제가 있어 마음에 들어 하지 않는다.
③ 남자는 전화해서 문제를 설명하라고 Riley에게 조언해 주었다.
④ Riley는 온라인으로 노트북을 샀다.
⑤ Riley는 환불을 받을 수 있을 것이다.

[11~12] 다음 대화를 읽고 물음에 답하시오.

W: ⓐJake, here's a package for you.

M: It's my helmet. I bought it at an online (A)_____ (use) store a few days ago.

W: Oh, open it and let me (B)_____ (see) it.

M: Okay. *(pause)* Oh, this outer part is a little (C)_____ (break). ⓑThe seller said that it's perfectly fine though.

W: ⓒDidn't you check the pictures of the helmet before you bought it?

M: No, I just trusted the seller. ⓓI must have checked a bit more.

W: ⓔYou should call the seller and ask for a refund.

11 빈칸 (A)~(C)에 괄호 안의 단어를 문맥에 맞게 고쳐 빈칸을 채우시오.

➡ (A) _____ (B) _____ (C) _____

12 밑줄 친 ⓐ~ⓔ 중 흐름상 또는 어법상 어색한 것을 고르시오.

① ⓐ ② ⓑ ③ ⓒ ④ ⓓ ⑤ ⓔ

13 다음 문장에 공통으로 들어갈 알맞은 말을 고르시오. (대 · 소문자 구분 안 함.)

• _____ you go up a mountain, it gets cooler.
• Treat me _____ a friend.
• Leave the documents _____ they are.

① when ② since ③ as
④ that ⑤ if

[14~15] 다음 우리말에 맞게 주어진 어휘를 활용하여 영작하시오.

14
우리가 땅을 만들기 위해서 더 많은 나무를 베어 냄에 따라, 더 많은 숲들이 지구에서 사라진다. (forests, trees, land, make, disappear, cut, on Earth, to)

➡ _____

_____

15
여러분의 몸이 소비하는 힘의 3분의 1은 여러분이 먹는 음식으로부터 나옵니다. (the power, food, consume, come, from, eat)

➡ _____

_____

[16~19] 다음 글을 읽고 물음에 답하시오.

Why do I buy things just because they are on sale?

Nathan goes window shopping and sees a pair of headphones. He checks the price and finds out that they are $200. He thinks that the headphones are too (A)_____. The sales person approaches him and says, "You can get a 20 percent discount on those headphones." Even though the discounted price is still not very low, Nathan decides to buy the headphones.

The situation described above is an example of the "anchoring effect." The price mentioned first affects our opinion of prices mentioned afterwards. For example, if we start with $200, then $160 will seem cheap in comparison. Furthermore, as the difference of the two prices becomes bigger, the effect will be more powerful. As such, the price mentioned first acts as an "anchor" that fixes our thoughts about the price of an item.

16 빈칸 (A)에 들어갈 말로 적절한 것을 모두 고르시오.

① costly ② pricy ③ low
④ bargain ⑤ expensive

17 How much is the discounted price of the headphones?

➡ _____

18 What acts as an anchor that fixes our thoughts about the price of an item?

➡ _____

19 위 글의 내용을 바르게 이해한 사람은?

① Ann: Like Nathan, I buy things just because they are famous among friends.

② Kirl: Nathan will buy the headphones whether or not they are on sale.

③ Lisa: The price acting as an anchor here is the discounted price.

④ Paul: The price mentioned later makes the price mentioned first seem more expensive.

⑤ Jake: The effect will be more influential if Nathan gets a 10 percent discount on the headphones.

[20~21] 다음 글을 읽고 물음에 답하시오.

Why do I want to buy what my friends bought?

Jeff goes to the shopping center and sees a pair of soccer shoes on display. He recognizes the shoes at a glance because more than half of the boys on his soccer team wear them. Although he already has many pairs of soccer shoes, he ends up buying another new pair.

We can use the "bandwagon effect" to explain Jeff's behavior. A bandwagon is a wagon in a parade that encourages people to jump aboard and enjoy the music. As more and more people get on the bandwagon, others are more likely to (A)_____. In this way, people tend to buy something just because other people have bought it.

20 위 글의 흐름상 빈칸 (A)에 들어갈 말로 가장 적절한 것은?

① get off or take off from it

② jump on or fight off each other

③ get on or follow it

④ move on and find other wagons

⑤ come along and get ahead of it

21 다음 중 밴드왜건 효과의 영향을 받은 사람은?

① Andrea: I bought another new sweater to complete my new look.

② Paul: I bought a yellow shirt to look fancier than other friends.

③ Chris: I bought a bike because it was on sale.

④ Dave: I bought several notes because I needed them.

⑤ Ethan: I bought a laptop computer because most of my friends have one.

[22~23] 다음 글을 읽고 물음에 답하시오.

What made Lisa search for new items immediately after buying a new coat?

(A) Soon after receiving the gift, he noticed that all of his furniture did not go well with his new gown.

(B) The "Diderot effect" may explain it. Denis Diderot, a French writer, received a new gown as a gift.

(C) So, he ended up replacing most of it. The Diderot effect, therefore, is the concept that purchasing a new item often leads to more unplanned purchases.

22 자연스러운 글이 되도록 (A)~(C)를 바르게 나열하시오.

➡ _____

23 위 글의 내용에 맞게 빈칸에 들어갈 말이 바르게 짝지어진 것은?

> The "Diderot effect" explains that there can be _____ because of _____.

① planned purchases – their expectancy

② unexpected expenditures – one new item

③ unplanned purchases – their greed

④ careful expenditures – their carefulness

⑤ unplanned explorations – one new item

Lesson

8

Wonders of Space Travel

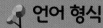 의사소통 기능

- 어떤 일이 실제로 가능한지 묻기
  A: Is it possible to lie down to sleep in space?
  B: Yes, it is.
- 이루어지기를 바라는 일 표현하기
  A: I wish I could have a pet robot.
  B: Me, too.

 언어 형식

- 가정법 과거
  If such wormholes **existed** in space, we **could get** to somewhere!

- 'with + 명사 + 분사'
  Wormholes may contain two mouths, **with a throat connecting** the two.

Words & Expressions

Key Words

- **achieve** [ətʃíːv] 동 달성하다, 성취하다
- **apply** [əplái] 동 적용하다, 응용하다
- **as** [əz] 접 ~(이)듯이, ~(이)다시피
- **astronaut** [ǽstrənɔ̀ːt] 명 우주 비행사
- **attach** [ətǽtʃ] 동 붙이다
- **bend** [bend] 동 굽히다, 구부리다
- **bottom** [bátəm] 명 맨 아랫부분, 바닥
- **celebrate** [séləbrèit] 동 축하하다
- **changeable** [tʃéindʒəbl] 형 바뀔 수 있는, 변덕스러운
- **connect** [kənékt] 동 연결되다, 이어지다
- **contain** [kəntéin] 동 ~이 들어 있다, 포함하다
- **cotton candy** 솜사탕
- **crush** [krʌʃ] 동 눌러 부수다, 찌부러뜨리다
- **detect** [kitékt] 동 감지하다, 발견하다
- **distance** [dístəns] 명 거리
- **dot** [dɑt] 명 점
- **eatable** [íːtəbl] 형 먹을 수 있는
- **eventually** [ivéntʃuəli] 부 결국
- **exist** [igzíst] 동 존재하다
- **exploration** [èkspləréiʃən] 명 탐사, 탐구
- **extend** [iksténd] 동 (팔, 다리를) 뻗다
- **gravity** [grǽvəti] 명 중력
- **impossible** [impásəbl] 형 불가능한
- **incorrect** [ìnkərékt] 형 부정확한, 사실이 아닌
- **infinite** [ínfənət] 형 무한한
- **instantly** [ínstəntli] 부 즉시
- **layer** [léiər] 명 층
- **lean** [liːn] 동 몸을 숙이다, 굽히다
- **lower** [lóuər] 동 낮추다
- **Mars** [mɑːrz] 명 화성
- **measure** [méʒər] 동 측정하다
- **ongoing** [angóuiŋ] 형 계속 진행 중인
- **passenger** [pǽsəndʒər] 명 승객, 탑승객
- **persistent** [pərsístənt] 형 끈질긴, 집요한, 지속적인
- **physics** [fíziks] 명 물리학
- **planet** [plǽnit] 명 행성
- **punch** [pʌntʃ] 동 구멍을 뚫다
- **researcher** [risə́ːrtʃər] 명 연구자, 조사자
- **root** [ruːt] 명 뿌리
- **shortcut** [ʃɔ́ːrtkət] 명 지름길
- **spaceship** [speisʃip] 명 우주선
- **sunrise** [sʌ́nraiz] 명 일출
- **surface** [sə́ːrfis] 명 표면
- **telescope** [téləskòup] 명 망원경
- **theory** [θíːəri] 명 이론, 학설
- **throat** [θrout] 명 목구멍
- **tough** [tʌf] 형 힘든, 어려운
- **unstable** [ənstéibəl] 형 불안정한
- **vast** [væst] 형 거대한, 광대한
- **waterless** [wɔ́ːtərlis] 형 물기 없는
- **weigh** [wei] 동 무게가 나가다
- **wipe** [waip] 동 닦다
- **worm** [wəːrm] 명 벌레
- **wormhole** [wə́ːrmhoul] 명 벌레 먹은 구멍, (우주의) 웜홀

Key Expressions

- **according to~** ~에 따르면
- **at first** 처음에는
- **at the bottom of ~** ~의 아래에
- **at the speed of ~** ~의 속도로
- **balance on ~** 위에서 균형을 잡다
- **be expected to+동사원형** ~가 …할 것으로 예상되다
- **billions of** 수십억의
- **different from** ~와 다른
- **far away from** ~에서 멀리 떨어져
- **figure out** ~을 알아내다, 생각해 내다
- **float around** 떠다니다
- **for a second** 잠시
- **in theory** 이론상으로는, 원칙상으로는
- **in the blink of an eye** 눈 깜박할 사이에
- **lie down** 눕다, 누워 있다
- **look back on** ~을 되돌아보다
- **match up** 맞추다
- **natural resources** 천연 자원
- **print out** (프린터로) 출력하다
- **such+a[an]+형용사+명사** 그렇게 ~한
- **too ~ to+동사원형** 너무 ~해서 …할 수 없다
- **Who knows?** 혹시 모르지. 어쩌면.

Word Power

※ 서로 비슷한 뜻을 가진 어휘

- □ **achieve** 달성하다, 성취하다 – **accomplish** 이루다, 성취하다
- □ **celebrate** 축하하다 – **commemorate** 기념하다, 축하하다
- □ **detect** 감지하다, 발견하다 – **discover** 발견하다, 알아채다
- □ **extend** (팔, 다리를) 뻗다 – **expand** 확대하다, 팽창하다
- □ **unstable** 불안정한 – **changeable** 변덕스러운

- □ **attach** 붙이다 – **stick** 붙이다
- □ **contain** 포함하다 – **include** 포함하다, 포함시키다
- □ **eatable** 먹을 수 있는 – **edible** 먹을 수 있는
- □ **persistent** 끈질긴, 지속적인 – **continuous** 끊임없는, 연속적인
- □ **vast** 거대한, 광대한 – **huge** 막대한, 거대한

※ 서로 반대의 뜻을 가진 어휘

- □ **attach** 붙이다 ↔ **detach** 떼다, 분리하다
- □ **connect** 연결되다, 이어지다 ↔ **disconnect** 연결을 끊다
- □ **impossible** 불가능한 ↔ **possible** 가능한
- □ **infinite** 무한한 ↔ **finite** 한정의, 유한의
- □ **unstable** 불안정한 ↔ **stable** 안정된

- □ **bottom** 맨 아랫부분, 바닥 ↔ **top** 꼭대기, 정상
- □ **eatable** 먹을 수 있는 ↔ **inedible** 먹을 수 없는
- □ **incorrect** 부정확한, 사실이 아닌 ↔ **correct** 맞는, 정확한
- □ **tough** 힘든, 어려운 ↔ **easy** 쉬운, 수월한
- □ **vast** 거대한, 광대한 ↔ **tiny** 아주 조그마한, 작은

※ 접두사 im-[in-]

- □ **im–** + **partial** → **impartial** 공정한
- □ **im–** + **possible** → **impossible** 불가능한

- □ **im–** + **patient** → **impatient** 안달하는
- □ **in–** + **active** → **inactive** 활발하지 않은, 소극적인

※ 접미사 -able

- □ **comfort** + **–able** → **comfortable** 편안한
- □ **account** + **–able** → **accountable** 셀 수 있는
- □ **desire** + **–able** → **desirable** 바람직한, 가치 있는
- □ **compare** + **–able** → **comparable** 비슷한, 비교할 만한

- □ **avail** + **–able** → **available** 사용가능한
- □ **reason** + **–able** → **reasonable** 합리적인
- □ **rely** + **–able** → **reliable** 신뢰할 만한

English Dictionary

- □ **achieve** 달성하다, 성취하다
  → to succeed in finishing something or reaching an aim, especially after a lot of work or effort
  특히 어떤 일이나 노력 후에 일을 끝내거나 목적을 달성하는 데 성공하다

- □ **connect** 연결되다, 이어지다
  → to join or be joined with something else
  다른 어떤 것과 합치거나 합쳐지다

- □ **detect** 감지하다, 발견하다
  → to notice something that is partly hidden or not clear, or to discover something, especially using a special method
  부분적으로 숨겨져 있거나 명확하지 않은 것을 알게 되거나 혹은 특히 특별한 방법을 통해 무언가를 발견하다

- □ **distance** 거리
  → the amount of space between two places
  두 장소 사이의 공간의 총계

- □ **exploration** 탐사, 탐구
  → the activity of searching and finding out about something
  어떤 것에 대하여 탐색하고 알아내는 활동

- □ **gravity** 중력
  → the force that attracts objects towards one another, especially the force that makes things fall to the ground
  물체를 서로 당기는 힘으로, 특히 사물을 땅으로 떨어지게 하는 힘

- □ **ongoing** 계속 진행 중인
  → continuing to exist or develop, or happening at the present moment
  현재 계속 존재하거나 전개되고 있는 혹은 일어나고 있는

- □ **planet** 행성
  → an extremely large, round mass of rock and metal, such as Earth, or of gas, such as Jupiter, that moves in a circular path around the sun or another star
  태양이나 다른 별 주위를 순환하는, 지구 같은 바위와 금속으로 이루어진 혹은 목성 같은 가스로 이루어진 광장히 크고 둥근 것

- □ **unstable** 불안정한
  → not solid and firm and therefore not strong, safe, or likely to last
  단단하거나 견고하지 않아서 강하거나 안전하거나 오래 지속될 것 같지 않는

- □ **vast** 거대한, 광대한
  → extremely big 굉장히 큰

01 다음 중 접두사 -in의 의미가 다른 하나를 고르시오.

① infinite   ② incorrect

③ insecure   ④ insight

⑤ inexpensive

02 다음 짝지어진 단어의 관계가 〈보기〉와 같은 것끼리 짝지어진 것을 고르시오.

┌─ 보기 ┐

vast – huge

ⓐ achieve – accomplish

ⓑ persistent – occasional

ⓒ tough – easy

ⓓ bottom – top

ⓔ attach – stick

① ⓐ, ⓑ   ② ⓑ, ⓒ   ③ ⓒ, ⓓ
④ ⓓ, ⓔ   ⑤ ⓐ, ⓔ

03 다음 밑줄 친 부분의 의미로 알맞지 않은 것은?

① A wormhole can connect two different universes. ((우주의) 웜홀)

② There are many theories about why the dinosaurs went extinct. (이론, 학설)

③ They stick a tube into a water pack, and drink it. (막대기)

④ Every passenger must wear a seatbelt. (승객)

⑤ Earth is the third closest planet to the sun. (행성)

04 빈칸 (A)~(C)에 들어갈 말이 바르게 짝지어진 것을 고르시오.

• How is life in space different (A)_____ that on Earth?

• (B)_____ theory, wormholes exist.

• What did Einstein figure (C)_____ about space and time?

	(A)	(B)	(C)
①	in	In	of
②	in	About	out
③	from	In	out
④	from	About	of
⑤	from	On	of

05 다음 문장의 빈칸을 〈보기〉에 있는 어휘로 채울 수 없는 것을 고르시오.

┌─ 보기 ┐

bend   connect   detect   punch

① Beetles _____ their way by the stars.

② The point of SNS is to _____ with other people.

③ You should _____ your back to stretch your muscles.

④ This belt is too big, so I'll _____ an extra hole in it.

⑤ Instant noodles _____ a lot of salt.

01 다음 빈칸에 공통으로 들어갈 접미사를 쓰시오.

> • The food is eat_____ but not good.
> • The rules are very change_____.

02 다음 〈보기〉에서 알맞은 단어를 골라 빈칸에 쓰시오. (형태 변화 가능, 한 단어는 한 번만 사용 가능.)

> ┤ 보기 ├
> bottom   dot   layer   surface

(1) You can see a small black dot on the sun's _____.

(2) Mom removed the outer _____ of the onion.

(3) Thanks to their beaks, dolphins can hunt for fish at the _____ of the sea.

(4) My new skirt was blue with white _____.

03 다음 주어진 우리말에 맞게 빈칸을 채우시오. (철자가 주어진 경우 주어진 철자로 시작할 것.)

(1) 일기예보에 따르면 오늘 밤에는 기온이 영하로 내려간다고 한다.
➡ _____ the weather forecast, it'll freeze tonight.

(2) 우리 집은 공항에서 멀리 떨어져 있다.
➡ My home is f_____ a_____ f_____ an airport.

(3) 이 열기구를 타면, 너는 이 도시 전체를 떠다닐 수 있다.
➡ If you take this hot-air balloon, you can _____ the whole city.

(4) 유성은 눈 깜박할 사이에 떨어진다.
➡ Shooting stars fall _____.

(5) 그녀는 곧 그녀의 유럽 순회공연을 되돌아볼 필요가 있다.
➡ She needs to _____ her European tour soon.

04 다음 빈칸에 공통으로 들어갈 말을 쓰시오.

> • Even _____ the Hunminjeongum was mentioned in many books, no one knows where it really was.
> • _____ we eat the food before he comes back, he will be mad.

05 다음 빈칸에 들어갈 말을 〈보기〉에서 찾아 쓰시오.

> ┤ 보기 ├
> changeable   eatable   impossible
> incorrect

(1) The food at that restaurant isn't _____.

(2) You can't pass the test with so many _____ answers.

(3) It is _____ to live without water.

(4) The weather in London is very _____.

Conversation

① 어떤 일이 실제로 가능한지 묻기

> **A:** Is it possible to lie down to sleep in space? 우주에서 누워 자는 게 가능할까요?
>
> **B:** Yes, it is. Astronauts attach their sleeping bag to a wall. 그럼요. 우주비행사들은 침낭을 벽에 붙여요.

■ 어떤 일이 실제로 가능한지 묻는 표현으로 'Is it possible to ~?'를 쓸 수 있다. 같은 표현으로 'Are we able to ~?', 'Can we actually ~?', 'Is there a possibility that 주어+동사 ~?', 'Would it be possible ~?' 등이 있다.

■ Is it possible for the astronauts to lie down to sleep in space?
= Are the astronauts able to lie down to sleep in space?
= Can the astronauts actually lie down to sleep in space?
= Is there a possibility that the astronauts lie down to sleep in space?
= Would it be possible for the astronauts to lie down to sleep in space?

어떤 일이 실제로 가능한지 묻기

- Is it possible to 동사원형 ~?
- Are 주어 able to 동사원형 ~?
- Can 주어 (actually) 동사 ~?
- Is there a possibility that 주어+동사 ~?
- Would it be possible ~?

핵심 Check

1. 다음 대화의 밑줄 친 부분과 바꿔 쓸 수 <u>없는</u> 것은?

> **A:** <u>Is it possible to drink water in space?</u>
> **B:** Yes, it is. Astronauts stick a tube into a water pack and drink it.

① Are astronauts able to drink water in space?

② Can astronauts actually drink water in space?

③ Is there a possibility that astronauts drink water in space?

④ Would it be possible for astronauts to drink water in space?

⑤ Could astronauts drink water in space?

② 이루어지기를 바라는 일 표현하기

> **A:** I wish I could have a pet robot. 애완 로봇이 있으면 참 좋겠다.
> **B:** Me, too. I'm sure that's every teenager's wish. 나도 그래. 그건 모든 10대들의 꿈일 거야.

■ 어떤 일이 이루어지기를 바라는 표현으로 'I wish I could ~.'를 쓸 수 있다. 이는 가능성이 낮거나 이루어지기 힘든 일에 대해 '할 수 있으면 좋겠다'라는 바람의 의미로 쓰인다. 같은 표현으로 '~ would be a dream come true.', 'How I wish I could ~!', 'It would be great if I could ~.' 등이 있다.

■ I wish I could have a pet robot.
 = Having a pet robot would be a dream come true.
 = It would be great if I could have a pet robot.
 = How I wish I could have a pet robot!

이루어지기를 바라는 일 표현하기

- I wish I could ~.
- ~ would be a dream come true.
- It would be great if 주어 could ~.

■ I wish I could ~. vs. I hope I can ~.
 두 표현은 바라는 일을 나타내는 비슷한 의미로 이해할 수 있지만 'I wish I could ~.'는 가정법, 즉 실제로는 일어날 수 없는 일에 대한 바람과 소망을 나타내는 반면에, 'I hope I can ~.'은 실제로 일어날 가능성이 있는 일에 대한 바람과 소망을 나타낸다는 차이가 있다.

- I wish I could live up to 200 years old.
- I hope I will be able to buy that house some day.

핵심 Check

2. 다음 대화의 밑줄 친 부분을 영작한 문장으로 적절하지 <u>않은</u> 것은?

> **A:** <u>난 수학 천재가 되었으면 좋겠어.</u>
> **B:** Me, too. I'm sure you could if you study hard.

① Being a math genius would be a dream come true.
② It would be great if I could be a math genius.
③ I thought I could be a math genius.
④ I wish I could be a math genius.
⑤ How I wish I could be a math genius!

Listen & Talk 1 A-1

M: Welcome back to Earth, Irene. What was your favorite part about ❶ being in the space station?

W: I could see a beautiful ❷sunrise 16 times a day. It was great.

M: ❸Is it possible to see the sunrise several times a day in space?

W: Yes, ❹it's possible because we moved around Earth every 90 minutes in the station.

M: Wow, that's amazing!

M: 지구에 돌아오신 것을 환영합니다, Irene 씨. 우주 정거장에서 보낸 시간 중 최고의 기억이 무엇인가요?

W: 저는 하루에 16번씩 아름다운 일출을 볼 수 있었어요. 그것은 굉장했죠.

M: 우주에서는 하루에 일출을 여러 번 보는 게 가능한가요?

W: 네, 가능해요. 왜냐하면 우주 정거장이 지구 주위를 90분마다 돌았거든요.

M: 와, 놀랍네요!

❶ 전치사 about 다음에는 명사나 동명사가 올 수 있다. be동사 다음에 장소를 나타내는 부사구가 오면 '있다, 존재하다'의 의미로 해석한다.

❷ sunrise: 일출(↔ sunset: 일몰)

❸ 'Is it possible to 동사원형 ~?'은 '~하는 것이 가능한가요?'의 의미로 상대방에게 가능성을 묻는 표현이다. possible 대신에 likely, probable을 사용할 수 있다. 같은 의미로 'Are 주어 able to 동사원형 ~?', 'Can 주어 (actually) 동사 ~?', 'Is there a possibility that 주어+동사 ~?', 'Would it be possible ~?' 등이 있다.

❹ 'It is possible[likely/probably] ~.' 등을 사용해 가능성 정도를 표현할 수 있다.

Check(√) True or False

(1) Irene has been to the space station.   T ☐ F ☐

(2) At the space station, Irene could see a sunrise only twice a day.   T ☐ F ☐

Listen & Talk 2 A-1

M: Look at these colorful pictures of the universe.

W: Oh, ❶they're beautiful. ❷I wish I could see Earth from space with my own eyes.

M: Actually, you can ❸do that at the National Youth Space Center.

W: Really?

M: Yeah, you can use the VR glasses. ❹I heard that you ❺feel like you are actually in space!

M: 이 다채로운 색깔의 우주 사진들을 좀 봐.

W: 오, 그것들은 아름다워. 내가 지구를 우주에서 직접 내 눈으로 볼 수 있으면 좋을 텐데.

M: 사실 넌 국립 청소년 우주 센터에서 그걸 해 볼 수 있어.

W: 정말?

M: 응, 가상 현실(VR) 안경을 써 볼 수 있거든. 실제로 우주에 있는 것 같은 기분이 든다고 들었어!

❶ they는 앞 문장의 'these colorful pictures of the universe(다채로운 색깔의 우주 사진들)'을 의미한다.

❷ 'I wish I could ~.'는 '내가 ~할 수 있으면 좋겠다.'의 뜻으로 현재 사실과 반대되거나 현재 이룰 수 없는 소망을 말할 때 사용한다. '~ would be a dream come true.', 'It would be great if 주어 could ~.'등으로 바꿔 쓸 수 있다.

❸ do that은 앞 문장의 'see Earth from space with your own eyes'를 받는다.

❹ 'I heard that 주어+동사 ~.'는 '~에 대해 들었다'의 뜻으로 알고 있거나 들은 것에 대해 말할 때 쓰는 표현이다.

❺ feel like 다음에는 동명사나 절이 올 수 있다. 여기서는 주어와 동사가 있는 절의 형식이 like 다음에 왔다. '~ 같이 느끼다, ~ 같은 기분이 든다'의 의미이다.

Check(√) True or False

(3) They are looking at the pictures of the universe.   T ☐ F ☐

(4) People can see Earth from space by using the VR glasses at the National Youth Space Center.   T ☐ F ☐

Listen & Talk 1 A-2

M: Irene, what was the best food ❶you ate in the space station?

W: Hmm... . ❷We grew some vegetables and ate them every day. They were ❸pretty fresh and tasty!

M: Wow, ❹is it possible to grow vegetables in the space station?

W: Yes. ❺Since there's no gravity in space, we had to grow them in special bags. The bags ❻helped the roots to grow.

M: How interesting!

M: Irene 씨, 우주 정거장에서 드셨던 것 중 최고의 음식은 무엇이었나요?

W: 음… . 우리는 채소를 키워서 매일 그걸 먹었어요. 그것은 매우 신선하고 맛있었어요!

M: 와, 우주 정거장에서 채소를 키우는 것이 가능한가요?

W: 네. 우주에는 중력이 없기 때문에, 우리는 그것을 특수한 봉지 안에서 키워야 했어요. 그 봉지는 뿌리가 자라는 데 도움을 줬어요.

M: 참 흥미롭네요!

❶ the best food와 you ate 사이에 목적격 관계대명사 which나 that이 생략되어 있다.

❷ grew와 ate는 접속사 and로 연결되어 있다. them은 vegetables를 의미한다.

❸ pretty는 부사로 '매우'의 의미이며 형용사인 fresh(신선한)와 tasty(맛있는)를 수식하고 있다.

❹ 'Is it possible to 동사원형 ～?'은 무언가가 가능한지 여부를 묻는 표현으로 'Is it possible that 주어+동사 ～?'로 바꿔 쓸 수 있다.

❺ since는 이유의 접속사로 '～ 때문에'라고 해석하며 because나 as로 바꿔 쓸 수 있다.

❻ 'help+목적어+목적격보어'는 '～에게 …하도록 도움을 주다'이며 목적어와 목적격보어의 관계가 능동일 때 목적격보어에는 동사원형이나 to부정사가 올 수 있다.

Check(√) True or False

(5) In the space staion, Irene couldn't eat vegetables at all.   T ☐ F ☐

(6) It was possible that Irene grow vegetables in the space station.   T ☐ F ☐

Listen & Talk 2 C

A: ❶I wish I could have a pet robot.

B: Me, too. ❷I'm sure that's every teenager's wish.

A: 난 애완 로봇을 가질 수 있으면 좋을 텐데.

B: 나도. 나는 그것이 모든 십대들의 바람이라고 확신해.

❶ 현재 사실과 반대되는 일에 대한 소망이나 유감을 나타낼 때 'I wish+주어+could+동사원형 ～.'으로 쓰며 '～라면 좋을 텐데'라고 해석한다. 'I wish+주어+동사의 과거형 ～.'으로도 나타내며 be동사는 보통 were를 쓴다. 바꿔 쓸 수 있는 표현으로 '～ would be a dream come true.', 'It would be great if 주어 could ～.' 등이 있다.

❷ '나는 ～라고 확신해.'라는 뜻으로 어떤 일에 대한 확신을 표현할 때, 'I'm sure (that) ～.' 또는 'I'm sure about ～.'라고 한다. 접속사 that 다음에는 절이, 전치사 about 다음에는 명사(구)가 오고, that은 생략할 수 있다.

Check(√) True or False

(7) A wants to have a pet robot.   T ☐ F ☐

(8) B isn't interested in a pet robot.   T ☐ F ☐

Listen & Talk 1 B

M: ❶Have you heard that NASA is going to send a 3D printer into space?

W: They're going to send a 3D printer into space? Why?

M: ❷I've heard that the 3D printer will ❸be used to print out food for astronauts.

W: ❹Is it possible to print out food using a 3D printer?

M: Yes, it's possible. It can print out a fresh pizza in ❺less than five minutes.

W: Really? ❻I wonder what it would taste like.

❶ 'Have you heard that 주어+동사 ∼?'는 '∼를 들어 본 적 있니?'의 의미로 알고 있는지 묻는 표현이다.

❷ 'I've heard that ∼.'은 '∼에 대해 들었다.'의 뜻으로 알고 있거나 들은 것에 대해 말할 때 쓰는 표현이다.

❸ be used to+동사원형: ∼하기 위해 사용되다 print out: (프린터로) 출력하다 astronaut: 우주 비행사

❹ 'Is it possible to+동사원형 ∼?'은 '∼하는 것이 가능한가요?'라는 의미로 가능 여부를 물을 때 사용하는 표현이다.

❺ less than: ∼보다 적은

❻ 궁금증을 표현할 때 '∼를 궁금해 하다'라는 의미를 가진 동사 wonder를 이용하여 'I wonder ∼.'라고 말한다. I wonder 뒤에는 간접의문의 어순인 '의문사+주어+동사'를 사용한다.

Listen & Talk 1 C

A: ❶Is it possible to lie down to sleep in space?

B: Yes, astronauts ❷attach their sleeping bag to a wall.

A: Sounds interesting. Life in space is so ❸different from ❹that on Earth.

❶ 'Is it possible to+동사원형 ∼?'은 무언가가 가능한지 여부를 묻는 표현이다. lie down: 눕다, 누워 있다

❷ attach A to B: A를 B에 붙이다

❸ different from: ∼와 다른

❹ that은 life를 받는 지시대명사이다.

Listen & Talk 2 B

W: Look at this man, Jake. He lived in space for one year.

M: It ❶must have been tough for him.

W: Right, but you know what's interesting? He grew 2 inches ❷while in space.

M: Really? How is that possible?

W: I'm not sure, but maybe it's because there's no gravity in space.

M: That's so cool. ❸I wish I could live in space. That way, I could become taller.

W: ❹I'm sure there are other ways ❺to become taller than going to space.

❶ 'must have+과거분사'는 과거 사실에 대한 강한 추측을 나타내는 표현으로 '∼이었음에 틀림이 없다'라는 의미를 가진다.

❷ while (he was) in space로 접속사 while 다음에 '주어와 be동사'가 생략되어 있다.

❸ 'I wish I could ∼.'는 소망이나 바람을 나타낼 때 사용하는 표현으로 '내가 ∼할 수 있다면 좋을 텐데.'라는 뜻이다. 'I wish+가정법 과거'의 형태로 현재 사실과 반대되는 소망을 나타낸다.

❹ 어떤 일에 대해 확실한 의견이 있을 때 'I'm sure (that) 주어+동사 ∼.'로 말할 수 있다.

❺ to become은 other ways를 수식하고 있으므로 '키가 더 커지는 다른 방법들'로 해석한다. (to부정사의 형용사적 용법)

Communication Step A

W: Hello, everyone, welcome to *All about Movies*! Today, we're going to talk about the top three things from movies ❶that we wish were real.

M: Let's start with number three, the flying skateboard from *Back to the Future*.

W: It's a cool item. ❷I wish I could have a flying skateboard.

M: Actually, ❸I read somewhere that this is not entirely impossible.

W: Really? ❹Is it actually possible to fly on a skateboard?

M: Yes. Some companies have ❺applied physics to create flying skateboards.

❶ that은 주격 관계대명사로 선행사는 the top three things from movies이다.

❷ 현재 사실과 반대되는 일에 대한 소망이나 유감을 나타낼 때 'I wish+주어+could+동사원형 ∼.'으로 쓰며 '∼라면 좋을 텐데'라고 해석한다. 'I wish+주어+동사의 과거형 ∼.'으로도 나타내며 be동사는 보통 were를 쓴다.

❸ somewhere는 부사로 '어딘가에서'의 의미이며, read의 목적어로 that절이 사용되었다.

❹ 'Is it possible to+동사원형 ∼?'은 '∼하는 것은 가능한가요?'라는 의미로 가능 여부를 물을 때 사용하는 표현이다.

❺ apply: 적용하다, 응용하다

● 다음 우리말과 일치하도록 빈칸에 알맞은 말을 쓰시오.

Listen & Talk 1 A

1. M: Welcome back _____ Earth, Irene. _____ was your favorite part about _____ in the space station?

   W: I _____ _____ a beautiful sunrise 16 _____ _____ _____. It was great.

   M: _____ _____ _____ _____ _____ the sunrise several times _____ _____ in space?

   W: Yes, it's _____ _____ we moved around Earth every 90 minutes in the station.

   M: Wow, that's _____!

2. M: Irene, what was _____ _____ _____ _____ _____ in the space station?

   W: Hmm…. We _____ some vegetables and _____ them every day. They were pretty _____ _____ _____!

   M: Wow, _____ _____ _____ _____ _____ _____ vegetables in the space station?

   W: Yes. _____ there's no gravity in space, we _____ grow them in special bags. The bags _____ _____ _____ grow.

   M: How interesting!

Listen & Talk 1 B

M: _____ _____ _____ _____ NASA is going to _____ a 3D printer into space?

W: They're going to send a 3D printer _____ _____? Why?

M: _____ _____ _____ _____ the 3D printer _____ _____ _____ _____ _____ _____ food for astronauts.

W: Is it _____ _____ _____ food using a 3D printer?

M: Yes, it's possible. It can print out a fresh pizza _____ _____ _____ five minutes.

W: Really? I wonder _____ _____ _____ _____ _____.

해석

1. M: 지구에 돌아오신 것을 환영합니다, Irene 씨. 우주 정거장에서 보낸 시간 중 최고의 기억이 무엇인가요?
   W: 저는 하루에 16번씩 아름다운 일출을 볼 수 있었어요. 그것은 굉장했죠.
   M: 우주에서는 하루에 일출을 여러 번 보는 게 가능한가요?
   W: 네, 가능해요. 왜냐하면 우주 정거장이 지구 주위를 90분마다 돌았거든요.
   M: 와, 놀랍네요!

2. M: Irene 씨, 우주 정거장에서 드셨던 것 중 최고의 음식은 무엇이었나요?
   W: 음… . 우리는 채소를 키워서 매일 그걸 먹었어요. 그것은 매우 신선하고 맛있었어요!
   M: 와, 우주 정거장에서 채소를 키우는 것이 가능한가요?
   W: 네. 우주에는 중력이 없기 때문에, 우리는 그것을 특수한 봉지 안에서 키워야 했어요. 그 봉지는 뿌리가 자라는 데 도움을 줬어요.
   M: 참 흥미롭네요!

M: 나사(NASA)가 3D 프린터를 우주로 보낼 거라는 이야기 들어 봤니?
W: 그들이 3D 프린터를 우주로 보낸다고? 왜?
M: 우주 비행사들이 먹을 음식을 출력하는 데 3D 프린터가 쓰일 거라고 들었어.
W: 3D 프린터를 이용해 음식을 출력하는 게 가능해?
M: 응, 가능해. 그것은 신선한 피자를 5분도 안 되어서 출력해 낼 수 있어.
W: 정말? 그게 어떤 맛일지 궁금하다.

Listen & Talk 2 A

1. M: Look at these colorful pictures of the universe.

   W: Oh, they're beautiful. _____ _____ _____ _____ Earth _____ space _____ _____ _____ _____.

   M: Actually, you can _____ _____ at the National Youth Space Center.

   W: Really?

   M: Yeah, you can use the VR glasses. I heard _____ you feel like you are actually _____ _____!

2. W: What are you watching?

   M: It's a documentary about life in space. Everything _____ so _____.

   W: Yes, _____ _____ there's _____ _____ in space.

   M: Right. _____ _____ _____ _____ float around like an _____!

   W: Really? I don't. It _____ _____.

Listen & Talk 2 B

W: Look at this man, Jake. He _____ _____ space for one year.

M: It _____ _____ _____ _____ for him.

W: Right, but you know what's interesting? He grew 2 inches _____ _____ _____.

M: Really? How is that _____?

W: I'm not sure, but maybe _____ _____ there's no _____ in space.

M: That's so cool. _____ _____ _____ _____ space. That way, I could _____ _____.

W: _____ _____ _____ are other _____ _____ _____ _____ than going to space.

해석

1. M: 이 다채로운 색깔의 우주 사진들을 좀 봐.
   W: 오, 그것들은 아름다워. 내가 지구를 우주에서 직접 내 눈으로 볼 수 있으면 좋을 텐데.
   M: 사실 넌 국립 청소년 우주 센터에서 그걸 해 볼 수 있어.
   W: 정말?
   M: 응, 가상 현실(VR) 안경을 써 볼 수 있거든. 실제로 우주에 있는 것 같은 기분이 든다고 들었어!

2. W: 너는 무엇을 보고 있니?
   M: 우주에서의 삶에 관한 다큐멘터리야. 모든 것이 너무 달라 보여.
   W: 응, 왜냐하면 우주에는 중력이 없기 때문이지.
   M: 맞아. 나도 우주 비행사처럼 떠다닐 수 있다면 좋을 텐데!
   W: 정말이니? 나는 아니야. 그건 불편해 보여.

W: 이 남자 좀 봐, Jake. 그는 우주에서 1년 동안 살았어.
M: 그는 분명히 힘들었을 거야.
W: 맞아, 하지만 흥미로운 게 뭔 줄 아니? 그가 우주에 있는 동안 키가 2인치 자랐어.
M: 정말? 어떻게 그게 가능해?
W: 확실하진 않지만, 아마 우주에 중력이 없기 때문일 거야.
M: 정말 멋지다. 내가 우주에서 살 수 있으면 좋을 텐데. 그러면 난 키가 더 커질 수 있을 텐데.
W: 우주에 가는 것 말고 키가 더 커지는 다른 방법들이 있을 거라고 확신해.

Communication Step A

W: Hello, everyone, welcome to *All about Movies*! Today, we're going _____ _____ _____ the top three things from movies _____ _____ _____ _____ _____ .

M: Let's _____ _____ number three, the flying skateboard from *Back to the Future*.

W: It's a cool item. _____ _____ _____ _____ _____ a flying skateboard.

M: Actually, I read _____ _____ this is not entirely impossible.

W: Really? _____ _____ _____ _____ _____ _____ on a skateboard?

M: Yes. Some companies _____ _____ physics to create flying skateboards.

Wrap Up

1. W: Mr. Scott, did you _____ your trip to space?

   M: Yes, it was _____ _____ _____ of my life.

   W: Can you tell us _____ _____ _____ _____ _____ during your trip?

   M: I flew in space _____ _____ and saw our blue planet, Earth.

   W: _____ _____ _____ _____ _____ _____ in space _____ _____ ?

   M: Yes, I _____ _____ to a special line, so it was safe.

   W: Sounds fantastic!

2. M: Hey, Cindy. I _____ _____ you went to the National Space Center last weekend. _____ was it?

   W: It was great, Chris. I experienced _____ _____ and astronauts' space life.

   M: Sounds fun. Did you meet _____ _____ in person?

   W: Yes, and I heard about their _____ stories.

   M: Oh, I wish I could become an _____ like them and _____ _____ .

W: 안녕하세요, 여러분, '영화에 대한 모든 것(All about Movies)'에 오신 것을 환영합니다! 오늘 우리는 실제로 가능하기를 바라는 영화 속 물건들 중에서 상위 세 개에 관해 이야기해 보려고 합니다.

M: 우선 3위부터 시작하자면, '백 투 더 퓨처'에 나온, 날아다니는 스케이트보드입니다.

W: 멋진 물건이에요. 제가 날아다니는 스케이트보드를 가질 수 있다면 좋을 텐데요.

M: 사실, 전 그것이 전혀 불가능한 일은 아니라고 어딘가에서 읽었어요.

W: 정말요? 스케이트보드를 타고 날아다니는 것이 실제로 가능해요?

M: 네. 몇몇 회사들이 날아다니는 스케이트보드를 만들기 위해 물리학을 적용했어요.

1. W: Scott 씨, 우주로의 여행은 즐거우셨나요?

   M: 네, 그것은 제 인생 최고의 경험이었어요.

   W: 여행 중 어떤 부분이 최고였는지 말씀해 주실 수 있나요?

   M: 혼자 우주를 날아서 우리의 푸른 행성인 지구를 보았어요.

   W: 우주에서 혼자 나는 것이 가능한가요?

   M: 네, 제 자신을 특수한 선에 연결해서 그건 안전했어요.

   W: 환상적이네요!

2. M: 안녕, Cindy. 지난 주말에 네가 국립 우주 센터에 갔다고 들었어. 어땠어?

   W: 굉장히 좋았어, Chris. 난 무중력 상태와 우주 비행사들의 우주 생활을 경험했어.

   M: 재미있었겠다. 너는 직접 진짜 우주인을 만났어?

   W: 응, 그리고 나는 그들의 모험 이야기를 들었어.

   M: 오, 나는 그들처럼 우주인이 돼서 화성을 탐험하고 싶어.

01 다음 중 의도하는 바가 나머지 넷과 <u>다른</u> 하나를 고르시오.

① I wish I could go to the same high school as my friends.

② If I go to the high school, I will be able to go to the same high school as my friends.

③ Going to the same high school as my friends would be a dream come true.

④ How I wish I could go to the same high school as my friends!

⑤ It would be great if I could go to the same high school as my friends.

[02~03] 다음 대화를 읽고 물음에 답하시오.

M: Welcome back to Earth, Irene. What was your favorite part about being in the space station?

W: I could see a beautiful sunrise 16 times a day. It was great.

M: (A)_____ see the sunrise several times a day in space?

W: Yes. (B)_____

M: Wow, that's amazing!

02 빈칸 (A)에 알맞은 말을 고르시오.

① Is it possible that   ② Is it necessary to

③ Is it possible to   ④ Is it probably that

⑤ Is it okay if

03 빈칸 (B)에 알맞은 말을 고르시오..

① Astronauts use special toothpaste, and drink it after brushing their teeth.

② Since there's no gravity in space, it's possible.

③ It's possible. It can print out a fresh pizza in less than five minutes.

④ It's possible because we grow vegetables in the space station.

⑤ It's possible because we moved around Earth every 90 minutes in the station.

[01~02] 다음 대화를 읽고 물음에 답하시오.

M: Look at these colorful pictures of the universe.
W: Oh, they're beautiful. I wish (A)_____ _____.
M: Actually, you can do that at the National Youth Space Center.
W: Really?
M: Yeah, you can use the VR glasses. I heard that you feel like you are actually in space!

01 빈칸 (A)에 알맞은 말을 고르시오.

① I can see other pictures of space
② you could use the VR glasses
③ I could see Earth from space with my own eyes
④ you could live in space
⑤ I can be good at all kinds of sports

02 위 대화를 읽고 답할 수 없는 질문을 모두 고르시오.

① Has the man been to the National Youth Space Center?
② What does the woman wish to do?
③ When are they going to the National Youth Space Center?
④ What are they looking at?
⑤ Where can the woman feel like she is actually in the space?

03 다음 중 짝지어진 대화가 어색한 것은?

① A: I wish I had a map of the area.
   B: Don't worry. There is an information desk over there.
② A: I wish I could have the robotic taxi from the movie *Total Recall*.
   B: Actually, I read somewhere that this is not entirely impossible.
③ A: I'm going to visit the museum this Saturday.
   B: I wish I could go there with you.
④ A: What would you do if you made a lot of money?
   B: It is not possible to make a lot of money.
⑤ A: I wish I could see the launch of satellite in person.
   B: So do I.

[04~05] 다음 대화를 읽고 물음에 답하시오.

A: (A)_____? (possible, space, wash, in, it, body, is, their, to)
B: Yes, astronauts use waterless soap, and wipe their body with a wet towel.
A: Sounds interesting. Life in space is so different (B)_____ that on Earth.

서답형
04 빈칸 (A)를 괄호 안에 주어진 단어를 알맞게 배열하여 채우시오.

➡ _____

서답형
05 빈칸 (B)에 알맞은 전치사를 쓰시오.

➡ _____

06 밑줄 친 ⓐ~ⓔ 중 흐름상 어색한 것을 고르시오.

> W: What are you watching?
> M: ⓐIt's a documentary about life in space. ⓑEverything seems so different.
> W: ⓒYes, it's because there's no gravity in space.
> M: Right. ⓓI wish I could float around like an astronaut!
> W: Really? I don't. ⓔIt looks comfortable.

① ⓐ   ② ⓑ   ③ ⓒ   ④ ⓓ   ⑤ ⓔ

[07~09] 다음 대화를 읽고 물음에 답하시오.

> W: Look at this man, Jake. He lived in space for one year.
> M: It (A)_____ tough for him.
> W: Right, but you know what's interesting? He grew 2 inches while in space.
> M: Really? How is that possible?
> W: I'm not sure, but maybe it's because there's no gravity in space.
> M: That's so cool. I wish I could live in space. That way, I could become taller.
> W: I'm sure there are other ways (B)_____ _____.

07 빈칸 (A)에 알맞은 말을 고르시오.

① must have been
② must be
③ should have been
④ should be
⑤ might be

08 빈칸 (B)에 알맞은 말을 고르시오.

① to live in space alone
② to become a famous star
③ to make a spacecraft
④ to become taller than going to space
⑤ to do space exploration

09 대화의 내용과 일치하지 <u>않는</u> 것을 고르시오.

① 남자와 여자가 보고 있는 남자는 우주에서 1년 동안 살았다.
② 남자는 키가 2인치 이상 더 크고 싶어한다.
③ 우주에서 1년 동안 산 남자는 키가 더 커졌다.
④ 남자는 키가 더 커지고 싶어서 우주에서 살기를 바라고 있다.
⑤ 여자는 우주에 있는 동안 키가 커졌던 이유를 중력이 없기 때문이라고 생각하고 있다.

[10~11] 다음 대화를 읽고 물음에 답하시오.

> W: Mr. Scott, did you enjoy your trip to space?
> M: Yes, it was the best experience of my life.
> W: Can you tell us what was the best part during your trip?
> M: I flew in space by myself and (A)_____ (see) our blue planet, Earth.
> W: (B) 우주에서 혼자 나는 것이 가능한가요? (possible, yourself, fly, by, it, space, is, in, to)
> M: Yes, I attached myself to a special line, so it was safe.
> W: Sounds fantastic!

서답형
10 다음 괄호 안의 단어를 문맥에 맞게 고쳐 빈칸 (A)를 채우시오.

➡ _____

서답형
11 밑줄 친 (B)의 우리말과 일치하도록 괄호 안에 주어진 단어를 알맞게 배열하시오.

➡ _____

[01~04] 다음 대화를 읽고 물음에 답하시오.

M: Irene, (A)_____? (우주 정거장에서 드셨던 것 중 최고의 음식은 무엇이었나요? was, ate, the, the, station, what, space, food, in, you, best)

W: Hmm... . We grew some vegetables and ate them every day. They were pretty fresh and tasty!

M: Wow, is it (B)_____ to grow vegetables in the space station?

W: Yes. Since there's no gravity in space, we had to grow (a)them in special bags. The bags helped the roots (C)_____(grow).

M: How interesting!

01 빈칸 (A)를 우리말에 맞춰 괄호 안에 주어진 단어를 알맞게 배열하시오.

➡ _____

_____

02 위 대화의 내용에 맞게 빈칸 (B)에 알맞은 말을 주어진 철자로 시작하여 쓰시오.

➡ p_____

03 빈칸 (C)를 괄호 안의 단어를 활용하여 채우시오.

➡ _____

04 밑줄 친 (a)them이 가리키는 것을 찾아 쓰시오.

➡ _____

05 밑줄 친 우리말을 주어진 단어를 이용해 영작하시오.

M: Look at these colorful pictures of the universe.

W: Oh, they're beautiful. 내가 지구를 우주에서 직접 내 눈으로 볼 수 있으면 좋을 텐데. (own, could, wish, I, with)

M: Actually, you can do that at the National Youth Space Center.

W: Really?

M: Yeah, you can use the VR glasses. I heard that you feel like you are actually in space!

➡ _____

_____

[06~07] 다음 대화를 읽고 물음에 답하시오.

M: Have you heard that NASA is going to send a 3D printer into space?

W: They're going to send a 3D printer into space? Why?

M: I've heard that the 3D printer will be used (A)_____ out food for astronauts.

W: (B) 3D 프린터를 이용해 음식을 출력하는 게 가능해? (print, using, possible, is, to)

M: Yes, it's possible. It can print out a fresh pizza in less than five minutes.

W: Really? I wonder what it would taste like.

06 빈칸 (A)를 print를 활용하여 채우시오.

➡ _____

07 밑줄 친 (B)의 우리말을 주어진 단어를 이용해 영작하시오.

➡ _____

Grammar

① 가정법 과거

If such wormholes **existed** in space, we **could get** to somewhere! 그런 웜홀들이 우주에 존재한다면, 우리는 어딘가에 빠르게 도달할 수 있을 텐데!

- '만약 ~한다면 …할 텐데'라는 의미로, 현재 사실을 반대로 가정하거나 실현 가능성이 없는 일에 대해서 가정할 때 쓰며, 'If+주어+were/동사의 과거형 ~, 주어+조동사의 과거형(would/should/could/might)+동사원형 …'의 형태로 쓴다. 가정법이라는 표시로 if절에 과거 동사를 사용할 뿐이며, 가정법 '과거'라고 해서 과거의 일에 반대되는 가정이 아님을 유의한다.

- **가정법 과거 문장은 현재시제의 직설법으로 바꿔 쓸 수 있다.**
  - If I **knew** Susan's phone number, I **could** call her. 내가 Susan의 전화번호를 안다면 그녀에게 전화할 텐데. (가정법 과거, 현재 사실의 반대 가정)
    = As I **don't** know Susan's phone number, I **can't** call her. 내가 Susan의 전화번호를 모르기 때문에 그녀에게 전화를 걸 수 없다.
    cf. If I **know** Susan's phone number, I **can** call her. 내가 Susan의 전화번호를 안다면, 그녀에게 전화를 걸 수 있다. (조건문, 사실)

- 'be' 동사는 주어의 인칭 및 수와 무관하게 'were'를 쓰지만, 구어체에서는 주어가 'I' 또는 3인칭 단수인 경우 'was'를 쓰기도 한다.
  - If I **were[was]** a bird, I'**d** fly to you. 내가 새라면 너한테 날아가련만.

- **가정법의 다양한 표현**
  - If there **were** no air, we **could** not live even a single day. 공기가 없다면, 우리는 단 하루도 살 수 없을 텐데. (가정법)
    = If it **were** not for air, we **could** not live even a single day.
    = **Were** it not for air, we **could** not live even a single day. (If 생략 후 도치)
    = **But for** air, we **could** not live even a single day. (but for = if it were not for)
    = **Without** air, we **could** not live even a single day. (without = if it were not for)
  ※ if절의 동사가 'were' 또는 'had'일 때 생략하여 쓸 수 있으며, 이때 주어와 동사가 도치된다.

 핵심 Check

1. 다음 괄호 안의 단어를 가정법 문장으로 바르게 배열하시오.

(you, I, I, if, would, looking, were, start, another job, for)

➡ _____

❷ with + 명사 + 분사

Wormholes may contain two mouths, **with** a throat **connecting** the two. 웜홀은 두 개의 입과 그 둘을 연결하는 목구멍을 지니고 있을 지도 모른다.

- 의미: '~이 …한 채, ~이 …하면서'라는 뜻으로 동시 동작이나 부가적인 상황을 생생하게 표현할 때 사용한다.
  - The girl ran **with** her hair **blowing** in the wind. (그 소녀는 바람에 머리가 날리면서 뛰어갔다.)
  - Jason thought about the days **with** his eyes **closed**. (Jason은 눈을 감은 채로 그 날들에 대해 생각했다.)
- 쓰임: 'with+명사+분사'에서, 명사가 분사의 의미상 주어 역할을 한다.
  - Jenny counted the stars **with** her finger **pointing** at each of them. (Jenny는 손가락으로 별들을 하나하나 가리키며 세었다.)
  - She sat **with** her legs **crossed**. (그녀는 다리를 꼬고 앉았습니다.)
- 명사와 분사가 능동 관계이면 현재 분사를, 수동 관계이면 과거 분사를 쓴다. (명사를 분사의 주어처럼 생각하여 능동과 수동의 관계를 파악한다.)
  - A dog came into the classroom **with** everyone **staring** at him. (개 한 마리가 모두가 쳐다보는 가운데 교실로 들어왔다.) → 모두가 쳐다보고 있으므로 능동 관계
  - Sit comfortably **with** your eyes **closed**. (눈을 감은 채, 편안하게 앉으세요.) → 눈이 감긴 상태이므로 수동 관계
- 명사와 분사 관계가 수동일 때 쓰이는 과거 분사는 본래 'with+명사+(being+)과거 분사'에서 being이 생략된 형태로 볼 수 있다.
  - He was sitting **with** his arms **(being) folded**. (그는 팔짱을 끼고 앉아 있었다.)

핵심 Check

2. 다음 괄호 안에 주어진 어휘를 빈칸에 알맞게 쓰시오.
   (1) He fell asleep with the TV _____ on. (turn)
   (2) She tried to do the dishes with the baby _____ . (cry)

01 다음 각 가정법 문장에서 어법상 <u>어색한</u> 단어를 한 개씩만 찾아 고치시오.

(1) If Paul has money, he could buy a new computer.

_____ ➡ _____

(2) If such wormholes existed in space, we can get to places billions of light-years away quickly!

_____ ➡ _____

(3) If I know her phone number, I would call her.

_____ ➡ _____

(4) I will have nothing to do with him, if I were you.

_____ ➡ _____

02 다음 빈칸에 알맞은 것은?

Julie went to work, _____ her legs broken.

① to   ② at   ③ with
④ during   ⑤ while

03 다음 빈칸에 들어갈 말로 알맞은 것은?

If I _____ you, I would go to bed earlier.

① be   ② am   ③ are
④ were   ⑤ have been

04 괄호 안에 주어진 단어를 활용하여 우리말을 영작할 때 빈칸에 알맞은 말을 쓰시오.

(1) Rachel은 다리를 꼬고 앉았다. (cross)

➡ Rachel sat _____.

(2) Paul은 시원한 바람을 얼굴에 맞으며 자전거를 타고 있다. (the cool wind, blow)

➡ Paul is riding a bike, _____ on his face.

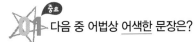
01 다음 중 어법상 <u>어색한</u> 문장은?

① If it were not for the knee injury, he would play.
② If I had wings, I could fly wherever I want.
③ If the weather were nice, I would go hiking.
④ If Lisa studied math a little harder, she will get a good grade.
⑤ If it didn't rain, I would go out to play basketball.

02 다음 중 빈칸에 알맞은 것은?

> Ella is playing the piano with her eyes _____.

① closing　② closed　③ close
④ to close　⑤ are closed

03 다음 문장의 밑줄 친 ①~⑤ 중 어법상 <u>어색한</u> 것은?

> If a spaceship ①<u>fly</u> into a wormhole, it ②<u>might</u> be ③<u>crushed</u> or ④<u>broken</u> into ⑤<u>pieces</u>.

04 다음 중 어법상 <u>어색한</u> 것은?

① Brian was leaning against the wall with his arms folded.
② Julie is riding her bike with her hair blowing in the wind.
③ John spoke with his mouth full.
④ Last night Maryanne fell asleep with the window open.
⑤ John slept with the TV turning on.

05 다음 중 같은 뜻의 문장으로 바르게 바꿔 쓴 것은?

① If I could travel abroad alone, I would take a trip to Africa.
  = I can travel abroad alone, so I take a trip to Africa.
② If Emma knew Eric's address, she would send him a letter.
  = As Emma didn't know Eric's address, she wouldn't send him a letter.
③ If I had much money, I could help people in need.
  = I don't have much money, so I can't help people in need.
④ I would be glad if Chad visited me.
  = Chad doesn't visit me, so I will be glad.
⑤ Sumi doesn't have a computer, so she wants to have one.
  = Sumi wants to have a computer if she had one.

06 다음 괄호 안에서 어법상 바른 것을 고르시오.

(1) If I (win / won) the lottery, I would buy the most expensive car.
(2) If he (has / had) a key, he could open the door.
(3) Ellie left the office, with her work (finishing / finished).
(4) The woman was running, with her hair (flying / flown) in the wind.

[07~08] 다음 우리말을 바르게 영작한 것을 고르시오.

07

만약 Sam이 일찍 일어나지 않는다면, 커피를 마실 수 없을 텐데.

① If Sam doesn't wake up early, he cannot drink coffee.
② If Sam doesn't wake up early, he could not drink coffee.
③ If Sam didn't wake up early, he could not drink coffee.
④ If Sam didn't wake up early, he cannot drink coffee.
⑤ If Sam hadn't woken up early, he could not have drunk coffee.

08

Tom은 셔츠를 밖으로 드러낸 채 걸어다니고 있었다.

① Tom was walking around by his shirt hanging out with.
② Tom was walking around with his shirt hanging out.
③ Tom was walking around his shirt with hanging out.
④ Tom was walking around hanging out with his shirt.
⑤ Tom was walking around with his shirt hung out.

 다음 두 문장을 한 문장으로 바르게 연결한 것은?

• Emma is crying.
• Tears are running down her face.

① Emma is crying with tears running down her face.
② Emma is crying with tears run down her face.
③ Emma is crying with tears ran down her face.
④ Emma is crying with tears to run down her face.
⑤ Emma is crying with tears runs down her face.

 다음 문장의 빈칸 (A)~(C)에 들어갈 말로 가장 적절한 것은?

• If there (A)_____ any taxi available now, I could take it.
• Were it not for computers, our lives (B)_____ be very inconvenient.
• If Harry (C)_____ enough money, he could buy a new bike.

	(A)	(B)	(C)
①	is	could	had
②	is	will	has
③	will be	could	had had
④	were	would	had
⑤	were	will	has

 다음 중 어법상 올바른 문장의 개수는?

ⓐ If I am a famous singer, I would meet my favorite stars.
ⓑ If Lily had some more money, she can buy a new computer.
ⓒ If I became a doctor, I could help many people.
ⓓ If you have super powers, what would you do?
ⓔ Do not speak with your mouth full.
ⓕ Mark remembered those days with his eyes closing.
ⓖ He sat alone, with his arms folding.

① 1개 ② 2개 ③ 3개 ④ 4개 ⑤ 5개

12 다음 문장과 같은 의미의 문장을 고르시오.

> If there were no laws of physics, the world would be crazy.

① The world will be crazy so there are laws of physics.

② There are no laws of physics, so the world won't be crazy.

③ Though there are laws of physics, the world will be crazy.

④ As there are no laws of physics, the world won't be crazy.

⑤ As there are laws of physics, the world won't be crazy.

13 다음 빈칸에 적절하지 <u>않은</u> 것을 고르시오.

> Jake is sitting on the sofa _____.

① with the TV on

② with his eyes closed

③ with his legs crossed

④ with the alarm rung

⑤ with a book in his hand

14 다음 우리말을 영작할 때, <u>어색한</u> 문장을 고르시오.

> 만일 옥수수가 없다면, 냉동 피자도 없을 텐데.

① But for corn, there would be no frozen pizza.

② If it were not for corn, there would be no frozen pizza.

③ If there are no corn, there would be no frozen pizza.

④ Were it not for corn, there would be no frozen pizza.

⑤ Without corn, there would be no frozen pizza.

서답형

15 with를 이용하여 두 문장을 한 문장으로 고쳐 쓸 때 빈칸에 알맞은 말을 쓰시오.

(1) • My sister was standing in the rain.
　　• She folded her umbrella.
　　= My sister was standing in the rain
　　_____ _____ _____ _____.

(2) • The student entered the library.
　　• She was holding a book in her hand.
　　= The student entered the library
　　_____ _____ _____ _____
　　_____ _____.

(3) • Taylor is waiting for a bus.
　　• Her hair is blowing in the wind.
　　= Taylor is waiting for a bus _____
　　_____ _____ _____ in the wind.

서답형

16 다음 문장에서 어법상 <u>어색한</u> 부분을 찾아서 한 단어만 고쳐 다시 쓰시오.

(1) If I can travel into the past, I would bring back all the latest technology.

　➡ _____
　_____

(2) If your coach were here, he will be proud of you.

　➡ _____
　_____

(3) Andy slept with the door closing.

　➡ _____

[01~02] 다음 우리말과 일치하도록 괄호 안에 주어진 어구를 바르게 배열하시오.

01

> 내가 우주에 간다면, 셀피를 찍을 텐데.
> (I, I, space, selfie, take, went, would, a, if, to)

➡ _____

02

> Chris는 한 쪽 눈을 감은 채 망원경으로 별을 바라보았다.
> (Chris, the stars, a telescope, eye, one, looked, closed, through, at, with)

➡ _____
_____

03 〈중요〉 다음 문장과 같은 뜻이 되도록 괄호 안에 주어진 어휘를 활용하여 단어 수에 맞게 빈칸을 채우시오.

> Without his idleness, he would be a good man.

(1) _____ his idleness, he would be a good man. (it, be, 5 단어)

(2) _____ his idleness, he would be a good man. (it, be, 4 단어)

(3) _____ his idleness, he would be a good man. (there, 4 단어)

(4) _____ his idleness, he would be a good man. (but, 2 단어)

(5) _____his idleness, he won't be a good man. (as, 3 단어, 직설법으로 쓸 것.)

04 다음 그림을 보고, 주어진 어휘를 이용하여 빈칸을 알맞게 채우시오.

> An astronaut is standing on a board with a pizza _____. (hand)

05 〈중요〉 다음 그림을 보고, 괄호 안에 주어진 단어를 빈칸에 알맞게 채우시오.

> If Sean _____(come) to the party, he could enjoy himself with us.

06 우리말에 맞게 빈칸에 알맞은 말을 쓰시오.

> TV를 켠 채로 공부하는 것은 좋지 않다.
> = It is not good to study with the TV _____ _____. (2 단어)

07 다음 주어진 문장과 뜻이 같도록 빈칸을 알맞게 채우시오.

> We can't live on a new planet, so we won't live on Dream Planet.
> → If we _____ _____ on a new planet, we _____ _____ on Dream Planet.

08 다음 우리말을 괄호 안에 주어진 어구들을 활용하여 영작하시오.

(1) 우리가 달에 산다면, 몸무게가 더 적게 나갈 텐데. (less, live, weigh)

➡ _____

(2) 만약 우리가 시간이 더 있다면, 너를 도와줄 수 있을 텐데. (have, more time)

➡ _____

(3) 팔을 뻗은 채, 고개를 바닥으로 숙이세요. (your arms, your head, the ground, lower, stretch, to)

➡ _____

_____

(4) Alice는 뺨에 눈물을 흘리며 서 있었다. (her cheeks, was standing, run down)

➡ _____

_____

09 다음 글에서 어법상 잘못 쓰인 것을 찾아 알맞게 고치시오. (3곳)

> If we can make a planet for future generations to live on, we will like to make a planet calling Zetopia. It would be a perfect planet for future generations.

➡ _____

10 다음 직설법 문장을 가정법 문장으로 고쳐 쓰시오.

(1) As I am not an architect, I can't build my own house.

➡ _____

_____

(2) Since Mom doesn't have an apple, she won't make me apple pie.

➡ _____

_____

(3) It doesn't rain, so we will go on a picnic.

➡ _____

(4) Because she didn't have enough time, she couldn't spend time with us.

➡ _____

_____

11 다음 문장에서 어법상 어색한 것을 찾아 바르게 고치시오.

(1) If there is a time machine in real life, I would go to the future.

➡ _____

(2) If people moved to it, they can communicate with animals on the planet.

➡ _____

(3) My sister smelled the flower, with her closed eyes.

➡ _____

(4) Cathy was singing, with the guitar played.

➡ _____

Reading

교과서

Wormholes: Fact or Theory?

Sci Teen: Hi, science fans. Today, we're going to talk about space travel. As we all know, there is nothing faster than light in the universe. So,
접속사(~이듯이, ~이다시피)
if we travel at the speed of light, we should be able to get to another
조건의 부사절을 이끄는 접속사(~라면)
planet in the blink of an eye, right?

Dr. Sci: That would be nice, but space is so vast that it is not possible. In
so ~ that ...: 너무 ~해서 ...하다
the movie, *Passengers*, a spaceship headed to a different planet travels
a spaceship에 수의 일치
at one-half the speed of light. So it should get to another planet very quickly, right? But, the passengers sleep for 120 years because it is expected to take that much time to get to a different planet.
It takes+시간+to V: V하는 데 ~만큼의 시간이 걸리다

Sci Teen: 120 years? Wow, that's a long time! Is there a faster way to travel through space?
to부정사의 형용사적 용법(way 수식)

Dr. Sci: Well, in order to answer that question, I'd like you to think
= so as to   *would like+목적어+to부정사*
about this apple for a second. Imagine a worm is on this apple. It detects something sweet at the bottom and wants to move from the
-thing으로 끝나는 부정대명사는 형용사의 수식을 뒤에서 받음
top to the bottom. For the worm, the apple's surface is as vast as our universe. Now the worm can either move around the outer layer or
either A or B: A 혹은 B 둘 중 하나
down a wormhole. Which do you think it will choose? Well, it would
think로 인해 의문사가 문두로 나간 간접의문문
choose the wormhole because it is a shortcut.

Sci Teen: Is there such a shortcut in the universe?

Dr. Sci: According to some researchers, yes. Einstein figured out that
명사절 접속사(figure out의 목적어를 이끔)
space and time are connected, and he called it space-time. He thought that space-time could actually be bent. When it is bent, parts that are
주격 관계대명사
far away from each other are suddenly closer.

---

wormhole: 벌레 먹은 구멍
theory: 이론, 학설
passenger: 승객, 탑승객
in the blink of an eye: 눈 깜박할 사이에
detect: 발견하다, 감지하다
bottom: 맨 아랫부분, 바닥
vast: 광대한, 거대한
layer: 층
shortcut: 지름길
researcher: 연구자
connect: 이어지다
bend: 굽히다, 구부리다
figure out: ~을 생각해 내다

확인문제

● 다음 문장이 본문의 내용과 일치하면 T, 일치하지 않으면 F를 쓰시오.

1   The apple is as enormous as our space to the worm. ☐

2   Einstein thought that space-time could actually be broken. ☐

3   A wormhole is not helpful for us to travel through space as fast as possible. ☐

To understand this, take a sheet of paper and make a small dot at the
<small>부사적 용법 중 목적(= in order to = so as to)</small>
top of the paper and another at the bottom of the paper. On a flat sheet of paper, the dots are far away from one another. Now, take the paper and fold it with the dots matched up. Punch a hole in the paper and
<small>with+목적어+과거분사(목적어가 ~된 채로)</small>
the dots will be instantly connected. Like this, wormholes in space may contain two mouths, with a throat connecting the two.
<small>with+목적어+현재분사(목적어가 ~하는 채로)</small>

Sci Teen: Just like a wormhole in the apple, right? If such wormholes existed in space, we could get to places billions of light-years away
<small>가정법 과거(If+주어+동사의 과거형, 주어+조동사의 과거형+동사원형): 현재 사실과 반대되는 일에 대한 가정</small>
quickly!

Dr. Sci: Yes, but it's too early to celebrate. Wormholes exist in theory only.

Sci Teen: So all we need to do is find one, right?
<small>주어부에 do동사가 있을 때 be동사의 보어로 to를 생략한 원형부정사 사용 가능</small>

Dr. Sci: Even if we find one, there are many things to consider before
<small>to부정사의 형용사적 용법(things 수식)</small>
actually going through one. A wormhole would be very unstable. If a spaceship flew into one, it might be crushed or broken into pieces.
<small>우주선이 웜홀로 날아 들어가는 것이 당장 현실적으로 불가능하므로 가정법 과거로 표현</small>

Sci Teen: Ouch! That's not a pretty picture. So, are we hopeless? Is traveling in space through a wormhole simply an idea that only exists in theory?
<small>주격 관계대명사</small>

Dr. Sci: I wouldn't say so. The debate about wormholes is still ongoing,
<small>토론이 지금도 계속되고 있음</small>
but with persistent exploration and research, I believe we will eventually find one and learn how to travel through it. Look back at
<small>a wormhole 지칭</small>
our history. We've achieved so many things that seemed impossible at
<small>= which(관계대명사)</small>
first. Who knows? Maybe you can be the one to find the answer!
<small>to부정사의 형용사적 용법(the one 수식) 웜홀을 통해 우주여행을 하는 방법에 대한 해답</small>

dot: 점
punch: 구멍을 뚫다
instantly: 즉시
contain: 포함하다
throat: 목구멍
far away from: ~에서 멀리 떨어져
match up: 맞추다
exist: 존재하다
celebrate: 축하하다
unstable: 불안정한
crush: 눌러 부수다, 찌부러뜨리다
billions of: 수십억의
ongoing: 계속 진행 중인
persistent: 끈질긴, 집요한
exploration: 탐사, 탐구
eventually: 결국
achieve: 달성하다, 성취하다
impossible: 불가능한
look back: 되돌아보다

 **확인문제**

● 다음 문장이 본문의 내용과 일치하면 T, 일치하지 <u>않으면</u> F를 쓰시오.

1 A wormhole in the universe is a shortcut that connects two places. ☐

2 Researchers have found a few wormholes in space. ☐

3 A wormhole is very stable, so we can travel through it safely. ☐

4 The debate about wormholes is in progress. ☐

● 우리말을 참고하여 빈칸에 알맞은 말을 쓰시오.

1 Sci Teen: Hi, science fans. Today, we're _____ _____ _____ _____ space travel.

2 _____ _____ _____ _____, there is _____ _____ _____ light in the universe.

3 So, if we _____ _____ the speed of light, we should _____ _____ _____ _____ _____ another planet _____ _____ _____ _____ an eye, right?

4 Dr. Sci: That would be nice, but space _____ _____ _____ _____ it is not possible.

5 In the movie, *Passengers*, a spaceship _____ _____ a different planet _____ at _____ the speed of light.

6 So it should _____ _____ _____ planet very quickly, right?

7 But, the passengers sleep _____ _____ _____ because it _____ _____ _____ _____ that much time to get to a different planet.

8 Sci Teen: 120 years? Wow, that's a long time! Is there _____ _____ _____ _____ through space?

9 Dr. Sci: Well, _____ _____ _____ _____ answer that question, I'd like _____ _____ _____ about this apple for a second.

10 Imagine a worm is _____ _____ _____. It detects _____ _____ at the bottom and _____ _____ _____ from the top to the bottom.

11 For the worm, the apple's surface is _____ _____ our universe.

12 Now the worm can _____ _____ _____ the outer layer _____ _____ a wormhole.

13 _____ _____ _____ _____ it will choose? Well, it would choose the wormhole _____ _____ _____ _____.

14 Sci Teen: Is there _____ _____ _____ in the universe?

15 Dr. Sci: According to some researchers, yes. Einstein _____ _____ that space and time _____ _____, and he called it _____.

1	Sci Teen: 안녕하세요, 과학 팬 여러분. 오늘 우리는 우주여행에 대해 이야기할 것입니다.
2	우리가 모두 알다시피, 우주에서 빛보다 더 빠른 것은 없습니다.
3	그래서 만약 우리가 빛의 속도로 여행을 한다면, 우리는 다른 행성에 눈 깜박할 사이에 도달할 수 있어야 해요, 그렇죠?
4	Dr. Sci: 그렇다면 좋겠지만, 우주는 너무 광활해서 그건 불가능하답니다.
5	영화 〈Passengers〉에서 다른 행성으로 향하는 우주선이 빛의 속도의 절반으로 이동합니다.
6	그러면 그들은 다른 행성에 매우 빨리 도달해야겠지요, 그렇죠?
7	하지만 승객들은 120년 동안 잠을 자게 되는데, 왜냐하면 다른 행성에 도달하는 데 그만큼 많은 시간이 걸릴 것으로 예상되기 때문입니다.
8	Sci Teen: 120년이요? 우아, 그건 정말 긴 시간이네요! 우주를 여행하는 더 빠른 방법이 있나요?
9	Dr. Sci: 글쎄요, 그 질문에 답하기 위해서 여러분이 이 사과에 대해 잠깐 생각해 보기 바랍니다.
10	한 마리 벌레가 이 사과 위에 있다고 상상해 보세요. 그것은 맨 아래에 있는 달콤한 무언가를 감지하고 맨 위에서 아래로 이동하기를 원합니다.
11	그 벌레에게 사과의 표면은 우리의 우주만큼이나 광대합니다.
12	이제 그 벌레는 바깥 표면의 껍질을 돌아서 이동하거나 벌레 구멍 아래로 이동할 수 있습니다.
13	그것이 어떤 것을 선택할 거라고 생각하십니까? 음, 그것은 벌레 구멍을 선택할 것인데 왜냐하면 그것이 지름길이기 때문입니다.
14	Sci Teen: 우주에 그런 지름길이 있나요?
15	Dr. Sci: 몇몇 연구자들에 따르면, 그렇습니다. 아인슈타인은 공간과 시간이 연결되어 있다는 것을 생각해 냈고, 그것을 시공간이라고 불렀습니다.

16 He thought that _____ _____ _____ _____ _____ _____ . When it is bent, parts _____ _____ _____ from each other _____ suddenly closer.

17 _____ _____ this, _____ a sheet of paper and _____ a small dot _____ _____ _____ _____ the paper and _____ at the _____ of the paper.

18 _____ _____ _____ _____ of paper, the dots are _____ _____ from one another.

19 Now, take the paper and _____ it _____ the dots _____ . _____ a hole in the paper and _____ _____ will _____ instantly _____ .

20 Like this, wormholes in space may _____ _____ , with a throat _____ the two.

21 Sci Teen: _____ _____ a wormhole in the apple, right? If such wormholes _____ in space, we could _____ _____ billions of light-years _____ quickly!

22 Dr. Sci: Yes, but it's _____ _____ _____ _____ . Wormholes _____ in theory only.

23 Sci Teen: So _____ we need _____ _____ is _____ _____ , right?

24 Dr. Sci: _____ _____ we find one, there are many things _____ _____ before actually _____ _____ _____ .

25 A wormhole _____ _____ very _____ . If a spaceship _____ _____ one, it might _____ or _____ into pieces.

26 Sci Teen: Ouch! That's not _____ _____ _____ . So, are we _____ ?

27 Is traveling in space _____ a wormhole simply an idea _____ only _____ in theory?

28 Dr. Sci: I _____ _____ so. The debate about wormholes _____ still _____ , but _____ _____ _____ and _____ , I believe we will eventually find _____ and _____ _____ _____ through it.

29 _____ _____ _____ our history. We've achieved _____ _____ _____ seemed impossible at first.

30 Who _____ ? Maybe you can be the one _____ _____ _____ _____ !

16 '그는 시공간이 실제로 구부러질 수 있다고 생각했습니다. 그것이 구부러질 때 서로 멀리 떨어져 있는 부분들이 갑자기 더 가까워질 수 있습니다.

17 이것을 이해하기 위해서, 종이를 한 장 갖고 와서 그 종이의 윗부분에 작은 점을 찍고 또 다른 점을 그 종이의 아랫부분에 찍어 보세요.

18 펼쳐 놓은 종이에서 그 점들은 서로 멀리 떨어져 있습니다.

19 이제 그 종이를 들고 점들이 맞춰지도록 그것을 접으세요. 종이에 구멍을 뚫으면 그 점들이 즉시 연결될 것입니다.

20 이와 마찬가지로 우주의 웜홀은 두 개의 입과 그 둘을 연결하는 목구멍을 지니고 있을 겁니다.

21 Sci Teen: 사과에 있는 벌레 구멍처럼요, 그렇죠? 그런 웜홀이 우주에 존재한다면 우리는 수십억 광년 떨어져 있는 곳에 빠르게 도달할 수 있을 텐데요!

22 Dr. Sci: 그렇죠, 하지만 축하하기에는 너무 이릅니다. 웜홀은 이론상에서만 존재합니다.

23 Sci Teen: 그러면 우리가 해야 할 것이라고는 그것을 찾는 거네요, 그렇죠?

24 Dr. Sci: 우리가 그것을 찾는다고 하더라도 실제로 그걸 통과하여 가기 전에 고려해야 할 것들이 많이 있습니다.

25 웜홀은 매우 불안정할 것입니다. 만약 우주선이 그 안으로 날아가게 되면, 그것은 부서지거나 산산조각이 날 수도 있습니다.

26 Sci Teen: 어이쿠! 그건 좋은 광경이 아니네요. 그럼 우리는 가망이 없는 건가요?

27 우주에서 웜홀을 통하여 여행을 하는 것은 단지 이론상으로만 존재하는 아이디어인가요?

28 Dr. Sci: 그렇게 말하지는 않겠어요. 웜홀에 대한 논쟁은 여전히 진행 중이긴 하지만, 끊임없는 탐구와 연구로 우리가 결국 하나를 찾아 그것을 통해 여행하는 법을 배울 수 있을 거라고 믿습니다.

29 우리의 역사를 돌아보세요. 우리는 처음에는 불가능해 보였던 아주 많은 것들을 달성해 왔습니다.

30 누가 알겠어요? 아마도 여러분이 그 답을 찾아내는 그 사람이 될 수 있을지도요!

● 우리말을 참고하여 본문을 영작하시오.

1 Sci Teen: 안녕하세요, 과학 팬 여러분. 오늘 우리는 우주여행에 대해 이야기할 것입니다.
➡ _____

2 우리가 모두 알다시피, 우주에서 빛보다 더 빠른 것은 없습니다.
➡ _____

3 그래서 만약 우리가 빛의 속도로 여행을 한다면, 우리는 다른 행성에 눈 깜박할 사이에 도달할 수 있어야 해요, 그렇죠?
➡ _____

4 Dr. Sci: 그렇다면 좋겠지만, 우주는 너무 광활해서 그건 불가능하답니다.
➡ _____

5 영화 〈Passengers〉에서 다른 행성으로 향하는 우주선이 빛의 속도의 절반으로 이동합니다.
➡ _____
_____

6 그러면 그들은 다른 행성에 매우 빨리 도달해야겠지요, 그렇죠?
➡ _____

7 하지만 승객들은 120년 동안 잠을 자게 되는데, 왜냐하면 다른 행성에 도달하는 데 그만큼 많은 시간이 걸릴 것으로 예상되기 때문입니다.
➡ _____
_____

8 Sci Teen: 120년이요? 우아, 그건 정말 긴 시간이네요! 우주를 여행하는 더 빠른 방법이 있나요?
➡ _____

9 Dr. Sci: 글쎄요, 그 질문에 답하기 위해서 여러분들이 이 사과에 대해 잠깐 생각해 보기 바랍니다.
➡ _____

10 한 마리 벌레가 이 사과 위에 있다고 상상해 보세요. 그것은 맨 아래에 있는 달콤한 무언가를 감지하고 맨 위에서 아래로 이동하기를 원합니다.
➡ _____
_____

11 그 벌레에게 사과의 표면은 우리의 우주만큼이나 광대합니다.
➡ _____

12 이제 그 벌레는 바깥 표면의 껍질을 돌아서 이동하거나 벌레 구멍 아래로 이동할 수 있습니다.
➡ _____

13 그것이 어떤 것을 선택할 거라고 생각하십니까? 음, 그것은 벌레 구멍을 선택할 것인데 왜냐하면 그것이 지름길이기 때문입니다.
➡ _____
_____

14 Sci Teen: 우주에 그런 지름길이 있나요?
➡ _____

15 Dr. Sci: 몇몇 연구자들에 따르면, 그렇습니다. 아인슈타인은 공간과 시간이 연결되어 있다는 것을 생각해 냈고, 그것을 시공간이라고 불렀습니다.
➡ _____
_____

16 그는 시공간이 실제로 구부러질 수 있다고 생각했습니다. 그것이 구부러질 때 서로 멀리 떨어져 있는 부분들이 갑자기 더 가까워질 수 있습니다.

➡ _____

17 이것을 이해하기 위해서, 종이를 한 장 갖고 와서 그 종이의 윗부분에 작은 점을 찍고 또 다른 점을 그 종이의 아랫부분에 찍어 보세요.

➡ _____

18 펼쳐 놓은 종이에서 그 점들은 서로 멀리 떨어져 있습니다.

➡ _____

19 이제 그 종이를 들고 점들이 맞춰지도록 그것을 접으세요. 종이에 구멍을 뚫으면 그 점들이 즉시 연결될 것입니다.

➡ _____

➡ _____

20 이와 마찬가지로 우주의 웜홀은 두 개의 입과 그 둘을 연결하는 목구멍을 지니고 있을 겁니다.

➡ _____

21 Sci Teen: 사과에 있는 벌레 구멍처럼요, 그렇죠? 그런 웜홀이 우주에 존재한다면 우리는 수십억 광년 떨어져 있는 곳에 빠르게 도달할 수 있을 텐데요!

➡ _____

22 Dr. Sci: 그렇죠, 하지만 축하하기에는 너무 이릅니다. 웜홀은 이론상에서만 존재합니다.

➡ _____

23 Sci Teen: 그러면 우리가 해야 할 것이라고는 그것을 찾는 거네요, 그렇죠?

➡ _____

24 Dr. Sci: 우리가 그것을 찾는다고 하더라도 실제로 그걸 통과하여 가기 전에 고려해야 할 것들이 많이 있습니다.

➡ _____

25 웜홀은 매우 불안정할 것입니다. 만약 우주선이 그 안으로 날아가게 되면, 그것은 부서지거나 산산조각이 날 수도 있습니다.

➡ _____

26 Sci Teen: 어이쿠! 그건 좋은 광경이 아니네요. 그럼 우리는 가망이 없는 건가요?

➡ _____

27 우주에서 웜홀을 통하여 여행을 하는 것은 단지 이론상으로만 존재하는 아이디어인가요?

➡ _____

28 Dr. Sci: 그렇게 말하지는 않겠어요. 웜홀에 대한 논쟁은 여전히 진행 중이긴 하지만, 끊임없는 탐구와 연구로 우리가 결국 하나를 찾아 그것을 통해 여행하는 법을 배울 수 있을 거라고 믿습니다.

➡ _____

➡ _____

29 우리의 역사를 돌아보세요. 우리는 처음에는 불가능해 보였던 아주 많은 것들을 달성해 왔습니다.

➡ _____

30 누가 알겠어요? 아마도 여러분이 그 답을 찾아내는 그 사람이 될 수 있을지도요!

➡ _____

[01~03] 다음 글을 읽고 물음에 답하시오.

Sci Teen: Hi, science fans. Today, we're going to talk about space travel. As we all know, there is nothing faster than light in the universe. So, if we travel at the speed of light, we should be able to get to another planet in the blink of an eye, right?

Dr. Sci: (A)That would be nice, but space is so ⓐ_____ that it is not possible. In the movie, *Passengers*, a spaceship headed to a different planet travels at one-half the speed of light. So it should get to another planet very quickly, right? But, the passengers sleep for 120 years because it is expected to take that much time to get to a different planet.

01 위 글의 흐름상 빈칸 ⓐ에 들어갈 말로 가장 적절한 것은?

① empty ② small ③ vast
④ dangerous ⑤ dark

02 밑줄 친 (A)의 의미로 가장 적절한 것은?

① making space travel possible
② arriving at another planet in a blink
③ getting to another planet in the future
④ traveling the universe without any help
⑤ moving from one place to another whenever we want

서답형
03 What are they going to talk about today? Answer in English with a full sentence.

➡ _____

[04~06] 다음 글을 읽고 물음에 답하시오.

Sci Teen: 120 years? Wow, that's a long time!
　　(A)_____

Dr. Sci: Well, in order to answer that question, I'd like you to think about this apple for a second. Imagine a worm is on this apple. ⓐIt detects something sweet at the bottom and wants to move from the top to the bottom. For the worm, the apple's surface is as vast as our universe. Now the worm can either move around the outer layer or down a wormhole. Which do you think ⓑit will choose? Well, ⓒit would choose the wormhole because ⓓit is a shortcut.

04 빈칸 (A)에 들어갈 말로 가장 적절한 것은?

① Did someone find a wormhole?
② Do you know how to get to another planet?
③ Is there a safe way to travel through space?
④ How can we find a shortcut in our universe?
⑤ Is there a faster way to travel through space?

05 ⓐ~ⓓ에서 가리키는 것이 같은 것을 바르게 묶은 것은?

① ⓑ－ⓒ, ⓐ－ⓓ ② ⓐ, ⓑ－ⓒ－ⓓ
③ ⓒ, ⓐ－ⓑ－ⓓ ④ ⓐ－ⓑ－ⓒ, ⓓ
⑤ ⓑ－ⓓ, ⓐ－ⓒ

서답형
06 How big is the apple's surface for the worm? Answer in English.

➡ _____

[07~08] 다음 글을 읽고 물음에 답하시오.

Sci Teen: Is there such a shortcut in the universe?

Dr. Sci: According to some researchers, yes. Einstein figured out that space and time are connected, and he called it space-time. (①) He thought that space-time could actually be bent. (②) When it is bent, parts that are far away from each other are suddenly closer. (③) On a flat sheet of paper, the dots are far away from one another. (④) Now, take the paper and fold it with the dots matched up. Punch a hole in the paper and the dots will be instantly connected. (⑤) Like this, wormholes in space may contain two mouths, with a throat connecting the two.

07 (①)~(⑤) 중 주어진 문장이 들어가기에 가장 적절한 곳은?

> To understand this, take a sheet of paper and make a small dot at the top of the paper and another at the bottom of the paper.

①   ②   ③   ④   ⑤

08 Choose one that is TRUE.

① A short cut can't be found in the universe.

② There is no mouth in a wormhole.

③ Nothing can connect those mouths in wormholes.

④ Einstein thought bending space-time could be impossible.

⑤ Einstein thought space and time are connected.

[09~10] 다음 글을 읽고 물음에 답하시오.

Sci Teen: Just like a wormhole in the apple, right? If such wormholes existed in space, we could get to places billions of light-years away quickly!

Dr. Sci: Yes, but it's too early to celebrate. Wormholes exist in theory only.

Sci Teen: So all we need to do is find (A)<u>one</u>, right?

Dr. Sci: Even if we find one, there are many things to consider before actually going through one. A wormhole would be very unstable. If a spaceship flew into one, it might be crushed or broken into pieces.

Sci Teen: Ouch! That's not a pretty picture. So, are we hopeless? Is traveling in space through a wormhole simply an idea that only exists in theory?

Dr. Sci: I wouldn't say so. The debate about wormholes is still ongoing, but with persistent exploration and research, I believe we will eventually find one and learn how to travel through it. Look back at our history. We've achieved so many things that seemed impossible at first.

서답형

09 밑줄 친 (A)가 가리키는 것을 위 글에서 찾아 쓰시오.

➡ _____

서답형

10 What have we achieved? Answer in English.

➡ _____

_____

[11~13] 다음 글을 읽고 물음에 답하시오.

Sci Teen: Hi, science fans. Today, we're going to talk about space travel. As we all know, there is nothing faster than light in the universe. So, ⓐ만약 우리가 빛의 속도로 여행을 한다면, we should be able to get to another planet in the blink of an eye, right?

Dr. Sci: That would be nice, but space is so vast that it is not possible.
(A) But, the passengers sleep for 120 years because it is expected to take that much time to get to a different planet.
(B) So it should get to another planet very quickly, right?
(C) In the movie, *Passengers*, a spaceship headed to a different planet travels at one-half the speed of light.

11 주어진 단어를 바르게 나열하여 밑줄 친 우리말 ⓐ를 영어로 쓰시오.

(light / the / travel / if / of / speed / at / we)

➡ _____

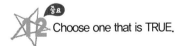 Choose one that is TRUE.

① They are talking about a spaceship.
② The conversation is for science fans.
③ Many things can travel as fast as light in the universe.
④ We can travel from a planet to another planet in the blink of an eye.
⑤ In the movie, *Passengers*, a spaceship travel at the speed of light.

13 자연스러운 글이 되도록 (A)~(C)를 바르게 나열하시오.

➡ _____

[14~15] 다음 글을 읽고 물음에 답하시오.

Sci Teen: 120 years? Wow, that's a long time! Is there a faster way (A)to travel through space?

Dr. Sci: Well, in order to answer that question, I'd like you to think about this apple for a second. Imagine a worm is on this apple. It detects something sweet at the bottom and wants to move from the top to the bottom. For the worm, the apple's surface is as vast as our universe. Now the worm can either move around the outer layer or down a wormhole. Which do you think it will choose? Well, it would choose the wormhole because it is a shortcut.

14 다음 중 밑줄 친 (A)와 쓰임이 같은 것은?

① It was kind of you to say so.
② He came in to find his wallet.
③ You must be upset to hear the news.
④ Is there any chance to meet her?
⑤ We'd like you to think about it.

15 On the apple, what does the worm detect? Answer in English.

➡ _____

_____

[16~18] 다음 글을 읽고 물음에 답하시오.

Sci Teen: Is there such a shortcut in the universe?
Dr. Sci: According to some researchers, yes. Einstein figured out that space and time

are connected, and he called it space-time. He thought that space-time could actually be ①bent. When it is bent, parts that are far away from each other are suddenly ②closer. To understand this, take a sheet of paper and make a small dot at the top of the paper and another at the bottom of the paper. On a ③flat sheet of paper, the dots are ④far away from one another. Now, take the paper and ⑤hold it with the dots matched up. Punch a hole in the paper and the dots will be instantly connected. Like this, wormholes in space may contain two mouths, with a throat connecting the two.

16 다음 중 위 글의 제목으로 가장 적절한 것은?

① A Wormhole: a Secret Way to the Mars
② Wormholes Disconnecting Universe
③ A Wormhole: a Shortcut of Universe
④ How to Find a Shortcut of Universe
⑤ What You Should Do to Find Wormholes

17 ①~⑤ 중 글의 흐름상 어색한 단어는?

① ② ③ ④ ⑤

18 If you punch a hole in the paper, what will happen? Answer in English.

➡ _____

_____

[19~21] 다음 글을 읽고 물음에 답하시오.

Sci Teen: Just like a wormhole in the apple, right? If ①such wormholes existed in space, we could get to places billions of light-years away quickly!

Dr. Sci: Yes, but it's too early ②to celebrate. Wormholes exist in theory only.

Sci Teen: So all we need to do is ③find one, right?

Dr. Sci: Even if we find one, there are many things to consider before actually going through one. A wormhole would be very (A)unstable. If a spaceship flew into one, it might be crushed or broken into pieces.

Sci Teen: Ouch! That's not a pretty picture. So, are we hopeless? Is traveling in space through a wormhole simply an idea that only ④exists in theory?

Dr. Sci: I wouldn't say so. The debate about wormholes ⑤are still ongoing, but with persistent exploration and research, I believe we will eventually find one and learn how to travel through it. Look back at our history. We've achieved so many things that seemed impossible at first. Who knows? Maybe you can be the one to find the answer!

19 밑줄 친 (A)를 대신하여 쓸 수 있는 것은?

① constant ② insecure ③ vast
④ instant ⑤ exclusive

20 ①~⑤ 중 어법상 바르지 않은 것은?

① ② ③ ④ ⑤

21 빈칸에 공통으로 들어갈 말을 쓰시오.

Q: Then, traveling in space through a wormhole is _____, isn't it?

Dr. Sci: I wouldn't say so. We've achieved so many things that seemed _____ at first. We will eventually find one and learn how to travel through it.

[01~03] 다음 글을 읽고 물음에 답하시오.

Sci Teen: Hi, science fans. Today, we're going to talk about space travel. As we all know, there is nothing faster than light in the universe. So, if we travel at the speed of light, we should be able to get to another planet in the blink of an eye, right?

Dr. Sci: That would be nice, but space is so vast that it is not possible. In the movie, *Passengers*, a spaceship headed to a different planet travels at one-half the speed of light. So it should get to another planet very quickly, right? But, the passengers sleep for 120 years because it is expected to take that much time to get to a different planet.

01 How fast does the spaceship in the movie, *Passengers*, travel?

➡ _____

02 Why do the passengers in the movie, *Passengers*, sleep so long? Answer in English.

➡ _____
_____

03 위 글의 내용과 일치하도록 빈칸에 알맞은 말을 쓰시오. (한 칸에 하나의 단어만 쓰시오.)

| Space is too vast for us to _____ |
| _____ _____ _____ _____ |
| _____ although we travel at the speed |
| of light. |

[04~05] 다음 글을 읽고 물음에 답하시오.

Sci Teen: 120 years? Wow, that's a long time! Is there a faster way to travel through space?

Dr. Sci: Well, in order to answer that question, (A)여러분들이 이 사과에 대해 잠깐 생각해 보기 바랍니다. Imagine a worm is on this apple. It detects something sweet at the bottom and wants to move from the top to the bottom. For the worm, the apple's surface is as vast as our universe. Now the worm can either move around the outer layer or down a wormhole. Which do you think it will choose? Well, it would choose the ⓐ_____ because it is a shortcut.

04 위 글의 흐름상 빈칸 ⓐ에 들어갈 알맞은 말을 쓰시오.

➡ _____

05 주어진 어구를 활용하여 밑줄 친 우리말 (A)를 영어로 쓰시오.

| (would like / for a second) |

➡ _____

[06~08] 다음 글을 읽고 물음에 답하시오.

Sci Teen: Is there such a shortcut in the universe?

Dr. Sci: According to some researchers, yes. Einstein figured out that space and time are connected, and he called it space-time. He thought that space-time could actually be bent. When it is bent, parts that are far away from each other are suddenly closer. To understand (A)this, take a sheet of paper and make a small dot at the top of the paper and another at the bottom of the paper. On a flat sheet of paper, the dots are far away from one another. Now, take the paper and fold it with the dots matched up. Punch a hole in the paper and the dots will be instantly connected. Like this, wormholes in space may contain two mouths, with a throat connecting the two.

06 밑줄 친 (A)this가 의미하는 것을 우리말로 쓰시오.

➡ _____

_____

07 What do we need to do after making dots on a sheet of paper? Answer in English.

➡ _____

_____

08 위 글의 내용에 맞게 과학 노트를 완성하시오.

| _____ in space |
| Einstein thought space and time are _____ and space-time can be _____. When it is _____, parts far away from each other can become _____. |

[09~12] 다음 글을 읽고 물음에 답하시오.

Sci Teen: Just like a wormhole in the apple, right? If such wormholes existed in space, we could get to places billions of light-years away quickly!

Dr. Sci: Yes, but (A)it's too early to celebrate. Wormholes exist in theory only.

Sci Teen: So all we need to do is find one, right?

Dr. Sci: Even if we find one, there are many things to consider before actually going through one. A wormhole would be very unstable. If a spaceship flew into one, it might be crushed or broken into pieces.

Sci Teen: Ouch! That's not a pretty picture. So, are we hopeless? Is traveling in space through a wormhole simply an idea that only exists in theory?

Dr. Sci: I wouldn't say so. The debate about wormholes is still ongoing, but with persistent exploration and research, I believe we will eventually find one and learn how to travel through it. Look back at our history. We've achieved so many things that seemed impossible at first. Who knows? Maybe you can be the one to find the answer!

09 Write the reason why Dr. Sci says like the underlined (A). Use the phrase 'It is because.'

➡ _____

10 According to Dr. Sci, what will we do if we eventually find a wormhole? Answer in English.

➡ _____

11 If a spaceship flew into a wormhole, what would happen to it? Answer in English.

➡ _____

12 Is the debate about wormholes over?

➡ _____

After You Read A

A faster way to travel through space

① Idea from an apple

A wormhole is a shortcut for a worm to move from the top to the bottom.
　　　　　　　　　　　　　意미상의 주어　　형용사적 용법(shortcut 수식)

② Wormholes in space

Einstein thought space and time are connected and space-time can be bent.
　　　　　　　　　　　　　　　　과학적 사실이므로 현재 시제 사용

When it is bent, parts far away from each other can become closer.

Do wormholes really exist?

③ In theory, wormholes exist.

Wormholes would be unstable. A spaceship could be crushed or broken into
　　　　　　　추측　　　　　　　　　　　　　'가정에 대한 결과의 상상'
pieces.

Still I believe with persistent exploration and research we will find a
그럼에도, 하지만, 그러나(접속사처럼 쓰여 but. however보다 센 뜻을 나타냄.)

wormhole!

구문해설 • shortcut: 지름길 • worm: 벌레 • connect: 연결하다 • bend: 굽히다, 구부리다 • theory: 이론
• exist: 존재하다 • unstable: 불안정한 • spaceship: 우주선 • crush: 눌러 부수다, 찌부러뜨리다
• persistent: 끈질긴, 집요한, 지속적인 • exploration: 탐구

Language in Use

• Is the universe finite or infinite?
특정 어근에 im-[in-]을 붙이면 부정의 의미를 더한다. im-은 뒤에 오는 어근의 철자가 m. p. b로 시작할 때 붙일 수 있다.(in→finite = infinite)

• Luckily, the driver is in a stable condition after the accident.
동사 뒤에 –able을 붙이면 '~할 수 있는'이라는 의미의 형용사가 된다. (stay+–able = stable)

Think & Write C

If I could make a planet for us to live on in the future, I would like to make
　　　　　　　　　　to부정사의 의미상 주어　　a planet 수식
a planet called Atlas. It would be a beautiful green planet. Its size would be
과거분사(~라고 불리는)
bigger than the moon, but smaller than Earth. The temperature of it would be
　　　　　　　　　　　　　　　　　　　　　　　　　Atlas 지칭
about 30℃. It would have beautiful nature. Interestingly, if people moved to it,
대략
they could communicate with animals on this planet.

구문해설 • would like to V: V하고 싶다 • temperature: 온도 • nature: 자연 • communicate: 의사소통
하다

Words & Expressions

01 다음 중 반의어의 연결이 어색한 것은?

① sensitive – insensitive
② active – inactive
③ stable – unstable
④ correct – imcorrect
⑤ possible – impossible

02 다음 괄호 안의 단어를 우리말에 맞게 변형하여 빈칸에 쓰시오.

> 그 인형은 움직일 수 있는 팔과 다리를 가지고 있다.
> → The doll has _____ arms and legs.
> (move)

03 다음 괄호 안의 단어를 문맥에 맞게 고쳐 쓰시오.

> Space _____ seems exciting to me. (explore)

04 다음 빈칸 (A)와 (B)에 들어갈 말이 알맞게 짝지어진 것은?

> • This puzzle is (A)_____ complicated for me to put together.
> • I've never seen (B)_____ a thrilling game.

	(A)	(B)		(A)	(B)
①	so	so	②	so	such
③	too	so	④	too	such
⑤	too	too			

05 다음 빈칸에 공통으로 들어갈 말을 쓰시오.

> • They are quite different (A)_____ each other in many ways.
> • My house is not far away (B)_____ here.

Conversation

06 자연스러운 대화가 되도록 (A)~(D)를 배열한 것을 고르시오.

> (A) Yes, it's possible because we moved around Earth every 90 minutes in the station.
> (C) I could see a beautiful sunrise 16 times a day. It was great.
> (B) What was your favorite part about being in the space station?
> (D) Is it possible to see the sunrise several times a day in space?

① (B) – (A) – (C) – (D)
② (B) – (C) – (A) – (D)
③ (B) – (C) – (D) – (A)
④ (C) – (B) – (A) – (D)
⑤ (C) – (D) – (B) – (A)

[07~09] 다음 대화를 읽고 물음에 답하시오.

W: What are you watching? (①)
M: It's a documentary about life in space. (②)
W: Yes, it's because there's no gravity in space. (③)
M: Right. (④) 나도 우주 비행사처럼 떠다닐 수 있다면 좋을 텐데! (⑤)
W: Really? I don't. It looks uncomfortable.

07 ①~⑤ 중 주어진 문장이 들어갈 곳은?

> Everything seems so different.

①   ②   ③   ④   ⑤

08 위 대화에서 다음 영영풀이에 해당하는 단어를 찾아 쓰시오.

> the force that attracts objects towards one another, especially the force that makes things fall to the ground

➡ _____

09 밑줄 친 우리말과 일치하도록 주어진 어구를 이용하여 영작하시오.

> like, float around, wish, could

➡ _____

[10~12] 다음 대화를 읽고 물음에 답하시오.

W: Hello, everyone, welcome to *All about Movies*! Today, we're going to talk about the top three things from movies that we wish were real.

M: Let's start with number three, the flying skateboard from *Back to the Future*.

W: It's a cool item. I wish I could have a flying skateboard.

M: Actually, I read somewhere that this is not entirely (A)_____.

W: Really? Is it actually possible to fly on a skateboard?

M: Yes. Some companies have (B)_____ physics to create flying skateboards.

10 대화의 흐름상 빈칸 (A)에 들어갈 말을 대화의 단어를 이용해 쓰시오.

➡ _____

11 빈칸 (B)에 알맞은 말을 고르시오.

① worked   ② applied   ③ made

④ showed   ⑤ required

12 위 대화의 내용과 일치하지 <u>않는</u> 것을 고르시오

① 실제로 가능하기를 바라는 영화 속 물건들에 대해서 말하고 있다.

② 남자는 날아다니는 스케이트보드를 만들 수 있다는 것을 어딘가에서 읽었다.

③ 남자는 날아다니는 스케이트보드를 가지기를 원한다.

④ 날아다니는 스케이트보드가 실제로 가능하기를 바라는 영화 속 물건들 중 3위이다.

⑤ 몇몇 회사들이 날아다니는 스케이트보드를 만들기 위해 노력 중이다.

Grammar

13 다음 중 밑줄 친 if의 쓰임이 나머지와 <u>다른</u> 하나를 고르시오.

① <u>If</u> I were you, I would call her.

② I would live in London <u>if</u> I could live anywhere I wanted.

③ I don't know <u>if</u> there is anything else I can do.

④ What would you do <u>if</u> you became an adult now?

⑤ <u>If</u> I were not sick, I could go to the meeting.

14 다음 중 어법상 <u>어색한</u> 문장은?

① Mike was standing by the door with his arms folded.

② Mozart was playing the piano with his eyes closed.

③ Jenny counted the stars with her finger pointing at each of them.

④ Alice was waiting for him with her legs crossing.

⑤ The little poor girl spoke with tears in her eyes.

15 다음 주어진 문장을 가정법으로 바르게 고친 것은?

> As I don't become an adult now, I won't get a driver's license.

① If I became an adult now, I won't get a driver's license.

② If I became an adult now, I would get a driver's license.

③ If I became an adult now, I wouldn't get a driver's license.

④ If I had become an adult now, I would get a driver's license.

⑤ If I hadn't become an adult now, I wouldn't get a driver's license.

[16~17] 우리말에 맞게 주어진 어휘를 이용하여 빈칸에 알맞은 말을 쓰시오.

16

> 웜홀은 두 개의 입과 그 둘을 연결하는 목구멍을 지니고 있을 것이다.
> = Wormholes may contain two mouths, _____ the two. (connect)

17

> 만약 Joe가 거짓말하지 않는다면, 선생님은 화내지 않을 텐데.
> = If Joe _____, the teacher _____ angry. (be, lie)

18 다음 괄호 안에 주어진 단어를 어법에 맞게 빈칸에 쓰시오.

(1) The woman was sitting on the chair with her legs _____. (cross)

(2) The girl ran with her hair _____ in the wind. (blow)

(3) Henry sat on the sofa with his eyes _____. (close)

(4) I ran out of the house with my dog _____ me. (follow)

(5) Listen to me carefully with your book _____. (close)

19 다음 그림을 보고, 괄호 안에 주어진 단어를 빈칸에 알맞게 채우시오.

> If I _____ an astronaut, I _____
> _____ space travel. (become, enjoy)

20 다음 주어진 문장과 의미가 같은 것은?

> The children listened to their teacher with their eyes shining.

① Their teacher listened to the children and their eyes were shining.
② Their eyes shining made the children listen to their teacher.
③ The children listened to their teacher and their teacher shone her eyes.
④ The children listened to their teacher and their eyes were shining.
⑤ The children listened to their teacher and their eyes shine.

21 다음 중 어법상 <u>어색한</u> 것을 고르시오.

① Jean and Tom are listening to music with their eyes closing.
② We slept in the room, with the door closed.
③ Don't go out with the gas on.
④ The girls walked along, singing merrily.
⑤ Let the patient sit down on a chair with her injured arm raised higher than her heart.

Reading

[22~26] 다음 글을 읽고 물음에 답하시오.

Wormholes: Fact or Theory?

Sci Teen: Hi, science fans. Today, we're going to talk about space travel. As we all know, there is nothing faster than light in the universe. So, if we travel at the speed of light, we should be able to get to another planet in the blink of an eye, right?

Dr. Sci: That would be nice, but space is so vast that it is not possible. In the movie, *Passengers*, a spaceship headed to a different planet travels at one-half the speed of light. So it should get to another planet very quickly, right? But, the passengers sleep for 120 years because it is expected to take that much time to get to a different planet.

Sci Teen: 120 years? Wow, that's a long time! Is there a faster way to travel through space?

Dr. Sci: Well, in order to answer that question, I'd like you to think about this apple for a second. Imagine a worm is on this apple. It detects something sweet at the bottom and wants to move from the top to the bottom. For the worm, the apple's surface is as vast as our universe. Now the worm can either move around the outer layer or down a wormhole. (A) <u>그것이 어떤 것을 선택할 거라고 생각하십니까?</u> Well, it would choose the wormhole ⓐ_____ it is a shortcut.

22 빈칸 ⓐ에 들어갈 말로 가장 적절한 것은?

① although ② because ③ if
④ unless ⑤ as if

23 주어진 단어를 바르게 나열하여 밑줄 친 우리말 (A)를 영어로 쓸 때 네 번째로 오는 단어는?

> (choose / which / will / think / it / do / you)?

① it ② which ③ you
④ think ⑤ do

24 What is the fastest thing in the universe? Answer in English with a full sentence.

➡ _____

25 If we travel at the speed of light, what does Sci Teen think should happen? Answer in English.

➡ _____

_____

_____

26 Choose one that is NOT true.

① What they are going to talk about is space travel.

② Dr. Sci explains what a wormhole is with an example.

③ Passengers in the movie, *Passengers*, travel to another planet while waking up.

④ A wormhole is considered to be a shortcut existing in the universe.

⑤ It is expected to take 120 years to move from one planet to another planet in the movie, *Passengers*.

[27~28] 다음 글을 읽고 물음에 답하시오.

> **Sci Teen:** Ouch! That's not a pretty picture. So, are we hopeless? Is traveling in space through a wormhole simply an idea that only exists in theory?
>
> **Dr. Sci:** I wouldn't say so. The debate about wormholes is still (A)ongoing, but with persistent exploration and research, I believe we will eventually find one and learn how to travel through it. Look back at our history. We've achieved so many things that seemed impossible at first. Who knows? Maybe you can be the one to find the answer!

27 밑줄 친 (A)를 대신하여 쓰일 수 있는 것은?

① upcoming　　　② promising
③ continuing　　　④ following
⑤ underlying

28 What is Dr. Sci's attitude toward the existence of a wormhole?

① critical　　　② pessimistic
③ encouraging　　　④ desperate
⑤ regretful

[29~31] 다음 글을 읽고 물음에 답하시오.

> If I could make a planet ①for us ②to live in the future, I would like to make a planet called Atlas. It would be a beautiful green planet. Its size would be bigger ③than the moon, but smaller than Earth. The temperature of it would be ④about 30℃. It would have beautiful nature. Interestingly, if people moved to it, they could communicate with animals ⑤on this planet.

29 ①~⑤ 중 어법상 바르지 않은 것은?

①　　②　　③　　④　　⑤

30 글쓴이가 만들 행성에 관하여 알 수 없는 것을 모두 고르시오.

① its name　　　② its size
③ its temperature　　　④ its location
⑤ how to get there

31 With what could people communicate on the planet 'Atlas'? Answer in English.

➡ _____

_____

01 밑줄 친 부분과 바꿔 쓸 수 있는 말을 접미사 -able을 이용하여 쓰시오.

> The political situation is still very <u>unstable</u>.

➡ _____

02 다음 빈칸에 들어갈 말을 〈보기〉에서 찾아 쓰시오.

> ┤ 보기 ├
> ongoing persistent tough unstable

(1) It was a _____ decision to move to Busan.

(2) What do you think about this _____ issue?

(3) That chair looks _____ to me.

(4) I have a _____ headache and neck pain.

03 다음 영영풀이가 나타내는 말을 고르시오.

> to succeed in finishing something or reaching an aim, especially after a lot of work or effort

① achieve   ② acquire
③ improve   ④ perform
⑤ obtain

04 다음 빈칸에 들어갈 말을 고르시오.

> The rules don't _____ to children.

① apply   ② weigh   ③ lower
④ lean   ⑤ attach

[05~06] 다음 대화를 읽고 물음에 답하시오.

M: Irene, what was the best food you ate in the space station?

W: Hmm... . We grew some vegetables and ate them every day. They were pretty fresh and tasty!

M: Wow, (a)is it possible to grow vegetables in the space station?

W: Yes. (A)_____ there's no gravity in space, we had to grow them in special bags. The bags helped the roots to grow.

M: How interesting!

05 빈칸 (A)에 알맞은 말을 고르시오.

① Since   ② Therefore
③ Although   ④ But
⑤ However

06 밑줄 친 문장 (a)와 같은 의미가 <u>아닌</u> 것을 고르시오.

① are you able to grow vegetables in the space station?

② can you grow vegetables in the space station?

③ maybe should you grow vegetables in the space station?

④ would it be possible to grow vegetables in the space station?

⑤ is there a possibility that you grow vegetables in the space station?

[07~09] 다음 대화를 읽고 물음에 답하시오.

M: Have you heard ⓐwhat NASA is going to send a 3D printer ⓑinto space?

W: They're going to send a 3D printer into space? Why?

M: I've heard that the 3D printer will be used ⓒprinting (A)_____ food for astronauts.

W: (B)_____ food using a 3D printer?

M: Yes, it's ⓓimpossible. It can print (C)_____ a fresh pizza in less than five minutes.

W: Really? I wonder ⓔthat it would taste like.

출제율 90%

07 빈칸 (A)와 (C)에 공통으로 들어갈 말을 쓰시오.

➡ _____

출제율 90%

08 빈칸 (B)에 알맞은 말을 고르시오.

① Is it a possibility that print out
② Is it possible to print out
③ Is that possible to printing out
④ Do you find it possible print out
⑤ Do you make possible to print out

출제율 95%

09 ⓐ~ⓔ 중 흐름상 또는 어법상 알맞은 것을 고르시오.

① ⓐ ② ⓑ ③ ⓒ ④ ⓓ ⑤ ⓔ

[10~11] 다음 대화를 읽고 물음에 답하시오.

M: Look at these colorful pictures of the universe.

W: Oh, they're beautiful. (①)

M: (②) Actually, you can do that at the National Youth Space Center. (③)

W: Really? (④)

M: Yeah, you can use the VR glasses. (⑤) I heard that (A)_____!

출제율 100%

10 ①~⑤ 중 주어진 문장이 들어갈 곳은?

I wish I could see Earth from space with my own eyes.

① ② ③ ④ ⑤

출제율 95%

11 빈칸 (A)에 알맞은 말을 고르시오.

① I wish to see the shooting star
② you grow vegetables in the space station
③ you see the beautiful sunrise several times a day
④ I lie down to sleep in space
⑤ you feel like you are actually in space

출제율 95%

12 주어진 문장 이후에 올 대화의 순서를 바르게 배열하시오.

What are you watching?

(A) Yes, it's because there's no gravity in space.
(B) Right. I wish I could float around like an astronaut!
(C) It's a documentary about life in space. Everything seems so different.
(D) Really? I don't. It looks uncomfortable.

➡ _____

13 다음 중 어법상 올바른 문장은?

① If I were the principal of my school, I will let students have PE class every day.

② If there were no cold air and warm air, a wind can not be made.

③ Without your help, I could not get along well enough.

④ If were it not for water, no living things could survive.

⑤ But for your advice, I will ruin my reputation.

14 다음 문장에서 어법상 어색한 부분을 찾아 고치시오.

(1) If Drake has a lot of money, he can start a business right now. But he's poor.

➡ _____

(2) Sit with your legs extending and lean forward.

➡ _____

15 다음 우리말을 괄호 안에 주어진 조건대로 영작하시오.

(1) 만약 Carrie가 시험에 통과한다면, 변호사가 될 텐데. (if로 시작) (같은 뜻을 as로 시작)

➡ _____

_____

(2) 우리가 빛의 속도로 여행한다면, 화성에 13분 안에 도착할 수 있을 텐데. (if로 시작) (같은 뜻을 since로 시작)

➡ _____

_____

(3) 그 종이를 들고 점들이 맞춰지도록 그것을 접으세요. (with 이용)

➡ _____

_____

16 다음 중 〈보기〉의 밑줄 친 부분과 바꿔 쓸 수 없는 것은?

┤ 보기 ├

The world would be a better place if there were no more wars.

① if it were not for more wars

② were it not for more wars

③ but for more wars

④ had there no more wars

⑤ without more wars

[17~21] 다음 글을 읽고 물음에 답하시오.

Sci Teen: Is there ⓐ_____ in the universe?

Dr. Sci: According to some researchers, yes. Einstein figured out ⓑthat space and time are connected, and he called it space-time. He thought that space-time could actually be bent. When it is bent, parts that are far away from each other are suddenly closer.

(A) On a flat sheet of paper, the dots are far away from one another. Now, take the paper and fold it with the dots matched up.

(B) To understand this, take a sheet of paper and make a small dot at the top of the paper and another at the bottom of the paper.

(C) Punch a hole in the paper and the dots will be instantly connected. Like this, wormholes in space may contain two mouths, with a throat connecting the two.

Sci Teen: Just like a wormhole in the apple, right? If such wormholes existed in space, we could get to places billions of light-years away quickly!

Dr. Sci: Yes, but it's too early to celebrate. Wormholes exist in theory only.

17 글의 흐름상 빈칸 ⓐ에 들어갈 말로 가장 적절한 것은?

① such a planet   ② a room to rest
③ so much noise   ④ such a big hole
⑤ such a shortcut

18 자연스러운 글이 되도록 (A)~(C)를 바르게 나열하시오.

➡ _____

19 밑줄 친 ⓑ와 쓰임이 다른 하나는?

① Did you just say that he had left for London?
② The news that he came back surprised me.
③ It was regretful that I didn't visit him more often.
④ The idea that he came up with is brilliant for us to use.
⑤ Have you heard about the rumor that Jane and Tom broke up?

20 다음과 같이 풀이되는 말을 위 글에서 찾아 쓰시오.

> a formal statement of the rules on which a subject of study is based

➡ _____

21 Choose one that is NOT true.

① It was thought that space-time could be bent.
② Einstein was the one who figured out space and time are connected.
③ A wormhole makes it possible to get to another planet safely.
④ Parts far away from each other can be closer if space-time is bent.
⑤ It is assumed that wormholes contain two mouths with a throat.

[22~23] 다음 글을 읽고 물음에 답하시오.

If I could make a planet for us to live (A)_____ in the future, I would like to make a planet called Atlas. It would be a beautiful green planet. Its size would be bigger than the moon, but smaller than Earth. The temperature of it would be about 30℃. It would have beautiful nature. Interestingly, if people moved to it, they could communicate with animals (B)_____ this planet.

22 빈칸 (A)와 (B)에 들어갈 말이 바르게 짝지어진 것은?

① in – at   ② on – on
③ about – at   ④ to – on
⑤ by – by

23 What is the name of the planet the writer wants to make?

➡ _____

서술형 실전문제

01 밑줄 친 우리말과 일치하도록 주어진 단어를 이용하여 영작하시오. (단어 변형 가능)

> **A:** <u>내가 우주 여행을 가면 좋을 텐데.</u>
> **B:** Me, too. I'm sure that's every teenager's wish.

➡ (1) _____
　　 (take, wish, could)

(2) _____
　　 (come true, would, take)

(3) _____
　　 (if, take, would, great)

02 다음 그림을 보고 〈보기〉의 단어를 이용하여 이루어지기를 바라는 일을 표현하는 문장 2개를 완성하시오.

> ┤ 보기 ├
> cooking show, wish, could, open,
> appear, own, also, restaurant

➡ (1) _____
(2) _____
_____

03 다음 그림을 보고 주어진 단어를 이용해 대화의 빈칸을 완성하시오.

> **A:** _____ to sleep in space?
> 　　(possible, down, 6 단어)
> **B:** Yes, astronauts attach _____ a wall. (attach, sleeping bag)
> **A:** Sounds interesting. Life in space is so different from that on Earth.

04 다음 문장을 주어진 조건대로 바꿔 쓰시오.

(1) If Mary heard the news, she would be happy. (as 이용)

➡ _____ .

(2) If my father knew the fact, he would not let me go there. (so 이용)

➡ _____
_____

(3) As the man can't speak English, I won't employ him. (if 이용)

➡ _____
_____

(4) Since the weather is not fine, Jini won't go on a picnic. (were 이용, if를 쓰지 말 것.)

➡ _____

(5) Half the pleasure of our daily lives could be lost if there were no television. (without을 문두에 쓸 것.)

➡ _____
_____

05 다음 두 문장을 with를 이용해서 한 문장으로 바꿔 쓰시오.

(1) • Mr. Jones is sitting on a chair.

    • He crossed his legs.

➡ _____

(2) • Bella laughed out loud.

    • She pointed her finger at me.

➡ _____

_____

(3) • It was a beautiful morning.

    • Little wind blows.

➡ _____

_____

[06~08] 다음 글을 읽고 물음에 답하시오.

> **Sci Teen:** Is there such a shortcut in the universe?
>
> **Dr. Sci:** According to some researchers, yes. Einstein figured out that space and time are connected, and he called it space-time. He thought that space-time could actually be bent. When it is bent, parts that are far away from each other are suddenly closer. To understand this, take a sheet of paper and make a small dot at the top of the paper and another at the bottom of the paper. On a flat sheet of paper, the dots are far away from one another. Now, take the paper and fold it with the dots (A)_____ up. Punch a hole in the paper and the dots will be instantly connected. Like this, wormholes in space may contain two mouths, with a throat connecting the two.

06 빈칸 (A)에 동사 match를 어법에 맞게 쓰시오.

➡ _____

07 What did Einstein figure out about space and time? Answer in English.

➡ _____

08 What connects two mouths of a wormhole? Answer in English with a full sentence.

➡ _____

[09~10] 다음 글을 읽고 물음에 답하시오.

> **Sci Teen:** Hi, science fans. Today, we're going to talk about space travel. As we all know, there is nothing faster than (A)_____ in the universe. So, if we travel at the speed of light, we should be able to get to another planet in the blink of an eye, right?
>
> **Dr. Sci:** That would be nice, but space is so vast that it is not possible. In the movie, *Passengers*, a spaceship (B)_____ to a different planet (C)_____ at one-half the speed of light. So it should get to another planet very quickly, right? But, the passengers sleep for 120 years because it is (D)_____ to take that much time to get to a different planet.

09 문맥상 빈칸 (A)에 알맞은 말을 위 글에서 찾아 쓰시오.

➡ _____

10 주어진 단어를 문맥과 어법에 맞게 빈칸 (B)~(D)에 쓰시오.

(travel / expect / head)

➡ (B)_____ (C)_____ (D)_____

01 I wish를 사용해 자신만의 소원 3가지 이상을 쓰시오.

(1) _____

(2) _____

(3) _____

02 다음 우리말을 가정법을 사용하여 영작하시오.

(1) 지구에 공기가 없다면, 하늘은 언제나 깜깜할 텐데.

➡ _____

(2) 중력이 없다면, 공기는 우주로 가 버릴 텐데. (주어진 조건에 맞춰 영작할 것.)
(a) there를 이용할 것. (b) if를 이용할 것. (c) if를 쓰지 말고 were를 이용할 것. (d) but을 이용할 것. (e) without을 이용할 것.

➡ _____

_____

_____

_____

_____

03 다음 질의응답을 참고하여 Jane이 구상한 행성에 대한 글을 완성하시오.

Q: What is the name of the planet? / And what color is it?

A: It's called Minas. It is a beautiful pink planet.

Q: How big is the planet? And what is the temperature of it?

A: Its size is bigger than the moon, but smaller than Earth. The temperature is about 20℃.

Q: What is special about the planet? If people moved to it, what would be good for them?

A: It has cotton candy mountains. If people moved to it, they could feel time pass slowly on this planet.

If I could make a planet for us to live on in the future, I would like to make a planet called _____. It would be a beautiful _____ planet. Its size would be _____ _____. The temperature of it would be about _____. It would have _____. Interestingly, if people moved to it, they could _____.

단원별 모의고사

01 빈칸에 전치사 in이 들어가지 <u>않는</u> 것을 <u>모두</u> 고르시오. (대·소문자 무시)

① _____ theory, it takes only 2 days to climb the mountain, but in practice it is impossible.

② Will you print _____ your report?

③ It disappeared _____ the blink of an eye.

④ I studied hard _____ order to pass the exam.

⑤ Lie _____ here and take a rest.

02 접두사 im-이나 in-을 붙여서 반의어를 만들 수 <u>없는</u> 것을 고르시오.

① partial ② patient ③ usual
④ credible ⑤ sensitive

03 다음 빈칸을 <보기>에 있는 어휘를 이용하여 채우시오. (형태 변화 가능)

┌─ 보기 ┐
attach crush exist extend
└────────┘

(1) Lie down on the floor and _____ your legs.

(2) You should _____ your photograph to the form.

(3) These cars were _____ in the accident.

(4) Do you believe life _____ on other planets?

04 다음 우리말에 맞도록 빈칸에 알맞은 말을 쓰시오. (철자가 주어진 경우 주어진 철자로 시작할 것.)

(1) 그 회사는 1주일에 수십억 달러를 쓴다.
➡ The company spends _____ _____ dollars a week.

(2) 그의 생일을 축하하기 위한 파티를 여는 게 어떠니?
➡ How about having a party to c_____ his birthday?

(3) 이 기계는 물 사용을 감지하는 센서가 있다.
➡ This machine has sensors to d_____ water use.

(4) 한참을 찾은 후에, 나는 잃어버렸던 우산을 결국 찾았다.
➡ After a long search, I e_____ the missing umbrella.

[05~06] 다음 대화를 읽고 물음에 답하시오.

A: Look at this movie. People are walking in the spaceship, just like on Earth.

B: That's because they can make "gravity" in the spaceship.

A: Is it possible to create gravity in space? If so, the space trip would be more (A) [comfortable / uncomfortable].

B: I heard it's not entirely (B)[possible / impossible]. Scientists are developing the technology.

A: Really? I wish I could travel long distance in a spaceship someday.

05 위 대화의 괄호 (A)와 (B)에서 적절한 것을 골라 쓰시오.

➡ (A) _____ (B) _____

06 위 대화에서 다음 영영풀이에 해당하는 단어를 찾아 쓰시오.

> the amount of space between two places

➡ _____

[07~09] 다음 대화를 읽고 물음에 답하시오.

> W: Look at this man, Jake. (①) He lived in space for one year.
> M: It must have been tough for him. (②)
> W: Right, but you know what's interesting? He grew 2 inches (A)_____ in space. (③)
> M: Really? How is that possible?
> W: I'm not sure, but maybe it's (B)_____ there's no gravity in space. (④)
> M: That's so cool. (a)내가 우주에서 살 수 있으면 좋을 텐데. (wish, could) (⑤)
> W: I'm sure there are other ways to become taller than going to space.

07 ①~⑤ 중 주어진 문장이 들어갈 곳은?

> That way, I could become taller.

①   ②   ③   ④   ⑤

08 빈칸 (A)와 (B)에 들어갈 말이 알맞게 짝지어진 것은?

	(A)	(B)
①	while	why
②	while	so
③	while	because
④	for	why
⑤	for	because

09 밑줄 친 (a)의 우리말과 일치하도록 주어진 단어를 이용해 영작하시오.

➡ _____

[10~12] 다음 대화를 읽고 물음에 답하시오.

> M: Hey, Cindy. (①) I heard that you went to the National Space Center last weekend. How was it?
> W: It was great, Chris. (②) I experienced zero gravity and astronauts' space life. (③)
> M: Sounds fun. (④)
> W: Yes, and I heard about their adventure stories. (⑤)
> M: Oh, (a)나는 그들처럼 우주인이 돼서 화성을 탐험하고 싶어. (could, Mars, I, I, an astronaut, explore, become, and, like, them, wish)

10 ①~⑤ 중 주어진 문장이 들어갈 곳은?

> Did you meet real astronauts in person?

①   ②   ③   ④   ⑤

11 밑줄 친 (a)의 우리말과 일치하도록 괄호 안에 주어진 단어를 알맞게 배열하시오.

➡ _____
_____

12 ⓐ~ⓓ 중 위 대화를 읽고 답할 수 있는 질문을 모두 고르시오.

> ⓐ What did Cindy do at the National Space Center?
> ⓑ Is it possible for Cindy to become an astronaut?
> ⓒ When did Cindy go to the National Space Center?
> ⓓ Did Cindy meet the astronauts?

➡ _____

13 다음 중 문장의 뜻이 나머지 넷과 <u>다른</u> 것은?

① If I had a magic lamp, I could wish for happiness and health.

② Had I a magic lamp, I could wish for happiness and health.

③ Since I have a magic lamp, I can wish for happiness and health.

④ As I don't have a magic lamp, I can't wish for happiness and health.

⑤ I don't have a magic lamp, so I can't wish for happiness and health.

14 다음 빈칸에 공통으로 알맞은 것은?

> • My little brother was crying _____ tears running down his face.
> • Brian looked at the children, _____ his arms folded.

① when   ② since   ③ if
④ with   ⑤ as

15 다음 중 밑줄 친 부분의 쓰임이 나머지 넷과 <u>다른</u> 것은?

① She said <u>if</u> she had a million dollars, she would buy a fancy house and a car.

② He had no idea <u>if</u> the students would like his gifts.

③ <u>If</u> Mike spoke English, he could make many foreign friends.

④ <u>If</u> I were the president, I would make more holidays.

⑤ We could go to a movie <u>if</u> my mom were not tired.

16 다음 문장에서 <u>틀린</u> 것을 고쳐 다시 쓰시오.

(1) They jogged with their dog followed them.

➡ _____

(2) Drake walked for a long time with his eyes fixing upon the floor.

➡ _____
_____

(3) The prince entered the hall with the people cheered.

➡ _____
_____

17 괄호 안에 주어진 어휘를 활용하여 우리말과 일치하도록 영작하시오.

(1) 내가 우주 비행사라면, 난 우주를 걸어다닐 텐데. (an astronaut, walk in space)

➡ _____

(2) 만약 비가 멈춘다면 우리는 야구를 할 수 있을 텐데. (stop, rain)

➡ _____

(3) 어머니를 다시 살아 돌아오시게 할 수 있으면 좋겠어요. (wish, bring back to, life)

➡ _____

(4) 윗팔에 무릎을 둔 채, 팔로 균형을 유지하세요. (balance, rest, the upper arms, on)

➡ _____

(5) 나의 선생님은 하루 종일 문을 닫은 채 일하셨다. (work, all day, close)

➡ _____
_____

[18~21] 다음 글을 읽고 물음에 답하시오.

Sci Teen: Is there a faster way to travel through space?

Dr. Sci: Well, in order to answer that question, I'd like you to think about this apple for a second. Imagine a worm is on this apple. It detects something sweet at the bottom and wants to move from the top to the bottom. For the worm, the apple's surface is as vast as our universe. Now the worm can either move around the outer layer or down a wormhole. Which do you think it will choose? Well, it would choose the wormhole because it is a shortcut.

Sci Teen: Is there such a shortcut in the universe?

Dr. Sci: According to some researchers, yes. Einstein figured out that space and time are connected, and he called it space-time. He thought that space-time could actually be bent. (①) When it is bent, parts that are far away from each other are suddenly closer. (②) To understand this, take a sheet of paper and make a small dot at the top of the paper and another at the bottom of the paper. (③) Now, take the paper and fold it with the dots matched up. (④) Punch a hole in the paper and the dots will be instantly connected. (⑤) Like this, wormholes in space may contain two mouths, (A)_____.

18 주어진 단어를 바르게 나열하여 빈칸 (A)에 들어갈 말을 완성하시오. 필요할 경우 어형을 바꾸시오.

> (the two / a throat / connect / with)

➡ _____

19 ①~⑤ 중 주어진 문장이 들어가기에 가장 적절한 곳은?

> On a flat sheet of paper, the dots are far away from one another.

①   ②   ③   ④   ⑤

20 What are the two ways for the worm to move from the top to the bottom of an apple? Answer in English.

➡ _____
_____

21 위 글을 읽고 답할 수 <u>없는</u> 것은?

① Why does the worm want to move to the bottom of the apple?

② Which way is better for the worm to choose to move to the bottom of the apple?

③ Who figured out that space and time are connected?

④ What happens to the dots if we punch a hole in the paper?

⑤ How did Einstein find out space and time are connected?

[22~25] 다음 글을 읽고 물음에 답하시오.

Sci Teen: Just like a wormhole in the apple, right? If such wormholes existed in space, we could get to places billions of light-years away quickly!

Dr. Sci: Yes, but it's too early to celebrate. Wormholes exist in theory only.

Sci Teen: So all we need to do is find one, right?

Dr. Sci: Even if we find one, there are many things to consider before actually going through one. A wormhole would be very unstable. If a spaceship flew into one, it might be crushed or broken into pieces.

Sci Teen: Ouch! That's not a pretty picture. So, are we hopeless? Is traveling in space through a wormhole simply an idea that only exists in theory?

Dr. Sci: I wouldn't say so. The debate about wormholes is still ongoing, but with persistent exploration and research, I believe we will eventually find one and learn how to travel through it. Look back at our history. We've achieved so many things that seemed impossible at first. Who knows? Maybe you can be the one to find (A)the answer!

22 빈칸에 들어갈 말로 가장 적절한 것은?

Q: Why do we need to consider many things before going through a wormhole?

A: It is because _____.

① there are too many wormholes
② lots of people want to go there
③ there is no place like a wormhole
④ a wormhole would be very unstable
⑤ a wormhole makes people comfortable

23 밑줄 친 (A)의 의미로 가장 적절한 것은?

① 웜홀의 기원을 연구하는 방법에 대한 답
② 웜홀을 통해 우주여행을 하는 방법에 대한 해답
③ 불가능한 것을 가능하게 만드는 것에 대한 해답
④ 웜홀을 증명하는 이론을 찾는 방법에 대한 답
⑤ 이론상에만 존재하는 웜홀의 존재를 증명하는 답

24 How will we find a wormhole and learn how to travel through it according to Dr. Sci? Answer in English.

➡ _____

_____

25 What could we do if wormholes existed in space? Answer in English.

➡ _____

_____

MEMO

INSIGHT
on the textbook

교과서 파헤치기

※ 다음 영어를 우리말로 쓰시오.

01 convenient

02 last

03 match

04 compete

05 allowance

06 purchase

07 release

08 affect

09 disappear

10 behavior

11 combine

12 replace

13 mention

14 aboard

15 discount

16 encourage

17 effect

18 compare

19 refund

20 spending

21 concept

22 endanger

23 complete

24 fix

25 striped

26 difference

27 immediately

28 tight

29 influence

30 lack

31 anchor

32 billion

33 overheated

34 consume

35 on display

36 in comparison

37 go well with

38 just because

39 keep track of

40 when it comes to

41 be likely to

42 more than half

43 at a glance

※ 다음 우리말을 영어로 쓰시오.

01 용돈 _____

02 결합하다 _____

03 즉시, 바로 _____

04 효과 _____

05 편리한, 간편한 _____

06 거래 _____

07 10억 _____

08 완성하다 _____

09 ~에 영향을 주다 _____

10 언급하다, 말하다 _____

11 소비하다, 소모하다 _____

12 닻; 닻을 내리다 _____

13 행동, 행위 _____

14 놓치다 _____

15 차이, 차이점 _____

16 비교하다 _____

17 부추기다, 조장하다 _____

18 경쟁하다 _____

19 위험에 빠뜨리다 _____

20 개념 _____

21 줄무늬가 있는 _____

22 환불 _____

23 출시하다, 발매하다 _____

24 ~에 영향을 주다 _____

25 부족, 결핍 _____

26 사라지다 _____

27 할인; 할인하다 _____

28 어울리다 _____

29 구매하다, 구입하다 _____

30 기르다, 키우다 _____

31 바꾸다, 교체하다 _____

32 지출 _____

33 꽉 조이는, 딱 붙는 _____

34 낭비하다, 소모하다 _____

35 진열된, 전시된 _____

36 한눈에, 즉시 _____

37 비교해 보면 _____

38 ~을 기록하다 _____

39 그러한 결과로 _____

40 단지 ~라는 이유로 _____

41 ~와 잘 어울리다 _____

42 ~에 관해서,
~에 대해 말하자면 _____

43 ~할 가능성이 있다,
~하기 쉽다 _____

※ 다음 영영풀이에 알맞은 단어를 <보기>에서 골라 쓴 후, 우리말 뜻을 쓰시오.

1 _____ : without delay: _____

2 _____ : a principle or idea: _____

3 _____ : to become impossible to see: _____

4 _____ : to buy property, goods, etc.: _____

5 _____ : to make something available to the public: _____

6 _____ : to be right for a particular person, situation, or occasion: _____

7 _____ : rather small and fit closely to your body: _____

8 _____ : to join together to make a single thing or group: _____

9 _____ : to use more of something than is necessary or useful: _____

10 _____ : suitable for your purposes and needs and causing the least difficulty:

_____

11 _____ : to support an activity or make it more likely: _____

12 _____ : an amount of money that is given to someone regularly or for a particular

purpose: _____

13 _____ : to use fuel, energy, or time, especially in large amounts or to eat or drink,

especially a lot of something: _____

14 _____ : to put someone or something at risk or in danger of being harmed,

damaged, or destroyed: _____

15 _____ : a condition of not having any or enough of something, especially

something necessary or wanted: _____

16 _____ : to have an influence on someone or something, or to cause a change in

someone or something: _____

보기			
lack	combine	affect	tight
convenient	disappear	encourage	concept
endanger	suit	consume	release
waste	immediately	allowance	purchase

※ 다음 우리말과 일치하도록 빈칸에 알맞은 말을 쓰시오.

해석

Listen & Talk 1 A

1. **M:** Hi, can I _____ you _____ anything?

   W: Yes, can I _____ _____ that cap _____ stars over there?

   M: Sure. _____ _____ _____ _____ it?

   W: The design is nice, _____ I don't think the color _____ me. Do you _____ it in black?

   M: Yes. I'll get _____ from the back. *(pause)* Here it is.

   W: Great. I'll _____ it.

2. **M:** Good morning. _____ _____ Kelly's Sporting Goods Store.

   W: Hi, _____ _____ _____ a backpack for hiking.

   M: These two are _____ _____ hikers. _____ _____ _____ _____ them?

   W: The _____ _____ _____ _____ _____ the blue _____. I'll take the _____ _____.

   M: Great _____.

1. M: 안녕하세요, 무엇을 도와 드릴까
      요?
   W: 네, 저기 별들이 그려진 모자를 써
      볼 수 있나요?
   M: 그럼요. 어떠세요?
   W: 디자인은 좋은데, 색이 제게 안 어
      울리는 것 같아요. 이거 검은색으
      로 있나요?
   M: 네. 제가 안쪽에서 가져다 드릴게
      요. (잠시 후) 여기 있어요.
   W: 좋아요. 그걸로 할게요.

2. M: 안녕하세요. Kelly의 스포츠 용품
      가게에 오신 것을 환영합니다.
   W: 안녕하세요, 저는 하이킹할 때 쓸
      배낭을 찾고 있어요.
   M: 이 두 개가 하이킹하시는 분들 사
      이에서 인기가 있어요. 어떠세요?
   W: 초록색 배낭이 파란색 배낭보다
      더 가볍네요. 더 가벼운 걸로 할게
      요.
   M: 탁월한 선택입니다.

Listen & Talk 1 B

W: Hi, Luke. Is that a new speaker?

M: Yes, I _____ it a _____ _____ _____.

W: It _____ cool. _____ _____ _____ _____ it?

M: It's _____. I can take it _____ and listen to music. The sound _____ is good, _____.

W: Great. _____ _____ does the battery _____?

M: _____ 2 hours. The battery _____ _____ long.

W: That's _____ _____.

M: Yeah, but I'm _____ _____ with it, _____.

W: 안녕, Luke. 그거 새 스피커니?
M: 응, 몇 주 전에 샀어.
W: 멋져 보인다. 그거 어때?
M: 편리해. 나는 그것을 어디든지 가져가
   서 음악을 들을 수 있어. 음질도 좋아.
W: 좋다. 배터리가 얼마나 오래가니?
M: 2시간 정도야. 배터리가 그렇게 오래
   가지 않아.
W: 그거 안타깝구나.
M: 응, 하지만 어쨌든 나는 꽤 만족해.

1. **M:** Oh, this coat is _____ _____.

   W: Why? _____ _____ _____ _____ _____ _____ ?

   M: It's too _____.

   W: Didn't _____ _____ _____ _____ _____ _____

      it?

   M: No. It was my size, _____ I just _____ it. I _____ _____

      _____ it _____.

2. **W:** Hey, Eric. Camilla and I _____ _____ _____ _____ _____ a

      movie. Do you want _____ _____ us?

   M: I'd _____ _____, but I can't. _____ _____ all of my

      _____ for this week.

   W: Didn't you just _____ _____ a few days _____? How

      did you spend it all?

   M: I'm not sure. I _____ _____ _____ _____ _____

      _____ _____.

1. **M:** 오, 이 코트는 너무 불편해.
   W: 왜? 무슨 문제가 있니?
   M: 너무 꽉 껴.
   W: 사기 전에 입어 보지 않았어?
   M: 아니. 내 사이즈여서 그냥 사 버렸어. 난 그것을 입어 봤어야 했어.

2. **W:** 안녕, Eric. Camilla랑 나는 영화를 보러 갈 거야. 우리랑 같이 갈래?
   M: 그러고 싶지만, 안 돼. 이번 주 용돈을 전부 써 버렸거든.
   W: 너 고작 며칠 전에 받지 않았어? 어떻게 다 써 버렸어?
   M: 잘 모르겠어. 내 지출을 기록했어야 했어.

M: Did you get a new phone, Jamie? It's just _____ _____.

W: Yeah, I got it last weekend _____ _____.

M: It was _____ _____? But it _____ _____ _____

   _____, hasn't it?

W: Right, but the store on Green Street _____ _____ a year-end

   _____.

M: Oh, I bought mine _____ _____ _____ !

W: Really? That's too bad. They're _____ them _____ a 40 percent

   _____.

M: I _____ _____ _____ _____ _____ _____ _____ buying

   mine.

M: 새 전화기를 샀니, Jamie? 내 것과 똑같다.
W: 응, 나는 이것을 지난주 할인할 때 샀어.
M: 그거 할인 중이었어? 하지만 그것은 막 출시되었잖아, 그렇지 않아?
W: 맞아, 하지만 Green가에 있는 가게에서 연말 할인 판매를 하더라.
M: 오, 나는 내 것을 정가를 주고 샀는데!
W: 정말? 그것 참 안됐다. 40퍼센트 할인하여 팔고 있어.
M: 내 것을 사기 전에 할인 판매를 확인했어야 했어.

Communication Step A

M: Hi, Riley. I _____ _____ _____ a laptop online. _____ do you _____ it?

W: Oh, I'm _____ _____ with _____.

M: _____? _____ wrong?

W: It makes too much noise and _____ _____. I should _____ _____ more _____.

M: Oh, then you should _____ _____ your money back.

W: The online store _____ _____ _____ _____ my money because _____ _____ it for a week.

M: How about _____ the online shop and _____ your problem?

W: Yeah, I think I should _____ that.

Wrap Up

1. M: Good morning. May I help you?

   W: _____ _____ _____ buy a T-shirt for my sister. She's eleven years old.

   M: _____ _____ _____ _____ _____ _____ _____? This character is quite popular _____ children.

   W: Well, she doesn't like animation characters _____ much. Can I see the blue _____?

   M: You mean this blue _____ T-shirt? _____ design is simple and cool.

   W: Yes, I think my sister will like it. I'll _____ it.

2. W: Jake, here's a _____ for you.

   M: It's my helmet. I _____ it at an _____ _____ _____ a few days _____.

   W: Oh, open it and _____ _____ _____ it.

   M: Okay. (pause) Oh, this outer part _____ _____ _____ _____. The seller _____ _____ it's perfectly fine though.

   W: Didn't you check the pictures of the helmet _____ you bought it?

   M: No, _____ _____ _____ the seller. I _____ _____ _____ _____ _____ _____.

   W: You _____ _____ the seller and _____ _____ _____.

M: 안녕, Riley. 네가 온라인으로 노트북을 샀다고 들었어. 그거 어때?

W: 아, 나는 별로 마음에 들지 않아.

M: 왜? 무슨 문제가 있어?

W: 소음이 너무 심하고 과열이 돼. 난 후기를 더 많이 읽어 봤어야 했어.

M: 오, 그럼 환불을 요청해 봐.

W: 내가 그것을 일주일 동안 사용했기 때문에 온라인 가게는 환불을 해 주지 않을 거야.

M: 온라인 가게에 전화해서 문제를 설명하는 건 어때?

W: 응, 그렇게 해야 할 것 같아.

1. M: 안녕하세요. 도와 드릴까요?

   W: 저는 여동생에게 티셔츠를 사 주고 싶어요. 그 애는 11살이에요.

   M: 이 빨간색 티셔츠는 어떠세요? 이 캐릭터는 아이들 사이에서 꽤 인기가 있어요.

   W: 글쎄요, 그 애는 만화 캐릭터를 그다지 좋아하지 않아요. 파란색 티셔츠 좀 볼 수 있을까요?

   M: 파란색 줄무늬 티셔츠 말씀이시죠? 그건 디자인이 단순하고 멋있어요.

   W: 네, 제 여동생이 좋아할 것 같아요. 그걸로 할게요.

2. W: Jake, 여기 네 소포가 있어.

   M: 그거 내 헬멧이야. 며칠 전에 온라인 중고 가게에서 샀어.

   W: 오, 열어서 보여 줘.

   M: 그래. (잠시 후) 아, 이 바깥 부분이 조금 깨졌어. 하지만 판매자는 이것이 완벽하게 괜찮다고 말했어.

   W: 사기 전에 헬멧 사진을 확인해 보지 않았니?

   M: 아니, 나는 그냥 판매자를 믿었어. 조금 더 확인을 했어야 했어.

   W: 너는 판매자에게 전화해서 환불을 요청해야 해.

※ 다음 우리말에 맞도록 대화를 영어로 쓰시오.

Listen & Talk 1 A

1. M: _____

   W: _____

   M: _____

   W: _____

   _____

   M: _____

   W: _____

2. M: _____

   W: _____

   M: _____

   W: _____

   M: _____

Listen & Talk 1 B

W: _____

M: _____

W: _____

M: _____

_____

W: _____

M: _____

W: _____

M: _____

1. M: 안녕하세요, 무엇을 도와 드릴까
      요?
   W: 네, 저기 별들이 그려진 모자를 써
      볼 수 있나요?
   M: 그럼요. 어떠세요?
   W: 디자인은 좋은데, 색이 제게 안 어
      울리는 것 같아요. 이거 검은색으
      로 있나요?
   M: 네. 제가 안쪽에서 가져다 드릴게
      요. (잠시 후) 여기 있어요.
   W: 좋아요. 그걸로 할게요.

2. M: 안녕하세요. Kelly의 스포츠 용품
      가게에 오신 것을 환영합니다.
   W: 안녕하세요, 저는 하이킹할 때 쓸
      배낭을 찾고 있어요.
   M: 이 두 개가 하이킹하시는 분들 사
      이에서 인기가 있어요. 어떠세요?
   W: 초록색 배낭이 파란색 배낭보다
      더 가볍네요. 더 가벼운 걸로 할게
      요.
   M: 탁월한 선택입니다.

W: 안녕, Luke. 그거 새 스피커니?
M: 응, 몇 주 전에 샀어.
W: 멋져 보인다. 그거 어때?
M: 편리해. 나는 그것을 어디든지 가져가
   서 음악을 들을 수 있어. 음질도 좋아.
W: 좋다. 배터리가 얼마나 오래가니?
M: 2시간 정도야. 배터리가 그렇게 오래
   가지 않아.
W: 그거 안타깝구나.
M: 응, 하지만 어쨌든 나는 꽤 만족해.

Listen & Talk 2 A

1. M: _____

   W: _____

   M: _____

   W: _____

   M: _____

2. W: _____

   M: _____

   W: _____

   M: _____

Listen & Talk 2 B

M: _____

W: _____

M: _____

W: _____

M: _____

W: _____

M: _____

1. M: 오, 이 코트는 너무 불편해.
   W: 왜? 무슨 문제가 있니?
   M: 너무 꽉 껴.
   W: 사기 전에 입어 보지 않았어?
   M: 아니. 내 사이즈여서 그냥 사 버렸어. 난 그것을 입어 봤어야 했어.

2. W: 안녕, Eric. Camilla랑 나는 영화를 보러 갈 거야. 우리랑 같이 갈래?
   M: 그러고 싶지만, 안 돼. 이번 주 용돈을 전부 써 버렸거든.
   W: 너 고작 며칠 전에 받지 않았어? 어떻게 다 써 버렸어?
   M: 잘 모르겠어. 내 지출을 기록했어야 했어.

M: 새 전화기를 샀니, Jamie? 내 것과 똑같다.
W: 응, 나는 이것을 지난주 할인할 때 샀어.
M: 그거 할인 중이었어? 하지만 그것은 막 출시되었잖아, 그렇지 않아?
W: 맞아, 하지만 Green가에 있는 가게에서 연말 할인 판매를 하더라.
M: 오, 나는 내 것을 정가를 주고 샀는데!
W: 정말? 그것 참 안됐다. 40퍼센트 할인하여 팔고 있어.
M: 내 것을 사기 전에 할인 판매를 확인했어야 했어.

Communication Step A

M: _____

W: _____

M: _____

W: _____

_____

M: _____

W: _____

M: _____

W: _____

Wrap Up

1. M: _____

W: _____

M: _____

_____

W: _____

M: _____

W: _____

2. W: _____

M: _____

W: _____

M: _____

_____

W: _____

M: _____

W: _____

M: 안녕, Riley. 네가 온라인으로 노트북을 샀다고 들었어. 그거 어때?
W: 아, 나는 별로 마음에 들지 않아.
M: 왜? 무슨 문제가 있어?
W: 소음이 너무 심하고 과열이 돼. 난 후기를 더 많이 읽어 봤어야 했어.
M: 오, 그럼 환불을 요청해 봐.
W: 내가 그것을 일주일 동안 사용했기 때문에 온라인 가게는 환불을 해 주지 않을 거야.
M: 온라인 가게에 전화해서 문제를 설명하는 건 어때?
W: 응, 그렇게 해야 할 것 같아.

1. M: 안녕하세요. 도와 드릴까요?
W: 저는 여동생에게 티셔츠를 사 주고 싶어요. 그 애는 11살이에요.
M: 이 빨간색 티셔츠는 어떠세요? 이 캐릭터는 아이들 사이에서 꽤 인기가 있어요.
W: 글쎄요, 그 애는 만화 캐릭터를 그다지 좋아하지 않아요. 파란색 티셔츠 좀 볼 수 있을까요?
M: 파란색 줄무늬 티셔츠 말씀이시죠? 그건 디자인이 단순하고 멋있어요.
W: 네, 제 여동생이 좋아할 것 같아요. 그걸로 할게요.

2. W: Jake, 여기 네 소포가 있어.
M: 그거 내 헬멧이야. 며칠 전에 온라인 중고 가게에서 샀어.
W: 오, 열어서 보여 줘.
M: 그래. (잠시 후) 아, 이 바깥 부분이 조금 깨졌어. 하지만 판매자는 이것이 완벽하게 괜찮다고 말했어.
W: 사기 전에 헬멧 사진을 확인해 보지 않았니?
M: 아니, 나는 그냥 판매자를 믿었어. 조금 더 확인을 했어야 했어.
W: 너는 판매자에게 전화해서 환불을 요청해야 해.

※ 다음 우리말과 일치하도록 빈칸에 알맞은 것을 골라 쓰시오.

1 Have you ever _____ _____ you've _____ things that you don't _____ want or need?

     A. bought   B. wondered   C. why   D. even

2 Let's consider _____ _____ us when it _____ to _____ things.

     A. affects   B. buying   C. what   D. comes

3 Why do I want to buy _____ _____ _____ _____?

     A. bought   B. my   C. what   D. friends

4 Jeff _____ to the shopping center and sees a _____ of soccer shoes _____ _____.

     A. display   B. goes   C. pair   D. on

5 He _____ the shoes at a glance _____ more than _____ of the boys on his soccer team _____ them.

     A. half   B. recognizes   C. wear   D. because

6 _____ he already has many pairs of soccer shoes, he _____ _____ buying _____ new pair.

     A. ends   B. although   C. up   D. another

7 We can use the "bandwagon _____" _____ _____ Jeff's _____.

     A. behavior   B. effect   C. explain   D. to

8 A bandwagon is a wagon in a _____ that _____ people to _____ _____ and enjoy the music.

     A. encourages   B. aboard   C. parade   D. jump

9 As more and more people get on the bandwagon, _____ are more _____ to _____ on or _____ it.

     A. others   B. get   C. follow   D. likely

10 In this _____, people _____ to buy something _____ because other people have _____ it.

     A. bought   B. way   C. just   D. tend

11 Why do I _____ a _____ of pants and a bag _____ I have _____ a new coat?

     A. bought   B. pair   C. after   D. buy

1 여러분은 원하거나 필요로 하지도 않는 것들을 자신이 왜 구입했는지 궁금해 한 적이 있는가?

2 물건들을 구입하는 것에 관하여 무엇이 우리에게 영향을 주는지 생각해 보자.

3 나는 왜 친구들이 산 것을 사고 싶은 걸까?

4 Jeff는 쇼핑센터에 가서 진열되어 있는 축구화 한 켤레를 보게 된다.

5 그의 축구팀에 있는 소년들의 반 이상이 그 축구화를 신기 때문에 그는 그 신발을 한눈에 알아챈다.

6 이미 그에게는 축구화가 많이 있지만 결국 그는 또 다른 새 축구화를 사 버리고 만다.

7 우리는 Jeff의 행동을 설명하기 위해 '밴드왜건 효과'를 이용할 수 있다.

8 밴드왜건(악대차)은 사람들이 올라타서 음악을 즐기게끔 부추기는 퍼레이드에 있는 사륜마차이다.

9 더 많은 사람들이 밴드왜건에 올라탈수록 다른 사람들이 더욱 그것에 올라타거나 그것을 따라가려 한다.

10 이런 식으로, 사람들은 단지 다른 사람들이 어떤 것을 샀다는 이유로 그것을 구매하는 경향이 있다.

11 나는 왜 새 코트를 구입한 후에 바지와 가방을 사는 걸까?

12 Lisa buys a coat _____ she really loves. _____, she _____ that her pants do not _____ her new coat.

    A. realizes   B. match   C. immediately   D. that

13 So, she _____ new pants that _____ _____ _____ her new coat.

    A. go   B. buys   C. with   D. perfectly

14 But she _____ that _____ of her bags _____ her new _____.

    A. clothes   B. none   C. match   D. sees

15 So, she buys a new bag. _____ of her money is spent _____ buying the new _____ to _____ her new look.

    A. most   B. on   C. complete   D. items

16 What _____ Lisa _____ for new items immediately _____ _____ a new coat?

    A. search   B. buying   C. made   D. after

17 The "Diderot effect" may _____ it. Denis Diderot, a French writer, _____ a new gown _____ a _____.

    A. received   B. explain   C. gift   D. as

18 Soon after receiving the gift, he _____ that all of his _____ did not _____ well with his new gown. So, he ended up _____ most of it.

    A. noticed   B. go   C. replacing   D. furniture

19 The Diderot effect, _____, is the concept that _____ a new item often _____ to more _____ purchases.

    A. leads   B. therefore   C. unplanned   D. purchasing

20 Why do I buy things _____ _____ they are _____ _____?

    A. sale   B. because   C. on   D. just

21 Nathan _____ _____ shopping and _____ a _____ of headphones.

    A. goes   B. sees   C. pair   D. window

---

12 Lisa는 정말 마음에 드는 코트를 산다. 그녀는 그녀의 바지가 새 코트와 어울리지 않는다는 것을 즉시 알아차린다.

13 그래서 그녀는 새 코트와 완벽하게 어울리는 새 바지를 구입한다.

14 하지만 그녀는 자신의 가방 중 어느 것도 새로운 옷들과 어울리지 않는다는 것을 알게 된다.

15 그래서 그녀는 새 가방을 산다. 그녀의 돈 대부분이 그녀의 새로운 모습을 완성하기 위하여 새로운 물품을 사는 데 쓰인다.

16 무엇이 Lisa로 하여금 새 코트를 산 후 즉시 새로운 물품을 찾게 했을까?

17 '디드로 효과'가 그것을 설명해 줄지도 모른다. 프랑스 작가인 Denis Diderot는 선물로 새 가운을 받았다.

18 그 선물을 받은 후에 곧 그는 그의 모든 가구가 새로운 가운과 어울리지 않는다는 것을 알아챘다. 그래서 그는 결국 대부분의 가구를 바꾸고 말았다.

19 그러므로 디드로 효과는 새로운 물품을 구입하는 것이 흔히 계획에 없던 더 많은 구매로 이어진다는 개념이다.

20 나는 왜 단지 할인 중이라는 이유로 물건을 구입하는 걸까?

21 Nathan은 진열된 상품을 구경하러 가서 헤드폰을 하나 본다.

22 He _____ the price and_____ _____ that they are $200. He thinks that the headphones are too _____.

    A. out   B. expensive   C. checks   D. finds

23 The _____ person _____ him and says, "You can get a 20 percent _____ _____ those headphones."

    A. discount   B. sales   C. on   D. approaches

24 Even _____ the _____ price is _____ not very _____, Nathan decides to buy the headphones.

    A. low   B. discounted   C. though   D. still

25 The situation _____ _____ is an _____ of the "anchoring _____."

    A. above   B. effect   C. example   D. described

26 The price _____ first _____ our _____ of _____ mentioned afterwards.

    A. prices   B. mentioned   C. opinion   D. affects

27 For example, if we start with $200, then $160 will _____ _____ _____ _____.

    A. comparison   B. seem   C. in   D. cheap

28 _____, as the difference of the two prices _____ _____, the effect will be more _____.

    A. bigger   B. furthermore   C. powerful   D. becomes

29 _____ _____, the price mentioned first acts as an "anchor" that _____ our _____ about the price of an item.

    A. thoughts   B. such   C. fixes   D. as

30 Just _____ Jeff and his friends, we tend to buy _____ without seriously _____ why we are _____ them.

    A. considering   B. buying   C. like   D. things

31 _____ these effects have _____, many things _____ our _____.

    A. shown   B. purchases   C. as   D. influence

32 The next _____ you decide to buy something, _____ for a moment _____ why you are _____ it.

    A. think   B. about   C. time   D. buying

22 그는 가격을 확인하고 그것이 **200**달러임을 알게 된다. 그는 그 헤드폰이 너무 비싸다고 생각한다.

23 점원이 그에게 다가와 "이 헤드폰에 **20**퍼센트 할인을 받을 수 있어요."라고 말한다.

24 비록 할인된 가격이 여전히 별로 저렴하지는 않지만 Nathan은 그 헤드폰을 사기로 결심한다.

25 위에 기술된 상황은 '앵커링 효과'의 한 예이다.

26 처음에 언급된 가격이 이후에 언급되는 가격에 대한 우리의 의견에 영향을 미친다.

27 예를 들어, 만약 우리가 **200**달러로 시작한다면, 비교해 볼 때 **160**달러는 저렴해 보일 것이다.

28 그뿐만 아니라, 두 가격의 차이가 커질수록 그 효과는 더욱 강력해질 것이다.

29 이와 같이 처음에 언급된 가격이 물건의 가격에 대한 우리의 생각을 고정하는 '닻'으로서 작동한다.

30 Jeff와 그의 친구들처럼, 우리는 우리가 왜 물건들을 사는지 진지하게 고려하지 않고 그것들을 구입하는 경향이 있다.

31 이러한 효과들이 보여 주듯이, 많은 것들이 우리의 구매에 영향을 미친다.

32 다음번에 여러분이 어떤 것을 구매하려고 결정할 때에는, 자신이 그것을 왜 사려는지 잠시 동안 생각해 보아라.

※ 다음 우리말과 일치하도록 빈칸에 알맞은 것을 골라 쓰시오.

1 Have you ever wondered _____ _____ _____ _____ _____ you don't even want or need?

2 Let's consider _____ _____ _____ when it _____ _____ _____ things.

3 Why do I want to buy _____ _____ _____ _____ _____ ?

4 Jeff _____ to the shopping center and _____ _____ _____ _____ soccer shoes _____ _____ .

5 He _____ the shoes at a glance _____ more than _____ _____ _____ _____ _____ on his soccer team _____ them.

6 _____ he already has _____ _____ _____ soccer shoes, he _____ _____ _____ _____ _____ new pair.

7 We can use the "_____ _____" _____ _____ Jeff's _____ .

8 A bandwagon is a wagon in a parade _____ _____ people _____ _____ _____ and enjoy the music.

9 As _____ _____ _____ _____ get on the bandwagon, _____ _____ more _____ _____ _____ _____ or _____ it.

10 _____ this _____ , people tend _____ something _____ other people _____ _____ _____ .

11 Why do I _____ _____ _____ _____ pants and a bag _____ I _____ _____ a new coat?

12 Lisa buys a coat _____ she really loves. _____ , she _____ _____ her pants do not _____ her new coat.

13 So, she buys new pants _____ _____ perfectly _____ her new coat.

14 But she sees _____ _____ _____ _____ _____ _____ her _____ _____ .

15 So, she _____ a new bag. _____ _____ _____ _____ _____ spent _____ buying the new items _____ her _____ .

16 What _____ Lisa _____ _____ _____ immediately _____ _____ a new coat?

1 여러분은 원하거나 필요로 하지도 않는 것들을 자신이 왜 구입했는지 궁금해 한 적이 있는가?

2 물건들을 구입하는 것에 관하여 무엇이 우리에게 영향을 주는지 생각해 보자.

3 나는 왜 친구들이 산 것을 사고 싶은 걸까?

4 Jeff는 쇼핑센터에 가서 진열되어 있는 축구화 한 켤레를 보게 된다.

5 그의 축구팀에 있는 소년들의 반 이상이 그 축구화를 신기 때문에 그는 그 신발을 한눈에 알아챈다.

6 이미 그에게는 축구화가 많이 있지만 결국 그는 또 다른 새 축구화를 사 버리고 만다.

7 우리는 Jeff의 행동을 설명하기 위해 '밴드왜건 효과'를 이용할 수 있다.

8 밴드왜건(악대차)은 사람들이 올라타서 음악을 즐기게끔 부추기는 퍼레이드에 있는 사륜마차이다.

9 더 많은 사람들이 밴드왜건에 올라탈수록 다른 사람들이 더욱 그것에 올라타거나 그것을 따라가려 한다.

10 이런 식으로, 사람들은 단지 다른 사람들이 어떤 것을 샀다는 이유로 그것을 구매하는 경향이 있다.

11 나는 왜 새 코트를 구입한 후에 바지와 가방을 사는 걸까?

12 Lisa는 정말 마음에 드는 코트를 산다. 그녀는 그녀의 바지가 새 코트와 어울리지 않는다는 것을 즉시 알아차린다.

13 그래서 그녀는 새 코트와 완벽하게 어울리는 새 바지를 구입한다.

14 하지만 그녀는 자신의 가방 중 어느 것도 새로운 옷들과 어울리지 않는다는 것을 알게 된다.

15 그래서 그녀는 새 가방을 산다. 그녀의 돈 대부분이 그녀의 새로운 모습을 완성하기 위하여 새로운 물품을 사는 데 쓰인다.

16 무엇이 Lisa로 하여금 새 코트를 산 후 즉시 새로운 물품을 찾게 했을까?

17 The "Diderot _____" may _____ _____. Denis Diderot, a French writer, _____ a new gown _____ a _____.

18 Soon _____ _____ the gift, he _____ _____ all of his _____ did not _____ _____ with his new gown. So, he ended up _____ _____ _____ _____ _____.

19 The Diderot effect, _____, is the concept _____ _____ _____ _____ _____ often _____ _____ more _____ _____.

20 Why do I buy things _____ _____ _____ _____ _____ _____ _____?

21 Nathan _____ _____ _____ and _____ a _____ of headphones.

22 He _____ the price and _____ _____ _____ they are $200. He thinks _____ the headphones are _____ _____.

23 The sales person _____ _____ and says, "You can get a 20 percent _____ _____ those headphones."

24 _____ _____ the discounted price _____ _____ not very _____, Nathan decides _____ _____ the headphones.

25 The situation _____ _____ is an _____ of the "_____ _____."

26 The price _____ first _____ our _____ _____ _____ _____ _____ afterwards.

27 _____ _____, if we start with $200, then $160 will _____ _____ _____ _____ _____.

28 _____, as _____ _____ of the two prices _____ _____, the effect will _____ _____ _____.

29 _____ _____, the price _____ _____ acts as an "_____" that _____ _____ _____ about the price of an item.

30 _____ _____ Jeff and his friends, we tend _____ _____ things _____ seriously _____ _____ _____ _____ them.

31 _____ these effects _____ _____, many things _____ _____ _____.

32 _____ _____ _____ you _____ _____ something, _____ for a moment _____ _____ _____ it.

---

17 '디드로 효과'가 그것을 설명해 줄지도 모른다. 프랑스 작가인 Denis Diderot는 선물로 새 가운을 받았다.

18 그 선물을 받은 후에 곧 그는 그의 모든 가구가 새로운 가운과 어울리지 않는다는 것을 알아챘다. 그래서 그는 결국 대부분의 가구를 바꾸고 말았다.

19 그러므로 디드로 효과는 새로운 물품을 구입하는 것이 흔히 계획에 없던 더 많은 구매로 이어진다는 개념이다.

20 나는 왜 단지 할인 중이라는 이유로 물건을 구입하는 걸까?

21 Nathan은 진열된 상품을 구경하러 가서 헤드폰을 하나 본다.

22 그는 가격을 확인하고 그것이 200달러임을 알게 된다. 그는 그 헤드폰이 너무 비싸다고 생각한다.

23 점원이 그에게 다가와 "이 헤드폰에 20퍼센트 할인을 받을 수 있어요."라고 말한다.

24 비록 할인된 가격이 여전히 별로 저렴하지는 않지만 Nathan은 그 헤드폰을 사기로 결심한다.

25 위에 기술된 상황은 '앵커링 효과'의 한 예이다.

26 처음에 언급된 가격이 이후에 언급되는 가격에 대한 우리의 의견에 영향을 미친다.

27 예를 들어, 만약 우리가 200달러로 시작한다면, 비교해 볼 때 160달러는 저렴해 보일 것이다.

28 그뿐만 아니라, 두 가격의 차이가 커질수록 그 효과는 더욱 강력해질 것이다.

29 이와 같이 처음에 언급된 가격이 물건의 가격에 대한 우리의 생각을 고정하는 '닻'으로서 작동한다.

30 Jeff와 그의 친구들처럼, 우리는 우리가 왜 물건들을 사는지 진지하게 고려하지 않고 그것들을 구입하는 경향이 있다.

31 이러한 효과들이 보여 주듯이, 많은 것들이 우리의 구매에 영향을 미친다.

32 다음번에 여러분이 어떤 것을 구매하려고 결정할 때에는, 자신이 그것을 왜 사려는지 잠시 동안 생각해 보아라.

※ 다음 문장을 우리말로 쓰시오.

1 Have you ever wondered why you've bought things that you don't even want or need?
➡ _____

2 Let's consider what affects us when it comes to buying things.
➡ _____

3 Why do I want to buy what my friends bought?
➡ _____

4 Jeff goes to the shopping center and sees a pair of soccer shoes on display.
➡ _____

5 He recognizes the shoes at a glance because more than half of the boys on his soccer team wear them.
➡ _____

6 Although he already has many pairs of soccer shoes, he ends up buying another new pair.
➡ _____

7 We can use the "bandwagon effect" to explain Jeff's behavior.
➡ _____

8 A bandwagon is a wagon in a parade that encourages people to jump aboard and enjoy the music.
➡ _____

9 As more and more people get on the bandwagon, others are more likely to get on or follow it.
➡ _____

10 In this way, people tend to buy something just because other people have bought it.
➡ _____

11 Why do I buy a pair of pants and a bag after I have bought a new coat?
➡ _____

12 Lisa buys a coat that she really loves. Immediately, she realizes that her pants do not match her new coat.
➡ _____

13 So, she buys new pants that go perfectly with her new coat.
➡ _____

14 But she sees that none of her bags match her new clothes.
➡ _____

15 So, she buys a new bag. Most of her money is spent on buying the new items to complete her new look.
➡ _____

16 What made Lisa search for new items immediately after buying a new coat?
➡ _____

17 The "Diderot effect" may explain it. Denis Diderot, a French writer, received a new gown as a gift.

➡ _____

18 Soon after receiving the gift, he noticed that all of his furniture did not go well with his new gown. So, he ended up replacing most of it.

➡ _____
_____

19 The Diderot effect, therefore, is the concept that purchasing a new item often leads to more unplanned purchases.

➡ _____

20 Why do I buy things just because they are on sale?

➡ _____

21 Nathan goes window shopping and sees a pair of headphones.

➡ _____

22 He checks the price and finds out that they are $200. He thinks that the headphones are too expensive.

➡ _____

23 The sales person approaches him and says, "You can get a 20 percent discount on those headphones."

➡ _____

24 Even though the discounted price is still not very low, Nathan decides to buy the headphones.

➡ _____

25 The situation described above is an example of the "anchoring effect."

➡ _____

26 The price mentioned first affects our opinion of prices mentioned afterwards.

➡ _____

27 For example, if we start with $200, then $160 will seem cheap in comparison.

➡ _____

28 Furthermore, as the difference of the two prices becomes bigger, the effect will be more powerful.

➡ _____

29 As such, the price mentioned first acts as an "anchor" that fixes our thoughts about the price of an item.

➡ _____

30 Just like Jeff and his friends, we tend to buy things without seriously considering why we are buying them.

➡ _____

31 As these effects have shown, many things influence our purchases.

➡ _____

32 The next time you decide to buy something, think for a moment about why you are buying it.

➡ _____

※ 다음 괄호 안의 단어들을 우리말에 맞도록 바르게 배열하시오.

1 (you / have / wondered / ever / you've / why / things / bought / that / don't / you / want / even / need? / or)

➡ _____

_____

2 (consider / let's / affects / what / when / us / comes / it / buying / to / things.)

➡ _____

3 (do / why / want / I / buy / to / what / friends / my / thought?)

➡ _____

4 (goes / Jeff / the / to / center / shoppiing / and / a / sees / pair / soccer / of / on / shoes / display.)

➡ _____

5 (recognizes / he / shoes / the / a / at / because / glance / more / half / than / the / of / boys / his / on / soccer / wear / team / them.)

➡ _____

_____

6 (he / although / has / already / many / of / pairs / shoes, / soccer / ends / he / buying / up / new / another / pair.)

➡ _____

7 (can / we / the / use / effect" / "bandwagon / to / Jeff's / explain / behavior.)

➡ _____

8 (bandwagon / a / is / wagon / a / in / parade / a / that / people / encourages / to / jump / and / aboard / the / enjoy / music.)

➡ _____

_____

9 (more / as / and / people / more / on / get / bandwagon, / the / are / others / likely / more / get / to / or / on / it. / follow)

➡ _____

10 (this / in / way, / tend / people / buy / to / just / something / other / because / people / bought / have / it.)

➡ _____

_____

11 (do / why / buy / I / pair / a / pants / of / and / bag / a / after / have / I / a / bought / coat? / new)

➡ _____

1 여러분은 원하거나 필요로 하지도 않는 것들을 자신이 왜 구입했는지 궁금해 한 적이 있는가?

2 물건들을 구입하는 것에 관하여 무엇이 우리에게 영향을 주는지 생각해 보자.

3 나는 왜 친구들이 산 것을 사고 싶은 걸까?

4 Jeff는 쇼핑센터에 가서 진열되어 있는 축구화 한 켤레를 보게 된다.

5 그의 축구팀에 있는 소년들의 반 이상이 그 축구화를 신기 때문에 그는 그 신발을 한눈에 알아챈다.

6 이미 그에게는 축구화가 많이 있지만 결국 그는 또 다른 새 축구화를 사 버리고 만다.

7 우리는 Jeff의 행동을 설명하기 위해 '밴드왜건 효과'를 이용할 수 있다.

8 밴드왜건(악대차)은 사람들이 올라타서 음악을 즐기게끔 부추기는 퍼레이드에 있는 사륜마차이다.

9 더 많은 사람들이 밴드왜건에 올라탈수록 다른 사람들이 더욱 그것에 올라타거나 그것을 따라가려 한다.

10 이런 식으로, 사람들은 단지 다른 사람들이 어떤 것을 샀다는 이유로 그것을 구매하는 경향이 있다.

11 나는 왜 새 코트를 구입한 후에 바지와 가방을 사는 걸까?

12 (buys / Lisa / coat / a / she / that / loves. / really // she / immediately, / that / realizes / her / do / pants / match / not / new / coat. / her)

➡ _____

_____

13 (she / so, / new / buys / that / pants / go / with / perfectly / her / coat. / new)

➡ _____

_____

14 (she / but / that / sees / none / her / of / bags / her / match / clothes. / new)

➡ _____

_____

15 (she / so, / a / buys / bag. / new // of / most / money / her / spent / is / buying / on / new / the / items / complete / to / new / her / look.)

➡ _____

_____

16 (made / what / search / Lisa / new / for / immediately / items / buying / after / new / a / coat?)

➡ _____

_____

17 ("Diderot / the / effect" / explain / may / it. // Diderot, / Denis / a / writer, / French / a / received / new / a / as / gown / gift.)

➡ _____

_____

18 (after / soon / the / receiving / gift, / noticed / he / all / that / his / of / did / furniture / not / well / go / his / with / gown. / new // so, / ended / he / up / most / replacing / it. / of)

➡ _____

_____

19 (Diderot / the / effect, / is / therefore, / concept / the / purchasing / that / new / a / often / item / to / leads / more / purchases. / unplanned)

➡ _____

_____

20 (do / why / buy / I / just / things / because / are / they / sale? / on)

➡ _____

12 Lisa는 정말 마음에 드는 코트를 산다. 그녀는 그녀의 바지가 새 코트와 어울리지 않는다는 것을 즉시 알아차린다.

13 그래서 그녀는 새 코트와 완벽하게 어울리는 새 바지를 구입한다.

14 하지만 그녀는 자신의 가방 중 어느 것도 새로운 옷들과 어울리지 않는다는 것을 알게 된다.

15 그래서 그녀는 새 가방을 산다. 그녀의 돈 대부분이 그녀의 새로운 모습을 완성하기 위하여 새로운 물품을 사는 데 쓰인다.

16 무엇이 Lisa로 하여금 새 코트를 산 후 즉시 새로운 물품을 찾게 했을까?

17 '디드로 효과'가 그것을 설명해 줄지도 모른다. 프랑스 작가인 Denis Diderot는 선물로 새 가운을 받았다.

18 그 선물을 받은 후에 곧 그는 그의 모든 가구가 새로운 가운과 어울리지 않는다는 것을 알아챘다. 그래서 그는 결국 대부분의 가구를 바꾸고 말았다.

19 그러므로 디드로 효과는 새로운 물품을 구입하는 것이 흔히 계획에 없던 더 많은 구매로 이어진다는 개념이다.

20 나는 왜 단지 할인 중이라는 이유로 물건을 구입하는 걸까?

21 (goes / Nathan / shopping / window / and / a / sees / of / pair / headphones.)

➡ _____

22 (checks / he / price / the / and / out / finds / they / that / $200. / are // thinks / he / that / headphones / the / too / are / expensive.)

➡ _____

23 (sales / the / person / him / approaches / says, / and / can / "you / a / get / percent / 20 / on / discount / headphones." / those)

➡ _____

24 (though / even / discounted / the / is / price / not / still / low, / very / decides / Nathan / buy / to / headphones. / the)

➡ _____

25 (situation / the / above / described / an / is / of / example / the / effect." / "anchoring)

➡ _____

26 (price / the / first / mentioned / affects / opinion / our / prices / of / afterwards. / mentioned)

➡ _____

27 (example, / for / we / if / with / start / $200, / $160 / then / will / cheap / seem / comparison. / in)

➡ _____

28 (as / furthermore, / the / of / difference / two / the / becomes / prices / bigger, / effect / the / will / more / be / powerful.)

➡ _____

29 (such, / as / price / the / first / mentioned / acts / an / as / that / "anchor" / our / fixes / about / thoughts / the / of / price / item. / an)

➡ _____

30 (like / just / and / Jeff / friends, / his / tend / we / buy / to / without / things / seriously / we / considering / why / buying / are / them.)

➡ _____

31 (these / as / have / effects / shown, / things / many / our / influence / purchases.)

➡ _____

32 (next / the / you / time / to / decide / something, / buy / for / think / moment / a / about / you / why / buying / are / it.)

➡ _____

21 Nathan은 진열된 상품을 구경하러 가서 헤드폰을 하나 본다.

22 그는 가격을 확인하고 그것이 200달러임을 알게 된다. 그는 그 헤드폰이 너무 비싸다고 생각한다.

23 점원이 그에게 다가와 "이 헤드폰에 20퍼센트 할인을 받을 수 있어요."라고 말한다.

24 비록 할인된 가격이 여전히 별로 저렴하지는 않지만 Nathan은 그 헤드폰을 사기로 결심한다.

25 위에 기술된 상황은 '앵커링 효과'의 한 예이다.

26 처음에 언급된 가격이 이후에 언급되는 가격에 대한 우리의 의견에 영향을 미친다.

27 예를 들어, 만약 우리가 200달러로 시작한다면, 비교해 볼 때 160달러는 저렴해 보일 것이다.

28 그뿐만 아니라, 두 가격의 차이가 커질수록 그 효과는 더욱 강력해질 것이다.

29 이와 같이 처음에 언급된 가격이 물건의 가격에 대한 우리의 생각을 고정하는 '닻'으로서 작동한다.

30 Jeff와 그의 친구들처럼, 우리는 우리가 왜 물건들을 사는지 진지하게 고려하지 않고 그것들을 구입하는 경향이 있다.

31 이러한 효과들이 보여 주듯이, 많은 것들이 우리의 구매에 영향을 미친다.

32 다음번에 여러분이 어떤 것을 구매하려고 결정할 때에는, 자신이 그것을 왜 사려는지 잠시 동안 생각해 보아라.

※ 다음 우리말을 영어로 쓰시오.

1 여러분은 원하거나 필요로 하지도 않는 것들을 자신이 왜 구입했는지 궁금해 한 적이 있는가?

➡ _____

2 물건들을 구입하는 것에 관하여 무엇이 우리에게 영향을 주는지 생각해 보자.

➡ _____

3 나는 왜 친구들이 산 것을 사고 싶은 걸까?

➡ _____

4 Jeff는 쇼핑센터에 가서 진열되어 있는 축구화 한 켤레를 보게 된다.

➡ _____

5 그의 축구팀에 있는 소년들의 반 이상이 그 축구화를 신기 때문에 그는 그 신발을 한눈에 알아챈다.

➡ _____

6 이미 그에게는 축구화가 많이 있지만 결국 그는 또 다른 새 축구화를 사 버리고 만다.

➡ _____

7 우리는 Jeff의 행동을 설명하기 위해 '밴드왜건 효과'를 이용할 수 있다.

➡ _____

8 밴드왜건(악대차)은 사람들이 올라타서 음악을 즐기게끔 부추기는 퍼레이드에 있는 사륜마차이다.

➡ _____

9 더 많은 사람들이 밴드왜건에 올라탈수록 다른 사람들이 더욱 그것에 올라타거나 그것을 따라가려 한다.

➡ _____

10 이런 식으로, 사람들은 단지 다른 사람들이 어떤 것을 샀다는 이유로 그것을 구매하는 경향이 있다.

➡ _____

11 나는 왜 새 코트를 구입한 후에 바지와 가방을 사는 걸까?

➡ _____

12 Lisa는 정말 마음에 드는 코트를 산다. 그녀는 그녀의 바지가 새 코트와 어울리지 않는다는 것을 즉시 알아차린다.

➡ _____

13 그래서 그녀는 새 코트와 완벽하게 어울리는 새 바지를 구입한다.

➡ _____

14 하지만 그녀는 자신의 가방 중 어느 것도 새로운 옷들과 어울리지 않는다는 것을 알게 된다.

➡ _____

15 그래서 그녀는 새 가방을 산다. 그녀의 돈 대부분이 그녀의 새로운 모습을 완성하기 위하여 새로운 물품을 사는 데 쓰인다.

➡ _____

16 무엇이 Lisa로 하여금 새 코트를 산 후 즉시 새로운 물품을 찾게 했을까?

➡ _____

17 '디드로 효과'가 그것을 설명해 줄지도 모른다. 프랑스 작가인 Denis Diderot는 선물로 새 가운을 받았다.

➡ _____

18 그 선물을 받은 후에 곧 그는 그의 모든 가구가 새로운 가운과 어울리지 않는다는 것을 알아챘다.
그래서 그는 결국 대부분의 가구를 바꾸고 말았다.

➡ _____
_____

19 그러므로 디드로 효과는 새로운 물품을 구입하는 것이 흔히 계획에 없던 더 많은 구매로 이어진다는 개념이다.

➡ _____
_____

20 나는 왜 단지 할인 중이라는 이유로 물건을 구입하는 걸까?

➡ _____

21 Nathan은 진열된 상품을 구경하러 가서 헤드폰을 하나 본다.

➡ _____

22 그는 가격을 확인하고 그것이 200달러임을 알게 된다. 그는 그 헤드폰이 너무 비싸다고 생각한다.

➡ _____

23 점원이 그에게 다가와 "이 헤드폰에 20퍼센트 할인을 받을 수 있어요."라고 말한다.

➡ _____

24 비록 할인된 가격이 여전히 별로 저렴하지는 않지만 Nathan은 그 헤드폰을 사기로 결심한다.

➡ _____

25 위에 기술된 상황은 '앵커링 효과'의 한 예이다.

➡ _____

26 처음에 언급된 가격이 이후에 언급되는 가격에 대한 우리의 의견에 영향을 미친다.

➡ _____

27 예를 들어, 만약 우리가 200달러로 시작한다면, 비교해 볼 때 160달러는 저렴해 보일 것이다.

➡ _____

28 그뿐만 아니라, 두 가격의 차이가 커질수록 그 효과는 더욱 강력해질 것이다.

➡ _____

29 이와 같이 처음에 언급된 가격이 물건의 가격에 대한 우리의 생각을 고정하는 '닻'으로서 작동한다.

➡ _____
_____

30 Jeff와 그의 친구들처럼, 우리는 우리가 왜 물건들을 사는지 진지하게 고려하지 않고 그것들을 구입하는
경향이 있다.

➡ _____
_____

31 이러한 효과들이 보여 주듯이, 많은 것들이 우리의 구매에 영향을 미친다.

➡ _____

32 다음번에 여러분이 어떤 것을 구매하려고 결정할 때에는, 자신이 그것을 왜 사려는지 잠시 동안 생각해
보아라.

➡ _____

※ 다음 우리말과 일치하도록 빈칸에 알맞은 말을 쓰시오.

Language in Use

1. _____ is difficult _____ _____ the results _____ _____.
2. We _____ children _____ _____ _____ _____.

1. 결과를 상세히 비교하는 것은 어렵다.
2. 우리는 아이들이 스스로 생각하도록 장려한다.

Grammar in Real Life B Look and Write

1. About _____ _____ the water _____ _____ _____ _____ animals in the U.S.
2. _____ _____ _____ the world's food _____ _____ —1.3 _____ _____ every year.
3. In Somalia, _____ _____ _____ _____ the children _____ _____ _____.
4. _____ fourteen percent of all people _____ know _____ _____ _____ _____ _____ _____ education.

1. 물의 절반 가량이 미국에서 동물을 키우기 위해 사용된다.
2. 세계 식량의 삼분의 일, 즉 매년 13억 톤이 낭비된다.
3. 소말리아에서는 단지 10퍼센트의 아이들이 학교에 다닌다.
4. 전체 인구의 약 14퍼센트는 교육의 부족으로 읽는 법을 알지 못한다.

Think & Write C

1. I _____ _____ _____ about _____.
2. First, I asked 10 students _____ _____ _____ _____ _____ _____.
3. Twenty percent of the students _____ _____ _____ every week and _____ _____ of the students _____ _____ _____ _____ _____.
4. Second, I asked them _____ they _____ _____ _____ _____ _____ _____ _____.
5. _____ _____ _____ _____ is spent on clothes and _____ _____ of the allowance _____ _____ _____ _____.
6. Lastly, I asked them _____ _____ _____ that they _____ _____ _____ _____.
7. _____ _____ _____ _____ _____ _____ that they should get a higher allowance.

1. 저는 용돈에 관하여 설문 조사를 했습니다.
2. 우선, 저는 10명의 학생들에게 그들이 얼마나 자주 용돈을 받는지 물었습니다.
3. 20퍼센트의 학생들은 매주 용돈을 받고, 70퍼센트의 학생들은 매달 용돈을 받습니다.
4. 두 번째로, 저는 학생들에게 어디에 용돈의 대부분을 쓰는지 물었습니다.
5. 대부분의 용돈은 옷에 쓰이고, 용돈의 4분의 1은 간식에 쓰입니다.
6. 마지막으로, 저는 학생들에게 그들이 더 많은 용돈을 받아야 한다고 생각하는지 물었습니다.
7. 학생들의 90퍼센트는 그들이 더 많은 용돈을 받아야 한다고 생각합니다.

구석구석 지문 Test

※ 다음 우리말을 영어로 쓰시오.

1. 결과를 상세히 비교하는 것은 어렵다.

   ➡ _____

2. 우리는 아이들이 스스로 생각하도록 장려한다.

   ➡ _____

Grammar in Real Life B Look and Write

1. 물의 절반 가량이 미국에서 동물을 키우기 위해 사용된다.

   ➡ _____

2. 세계 식량의 삼분의 일, 즉 매년 13억 톤이 낭비된다.

   ➡ _____

3. 소말리아에서는 단지 10퍼센트의 아이들이 학교에 다닌다.

   ➡ _____

4. 전체 인구의 약 14퍼센트는 교육의 부족으로 읽는 법을 알지 못한다.

   ➡ _____

Think & Write C

1. 저는 용돈에 관하여 설문 조사를 했습니다.

   ➡ _____

2. 우선, 저는 10명의 학생들에게 그들이 얼마나 자주 용돈을 받는지 물었습니다.

   ➡ _____

3. 20퍼센트의 학생들은 매주 용돈을 받고, 70퍼센트의 학생들은 매달 용돈을 받습니다.

   ➡ _____

   _____

4. 두 번째로, 저는 학생들에게 어디에 용돈의 대부분을 쓰는지 물었습니다.

   ➡ _____

5. 대부분의 용돈은 옷에 쓰이고, 용돈의 4분의 1은 간식에 쓰입니다.

   ➡ _____

6. 마지막으로, 저는 학생들에게 그들이 더 많은 용돈을 받아야 한다고 생각하는지 물었습니다.

   ➡ _____

7. 학생들의 90퍼센트는 그들이 더 많은 용돈을 받아야 한다고 생각합니다.

   ➡ _____

※ 다음 영어를 우리말로 쓰시오.

01 surface _____

02 bend _____

03 connect _____

04 sunrise _____

05 contain _____

06 shortcut _____

07 crush _____

08 distance _____

09 changeable _____

10 attach _____

11 tough _____

12 eatable _____

13 achieve _____

14 eventually _____

15 detect _____

16 extend _____

17 unstable _____

18 bottom _____

19 layer _____

20 vast _____

21 persistent _____

22 instantly _____

23 apply _____

24 exist _____

25 gravity _____

26 lean _____

27 punch _____

28 infinite _____

29 lower _____

30 exploration _____

31 measure _____

32 theory _____

33 ongoing _____

34 incorrect _____

35 look back _____

36 figure out _____

37 according to~ _____

38 far away from _____

39 lie down _____

40 in theory _____

41 at the bottom of ~ _____

42 different from _____

43 in the blink of an eye _____

※ 다음 우리말을 영어로 쓰시오.

01 연구자, 조사자

02 지름길

03 몸을 숙이다, 굽히다

04 계속 진행 중인

05 승객, 탑승객

06 부정확한, 사실이 아닌

07 눌러 부수다, 찌부러뜨리다

08 이론, 학설

09 낮추다

10 힘든, 어려운

11 무한한

12 적용하다, 응용하다

13 끈질긴, 집요한, 지속적인

14 맨 아랫부분, 바닥

15 존재하다

16 불안정한

17 거대한, 광대한

18 연결되다, 이어지다

19 달성하다, 성취하다

20 감지하다, 발견하다

21 먹을 수 있는

22 결국

23 바뀔 수 있는, 변덕스러운

24 탐사, 탐구

25 중력

26 붙이다

27 ~이 들어 있다, 포함하다

28 굽히다, 구부리다

29 즉시

30 층

31 측정하다

32 물리학

33 거리

34 축하하다

35 맞추다

36 눕다, 누워 있다

37 ~의 속도로

38 떠다니다

39 ~에 따르면

40 ~을 알아내다, 생각해 내다

41 되돌아보다

42 ~에서 멀리 떨어져

43 ~의 아래에

※ 다음 영영풀이에 알맞은 단어를 <보기>에서 골라 쓴 후, 우리말 뜻을 쓰시오.

1 _____ : extremely big: _____

2 _____ : to join or be joined with something else: _____

3 _____ : to fasten or join one thing to another: _____

4 _____ : the amount of space between two places: _____

5 _____ : not solid and firm and therefore not strong, safe, or likely to last: _____

6 _____ : to find out the size, length, or amount of something: _____

7 _____ : a professional cook, especially the most senior cook in a restaurant, hotel, etc.: _____

8 _____ : continuing to exist or develop, or happening at the present moment: _____

9 _____ : the time when the sun first appears in the sky in the morning: _____

10 _____ : a person who travels in a spacecraft into outer space: _____

11 _____ : to succeed in finishing something or reaching an aim, especially after a lot of work or effort: _____

12 _____ : to notice something that is partly hidden or not clear, or to discover something, especially using a special method: _____

13 _____ : the force that attracts objects towards one another, especially the force that makes things fall to the ground: _____

14 _____ : to do something special or enjoyable for an important event, occasion, holiday, etc.: _____

15 _____ : a person who is travelling in a car, bus, train, plane or ship and who is not driving it or working on it: _____

16 _____ : an extremely large, round mass of rock and metal, such as Earth, or of gas, such as Jupiter, that moves in a circular path around the sun or another star: _____

보기			
achieve	chef	sunrise	measure
celebrate	connect	passenger	vast
detect	unstable	gravity	ongoing
planet	distance	astronaut	attach

※ 다음 우리말과 일치하도록 빈칸에 알맞은 말을 쓰시오.

Listen & Talk 1 A

1. M: Welcome _____ _____ Earth, Irene. _____ was your favorite part about _____ in the space station?

   W: I _____ _____ a beautiful _____ 16 _____ _____ _____. It was great.

   M: _____ _____ _____ _____ _____ the sunrise several times _____ _____ in space?

   W: Yes, it's _____ _____ we _____ _____ Earth every 90 minutes in the station.

   M: Wow, that's _____!

2. M: Irene, what was _____ _____ _____ _____ _____ in the space station?

   W: Hmm…. . We _____ some vegetables and _____ them every day. They were pretty _____ _____ _____!

   M: Wow, _____ _____ _____ _____ _____ vegetables in the space station?

   W: Yes. _____ there's _____ _____ in space, we _____ _____ grow them in special bags. The bags _____ _____ _____ _____ _____.

   M: How interesting!

1. M: 지구에 돌아오신 것을 환영합니다, Irene 씨. 우주 정거장에서 보낸 시간 중 최고의 기억이 무엇인가요?

   W: 저는 하루에 16번씩 아름다운 일출을 볼 수 있었어요. 그것은 굉장했죠.

   M: 우주에서는 하루에 일출을 여러 번 보는 게 가능한가요?

   W: 네, 가능해요. 왜냐하면 우주 정거장이 지구 주위를 90분마다 돌았거든요.

   M: 와, 놀랍네요!

2. M: Irene 씨, 우주 정거장에서 드셨던 것 중 최고의 음식은 무엇이었나요?

   W: 음… . 우리는 채소를 키워서 매일 그걸 먹었어요. 그것은 매우 신선하고 맛있었어요!

   M: 와, 우주 정거장에서 채소를 키우는 것이 가능한가요?

   W: 네. 우주에는 중력이 없기 때문에, 우리는 그것을 특수한 봉지 안에서 키워야 했어요. 그 봉지는 뿌리가 자라는 데 도움을 줬어요.

   M: 참 흥미롭네요!

Listen & Talk 1 B

M: _____ _____ _____ _____ NASA is going to _____ a 3D printer _____ space?

W: They're _____ _____ _____ a 3D printer _____ _____?
   Why?

M: _____ _____ _____ the 3D printer _____ _____ _____ _____ _____ food for astronauts.

W: Is it _____ _____ _____ _____ food _____ a 3D printer?

M: Yes, it's possible. It can _____ _____ a fresh pizza _____ _____ _____ five minutes.

W: Really? I wonder _____ _____ _____ _____ _____ _____.

M: 나사(NASA)가 3D 프린터를 우주로 보낼 거라는 이야기 들어 봤니?

W: 그들이 3D 프린터를 우주로 보낸다고? 왜?

M: 우주 비행사들이 먹을 음식을 출력하는 데 3D 프린터가 쓰일 거라고 들었어.

W: 3D 프린터를 이용해 음식을 출력하는 게 가능해?

M: 응, 가능해. 그것은 신선한 피자를 5분도 안 되어서 출력해 낼 수 있어.

W: 정말? 그게 어떤 맛일지 궁금하다.

Listen & Talk 2 A

1. **M:** Look at these _____ pictures of the _____.

   W: Oh, they're beautiful. _____ _____ _____ _____
   _____ Earth _____ space _____ _____ _____
   _____.

   M: Actually, you can _____ _____ at the National Youth Space Center.

   W: Really?

   M: Yeah, you can use the VR glasses. I heard _____ you _____
   _____ you are _____ _____ _____!

2. **W:** What _____ you _____?

   M: It's a documentary about life in space. Everything _____ so
   _____.

   W: Yes, _____ _____ there's _____ _____ in space.

   M: Right. _____ _____ _____ _____ _____ _____ _____
   like an _____!

   W: Really? I don't. It _____ _____.

Listen & Talk 2 B

W: Look at this man, Jake. He _____ _____ space for one year.

M: It _____ _____ _____ _____ for him.

W: Right, but you know what's interesting? He grew 2 inches _____
_____ _____.

M: Really? How is that _____?

W: I'm _____ _____, but _____ _____ _____ there's no
_____ in space.

M: That's so cool. _____ _____ _____ _____ _____
_____ space. That way, I could _____ _____.

W: _____ _____ _____ are other _____ _____
_____ than _____ _____ _____.

1. M: 이 다채로운 색깔의 우주 사진들을 좀 봐.
W: 오, 그것들은 아름다워. 내가 지구를 우주에서 직접 내 눈으로 볼 수 있으면 좋을 텐데.
M: 사실 넌 국립 청소년 우주 센터에서 그걸 해 볼 수 있어.
W: 정말?
M: 응, 가상 현실(VR) 안경을 써 볼 수 있거든. 실제로 우주에 있는 것 같은 기분이 든다고 들었어!

2. W: 너는 무엇을 보고 있니?
M: 우주에서의 삶에 관한 다큐멘터리야. 모든 것이 너무 달라 보여.
W: 응, 왜냐하면 우주에는 중력이 없기 때문이지.
M: 맞아. 나도 우주 비행사처럼 떠다닐 수 있다면 좋을 텐데!
W: 정말이니? 나는 아니야. 그건 불편해 보여.

W: 이 남자 좀 봐, Jake. 그는 우주에서 1년 동안 살았어.
M: 그는 분명히 힘들었을 거야.
W: 맞아, 하지만 흥미로운 게 뭔 줄 아니? 그가 우주에 있는 동안 키가 2인치 자랐어.
M: 정말? 어떻게 그게 가능해?
W: 확실하진 않지만, 아마 우주에 중력이 없기 때문일 거야.
M: 정말 멋지다. 내가 우주에서 살 수 있으면 좋을 텐데. 그러면 난 키가 더 커질 수 있을 텐데.
W: 우주에 가는 것 말고 키가 더 커지는 다른 방법들이 있을 거라고 확신해.

Communication Step A

W: Hello, everyone, _____ _____ *All about Movies*! Today, we're going _____ _____ _____ the top three things from movies _____ _____ _____ _____ _____.

M: Let's _____ _____ number three, the flying skateboard from *Back to the Future*.

W: It's a cool item. _____ _____ _____ _____ _____ a flying skateboard.

M: Actually, I read _____ _____ this is not _____ _____.

W: Really? _____ _____ _____ _____ _____ _____ _____ on a skateboard?

M: Yes. Some companies _____ _____ physics _____ _____ flying skateboards.

Wrap Up

1. W: Mr. Scott, did you _____ your trip to space?

   M: Yes, it was _____ _____ _____ of my life.

   W: Can you tell us _____ _____ _____ _____ _____ your trip?

   M: I flew in space _____ _____ and saw our blue planet, Earth.

   W: _____ _____ _____ _____ _____ _____ in space _____ _____?

   M: Yes, I _____ _____ to a special line, _____ it was _____.

   W: Sounds fantastic!

2. M: Hey, Cindy. I _____ _____ you went to the National Space Center last weekend. _____ was it?

   W: It was great, Chris. I experienced _____ _____ and _____ _____ _____.

   M: Sounds fun. Did you meet _____ _____ in person?

   W: Yes, and I _____ about their _____ stories.

   M: Oh, I wish I could become an _____ like them and _____.

W: 안녕하세요, 여러분, '영화에 대한 모든 것(All about Movies)'에 오신 것을 환영합니다! 오늘 우리는 실제로 가능하기를 바라는 영화 속 물건들 중에서 상위 세 개에 관해 이야기해 보려고 합니다.

M: 우선 3위부터 시작하자면, '백 투 더 퓨처'에 나온, 날아다니는 스케이트보드입니다.

W: 멋진 물건이에요. 제가 날아다니는 스케이트보드를 가질 수 있다면 좋을 텐데요.

M: 사실, 전 그것이 전혀 불가능한 일은 아니라고 어딘가에서 읽었어요.

W: 정말요? 스케이트보드를 타고 날아다니는 것이 실제로 가능해요?

M: 네. 몇몇 회사들이 날아다니는 스케이트보드를 만들기 위해 물리학을 적용했어요.

1. W: Scott 씨, 우주로의 여행은 즐거우셨나요?

   M: 네, 그것은 제 인생 최고의 경험이었어요.

   W: 여행 중 어떤 부분이 최고였는지 말씀해 주실 수 있나요?

   M: 혼자 우주를 날아서 우리의 푸른 행성인 지구를 보았어요.

   W: 우주에서 혼자 나는 것이 가능한가요?

   M: 네, 제 자신을 특수한 선에 연결해서 그건 안전했어요.

   W: 환상적이네요!

2. M: 안녕, Cindy. 지난 주말에 네가 국립 우주 센터에 갔다고 들었어. 어땠어?

   W: 굉장히 좋았어, Chris. 난 무중력 상태와 우주 비행사들의 우주 생활을 경험했어.

   M: 재미있었겠다. 너는 직접 진짜 우주인을 만났어?

   W: 응, 그리고 나는 그들의 모험 이야기를 들었어.

   M: 오, 나는 그들처럼 우주인이 돼서 화성을 탐험하고 싶어.

※ 다음 우리말에 맞도록 대화를 영어로 쓰시오.

Listen & Talk 1 A

1. M: _____
   _____
   W: _____
   M: _____
   W: _____
   _____
   M: _____

2. M: _____
   W: _____
   M: _____
   W: _____
   _____
   M: _____

1. M: 지구에 돌아오신 것을 환영합니다, Irene 씨. 우주 정거장에서 보낸 시간 중 최고의 기억이 무엇인가요?
   W: 저는 하루에 16번씩 아름다운 일출을 볼 수 있었어요. 그것은 굉장했죠.
   M: 우주에서는 하루에 일출을 여러 번 보는 게 가능한가요?
   W: 네, 가능해요. 왜냐하면 우주 정거장이 지구 주위를 90분마다 돌았거든요.
   M: 와, 놀랍네요!

2. M: Irene 씨, 우주 정거장에서 드셨던 것 중 최고의 음식은 무엇이었나요?
   W: 음… . 우리는 채소를 키워서 매일 그걸 먹었어요. 그것은 매우 신선하고 맛있었어요!
   M: 와, 우주 정거장에서 채소를 키우는 것이 가능한가요?
   W: 네. 우주에는 중력이 없기 때문에, 우리는 그것을 특수한 봉지 안에서 키워야 했어요. 그 봉지는 뿌리가 자라는 데 도움을 줬어요.
   M: 참 흥미롭네요!

Listen & Talk 1 B

M: _____
W: _____
M: _____
W: _____
M: _____
W: _____

M: 나사(NASA)가 3D 프린터를 우주로 보낼 거라는 이야기 들어 봤니?
W: 그들이 3D 프린터를 우주로 보낸다고? 왜?
M: 우주 비행사들이 먹을 음식을 출력하는 데 3D 프린터가 쓰일 거라고 들었어.
W: 3D 프린터를 이용해 음식을 출력하는 게 가능해?
M: 응, 가능해. 그것은 신선한 피자를 5분도 안 되어서 출력해 낼 수 있어.
W: 정말? 그게 어떤 맛일지 궁금하다.

Listen & Talk 2 A

1. M: _____

   W: _____

   M: _____

   W: _____

   M: _____

   _____

2. W: _____

   M: _____

   W: _____

   M: _____

   W: _____

Listen & Talk 2 B

W: _____

M: _____

W: _____

M: _____

W: _____

M: _____

W: _____

1. M: 이 다채로운 색깔의 우주 사진들을 좀 봐.
   W: 오, 그것들은 아름다워. 내가 지구를 우주에서 직접 내 눈으로 볼 수 있으면 좋을 텐데.
   M: 사실 넌 국립 청소년 우주 센터에서 그걸 해 볼 수 있어.
   W: 정말?
   M: 응, 가상 현실(VR) 안경을 써 볼 수 있거든. 실제로 우주에 있는 것 같은 기분이 든다고 들었어!

2. W: 너는 무엇을 보고 있니?
   M: 우주에서의 삶에 관한 다큐멘터리야. 모든 것이 너무 달라 보여.
   W: 응, 왜냐하면 우주에는 중력이 없기 때문이지.
   M: 맞아. 나도 우주 비행사처럼 떠다닐 수 있다면 좋을 텐데!
   W: 정말이니? 나는 아니야. 그건 불편해 보여.

W: 이 남자 좀 봐, Jake. 그는 우주에서 1년 동안 살았어.
M: 그는 분명히 힘들었을 거야.
W: 맞아, 하지만 흥미로운 게 뭔 줄 아니? 그가 우주에 있는 동안 키가 2인치 자랐어.
M: 정말? 어떻게 그게 가능해?
W: 확실하진 않지만, 아마 우주에 중력이 없기 때문일 거야.
M: 정말 멋지다. 내가 우주에서 살 수 있으면 좋을 텐데. 그러면 난 키가 더 커질 수 있을 텐데.
W: 우주에 가는 것 말고 키가 더 커지는 다른 방법들이 있을 거라고 확신해.

Communication Step A

W: _____

_____

M: _____

W: _____

M: _____

W: _____

M: _____

W: 안녕하세요, 여러분, '영화에 대한 모든 것(All about Movies)'에 오신 것을 환영합니다! 오늘 우리는 실제로 가능하기를 바라는 영화 속 물건들 중에서 상위 세 개에 관해 이야기해 보려고 합니다.

M: 우선 3위부터 시작하자면, '백 투 더 퓨처'에 나온, 날아다니는 스케이트보드입니다.

W: 멋진 물건이에요. 제가 날아다니는 스케이트보드를 가질 수 있다면 좋을 텐데요.

M: 사실, 전 그것이 전혀 불가능한 일은 아니라고 어딘가에서 읽었어요.

W: 정말요? 스케이트보드를 타고 날아다니는 것이 실제로 가능해요?

M: 네. 몇몇 회사들이 날아다니는 스케이트보드를 만들기 위해 물리학을 적용했어요.

Wrap Up

1. W: _____

M: _____

W: _____

M: _____

W: _____

M: _____

W: _____

2. M: _____

W: _____

M: _____

W: _____

M: _____

1. W: Scott 씨, 우주로의 여행은 즐거우셨나요?

M: 네, 그것은 제 인생 최고의 경험이었어요.

W: 여행 중 어떤 부분이 최고였는지 말씀해 주실 수 있나요?

M: 혼자 우주를 날아서 우리의 푸른 행성인 지구를 보았어요.

W: 우주에서 혼자 나는 것이 가능한가요?

M: 네, 제 자신을 특수한 선에 연결해서 그건 안전했어요.

W: 환상적이네요!

2. M: 안녕, Cindy. 지난 주말에 네가 국립 우주 센터에 갔다고 들었어. 어땠어?

W: 굉장히 좋았어, Chris. 난 무중력 상태와 우주 비행사들의 우주 생활을 경험했어.

M: 재미있었겠다. 너는 직접 진짜 우주인을 만났어?

W: 응, 그리고 나는 그들의 모험 이야기를 들었어.

M: 오, 나는 그들처럼 우주인이 돼서 화성을 탐험하고 싶어.

※ 다음 우리말과 일치하도록 빈칸에 알맞은 것을 골라 쓰시오.

1 Sci Teen: Hi, science _____. Today, we're _____ to talk _____ space _____.
A. travel   B. going   C. fans   D. about

2 _____ we all know, there is _____ faster than _____ in the _____.
A. nothing   B. as   C. universe   D. light

3 So, if we _____ at the speed of light, we should be _____ to _____ to another planet in the _____ of an eye, right?
A. blink   B. travel   C. get   D. able

4 Dr. Sci: That would be nice, but _____ is so _____ it is not _____.
A. possible   B. vast   C. space   D. that

5 In the movie, *Passengers*, a spaceship _____ to a different planet _____ at _____ the speed of _____.
A. one-half   B. headed   C. light   D. travels

6 So it should _____ _____ _____ very quickly, right?
A. another   B. to   C. planet   D. get

7 But, the passengers sleep _____ 120 years because it is _____ to _____ that much time to _____ to a different planet.
A. expected   B. get   C. for   D. take

8 Sci Teen: 120 years? Wow, that's a long time! Is there a _____ _____ to _____ _____ space?
A. through   B. faster   C. travel   D. way

9 Dr. Sci: Well, _____ _____ to answer that question, I'd _____ you to _____ about this apple for a second.
A. order   B. think   C. in   D. like

10 Imagine a worm is on this apple. It detects _____ _____ at the bottom and want to _____ from the top to the _____.
A. sweet   B. bottom   C. something   D. move

11 For the _____, the apple's _____ is as _____ as our _____.
A. universe   B. surface   C. worm   D. vast

12 Now the worm can _____ move _____ the outer layer _____ _____ a wormhole.
A. or   B. down   C. either   D. around

13 Which do you _____ it will _____? Well, it would choose the wormhole _____ it is a _____.
A. shortcut   B. choose   C. because   D. think

14 Sci Teen: Is _____ _____ _____ in the universe?
A. a   B. there   C. shortcut   D. such

15 Dr. Sci: According to some researchers, yes. Einstein _____ _____ that space and time are _____, and he called it _____.
A. out   B. space-time   C. connected   D. figured

1 Sci Teen: 안녕하세요, 과학 팬 여러분. 오늘 우리는 우주여행에 대해 이야기할 것입니다.

2 우리가 모두 알다시피, 우주에서 빛보다 더 빠른 것은 없습니다.

3 그래서 만약 우리가 빛의 속도로 여행을 한다면, 우리는 다른 행성에 눈 깜박할 사이에 도달할 수 있어야 해요. 그렇죠?

4 Dr. Sci: 그렇다면 좋겠지만, 우주는 너무 광활해서 그건 불가능하답니다.

5 영화 〈Passengers〉에서 다른 행성으로 향하는 우주선이 빛의 속도의 절반으로 이동합니다.

6 그러면 그들은 다른 행성에 매우 빨리 도달해야겠지요, 그렇죠?

7 하지만 승객들은 120년 동안 잠을 자게 되는데, 왜냐하면 다른 행성에 도달하는 데 그만큼 많은 시간이 걸릴 것으로 예상되기 때문입니다.

8 Sci Teen: 120년이요? 우아, 그건 정말 긴 시간이네요! 우주를 여행하는 더 빠른 방법이 있나요?

9 Dr. Sci: 글쎄요, 그 질문에 답하기 위해서 여러분들이 이 사과에 대해 잠깐 생각해 보기 바랍니다.

10 한 마리 벌레가 이 사과 위에 있다고 상상해 보세요. 그것은 맨 아래에 있는 달콤한 무언가를 감지하고 맨 위에서 아래로 이동하기를 원합니다.

11 그 벌레에게 사과의 표면은 우리의 우주만큼이나 광대합니다.

12 이제 그 벌레는 바깥 표면의 껍질을 돌아서 이동하거나 벌레 구멍 아래로 이동할 수 있습니다.

13 그것이 어떤 것을 선택할 거라고 생각하십니까? 음, 그것은 벌레 구멍을 선택할 것인데 왜냐하면 그것이 지름길이기 때문입니다.

14 Sci Teen: 우주에 그런 지름길이 있나요?

15 Dr. Sci: 몇몇 연구자들에 따르면, 그렇습니다. 아인슈타인은 공간과 시간이 연결되어 있다는 것을 생각해 냈고, 그것을 시공간이라고 불렀습니다.

16 He thought that _____ could actually be _____. When it is bent, parts that are _____ _____ from each other are suddenly closer.

    A. bent   B. away   C. space-time   D. far

17 To _____ this, take a sheet of paper and make a small dot at the _____ of the paper and _____ at the _____ of the paper.

    A. top   B. understand   C. bottom   D. another

18 On a _____ _____ of paper, the dots are _____ _____ from one another.

    A. sheet   B. away   C. flat   D. far

19 Now, take the paper and _____ it with the dots _____ up. _____ a hole in the paper and the dots will be instantly _____.

    A. matched   B. connected   C. fold   D. punch

20 Like this, wormholes in space may _____ two _____, with a _____ _____ the two.

    A. connecting   B. contain   C. throat   D. mouths

21 Sci Teen: Just like a wormhole in the apple, right? If such wormholes _____ in space, we could _____ to billions of light-years _____ quickly!

    A. existed   B. places   C. away   D. get

22 Dr. Sci: Yes, but it's too _____ to _____. Wormholes in _____ only.

    A. theory   B. early   C. exist   D. celebrate

23 Sci Teen: So _____ we need to _____ is _____ _____, right?

    A. find   B. all   C. one   D. do

24 Dr. Sci: _____ if we find one, there are many things to _____ before _____ going _____ one.

    A. through   B. even   C. consider   D. actually

25 A wormhole would be very _____. If a spaceship _____ into one, it might be _____ or _____ into pieces.

    A. unstable   B. crushed   C. flew   D. broken

26 Sci Teen: Ouch! That's not a _____ _____. So, are we _____?

    A. hopeless   B. picture   C. pretty

27 Is _____ in space through a wormhole _____ an idea that only _____ in _____?

    A. simply   B. traveling   C. exists   D. theory

28 Dr. Sci: I wouldn't say so. The debate about wormholes is still _____, but with _____ _____ and _____, I believe we will eventually find one and learn how to travel through it.

    A. exploration   B. ongoing   C. research   D. persistent

29 _____ _____ at our history. We've achieved so many things that _____ _____ at first.

    A. seemed   B. back   C. impossible   D. look

30 Who knows? _____ you can _____ the one to _____ the _____!

    A. maybe   B. answer   C. find   D. be

---

16 '그는 시공간이 실제로 구부러질 수 있다고 생각했습니다. 그것이 구부러질 때 서로 멀리 떨어져 있는 부분들이 갑자기 더 가까워질 수 있습니다.

17 이것을 이해하기 위해서, 종이를 한 장 갖고 와서 그 종이의 윗부분에 작은 점을 찍고 또 다른 점을 그 종이의 아랫부분에 찍어 보세요.

18 펼쳐 놓은 종이에서 그 점들은 서로 멀리 떨어져 있습니다.

19 이제 그 종이를 들고 점들이 맞춰지도록 그것을 접으세요. 종이에 구멍을 뚫으면 그 점들이 즉시 연결될 것입니다.

20 이와 마찬가지로 우주의 웜홀은 두 개의 입과 그 둘을 연결하는 목구멍을 지니고 있을 겁니다.

21 Sci Teen: 사과에 있는 벌레 구멍처럼요. 그렇죠? 그런 웜홀이 우주에 존재한다면 우리는 수십억 광년 떨어져 있는 곳에 빠르게 도달할 수 있을 텐데요!

22 Dr. Sci: 그렇죠, 하지만 축하하기에는 너무 이릅니다. 웜홀은 이론상에서만 존재합니다.

23 Sci Teen: 그러면 우리가 해야 할 것이라고는 그것을 찾는 거네요, 그렇죠?

24 Dr. Sci: 우리가 그것을 찾는다고 하더라도 실제로 그걸 통과하여 가기 전에 고려해야 할 것들이 많이 있습니다.

25 웜홀은 매우 불안정할 것입니다. 만약 우주선이 그 안으로 날아가게 되면, 그것은 부서지거나 산산조각이 날 수도 있습니다.

26 Sci Teen: 어이쿠! 그건 좋은 광경이 아니네요. 그럼 우리는 가망이 없는 건가요?

27 우주에서 웜홀을 통하여 여행을 하는 것은 단지 이론상으로만 존재하는 아이디어인가요?

28 Dr. Sci: 그렇게 말하지는 않겠어요. 웜홀에 대한 논쟁은 여전히 진행 중이긴 하지만, 끊임없는 탐구와 연구로 우리가 결국 하나를 찾아 그것을 통해 여행하는 법을 배울 수 있을 거라고 믿습니다.

29 우리의 역사를 돌아보세요. 우리는 처음에는 불가능해 보였던 아주 많은 것들을 달성해 왔습니다.

30 누가 알겠어요? 아마도 여러분이 그 답을 찾아내는 그 사람이 될 수 있을지도요!

※ 다음 우리말과 일치하도록 빈칸에 알맞은 것을 골라 쓰시오.

1 Sci Teen: Hi, science fans. Today, we're _____ _____ _____ _____ _____ _____.

2 _____ _____ _____ _____ _____ _____, there is _____ _____ _____ in the universe.

3 So, if we _____ _____ the speed of light, we should _____ _____ _____ _____ _____ another planet _____ _____ _____ _____ an eye, _____?

4 Dr. Sci: That would be nice, but space _____ _____ _____ _____ it is _____ _____.

5 In the movie, *Passengers*, a spaceship _____ _____ a different planet _____ at _____ the speed of light.

6 So it should _____ _____ _____ _____ very quickly, right?

7 But, the passengers sleep _____ _____ _____ because it _____ _____ _____ that much time _____ _____ _____ a different planet.

8 Sci Teen: 120 years? Wow, that's a long time! Is there _____ _____ _____ _____ _____ _____ _____ space?

9 Dr. Sci: Well, _____ _____ _____ answer that question, I'd like _____ _____ _____ about this apple _____ _____ _____.

10 Imagine a worm is _____ _____ _____. It detects _____ _____ at the bottom and _____ _____ _____ _____ the top _____ the bottom.

11 For the worm, the apple's surface is _____ our universe.

12 Now the worm can _____ _____ _____ the outer layer _____ _____ a wormhole.

13 _____ _____ _____ _____ it will choose? Well, it would choose the wormhole _____ _____ _____ _____.

14 Sci Teen: Is there _____ _____ _____ _____ in the universe?

15 Dr. Sci: _____ _____ some researchers, yes. Einstein _____ _____ that space and time _____ _____, and he called it _____.

1 Sci Teen: 안녕하세요, 과학 팬 여러분. 오늘 우리는 우주여행에 대해 이야기할 것입니다.

2 우리가 모두 알다시피, 우주에서 빛보다 더 빠른 것은 없습니다.

3 그래서 만약 우리가 빛의 속도로 여행을 한다면, 우리는 다른 행성에 눈 깜박할 사이에 도달할 수 있어야 해요, 그렇죠?

4 Dr. Sci: 그렇다면 좋겠지만, 우주는 너무 광활해서 그건 불가능하답니다.

5 영화 〈Passengers〉에서 다른 행성으로 향하는 우주선이 빛의 속도의 절반으로 이동합니다.

6 그러면 그들은 다른 행성에 매우 빨리 도달해야겠지요, 그렇죠?

7 하지만 승객들은 **120**년 동안 잠을 자게 되는데, 왜냐하면 다른 행성에 도달하는 데 그만큼 많은 시간이 걸릴 것으로 예상되기 때문입니다.

8 Sci Teen: **120**년이요? 우아, 그건 정말 긴 시간이네요! 우주를 여행하는 더 빠른 방법이 있나요?

9 Dr. Sci: 글쎄요, 그 질문에 답하기 위해서 여러분이 이 사과에 대해 잠깐 생각해 보기 바랍니다.

10 한 마리 벌레가 이 사과 위에 있다고 상상해 보세요. 그것은 맨 아래에 있는 달콤한 무언가를 감지하고 맨 위에서 아래로 이동하기를 원합니다.

11 그 벌레에게 사과의 표면은 우리의 우주만큼이나 광대합니다.

12 이제 그 벌레는 바깥 표면의 껍질을 돌아서 이동하거나 벌레 구멍 아래로 이동할 수 있습니다.

13 그것이 어떤 것을 선택할 거라고 생각하십니까? 음, 그것은 벌레 구멍을 선택할 것인데 왜냐하면 그것이 지름길이기 때문입니다.

14 Sci Teen: 우주에 그런 지름길이 있나요?

15 Dr. Sci: 몇몇 연구자들에 따르면, 그렇습니다. 아인슈타인은 공간과 시간이 연결되어 있다는 것을 생각해 냈고, 그것을 시공간이라고 불렀습니다.

16 He thought that _____ _____ _____ _____ _____. When it is bent, parts _____ _____ _____ _____ _____ from each other _____ _____ _____.

17 _____ _____ this, _____ a sheet of paper and _____ a small dot _____ _____ _____ _____ the paper and _____ at the _____ of the paper.

18 _____ _____ _____ _____ of paper, the dots are _____ _____ _____ _____ one another.

19 Now, take the paper and _____ it _____ the dots _____ _____. _____ a hole in the paper and _____ _____ will _____ _____ _____.

20 Like this, wormholes in space may _____ _____ _____, with a _____ _____ the two.

21 Sci Teen: _____ _____ a wormhole in the apple, right? If such wormholes _____ in space, we could _____ _____ billions of light-years _____ quickly!

22 Dr. Sci: Yes, but it's _____ _____ _____ _____. Wormholes _____ _____ _____ only.

23 Sci Teen: So _____ we need _____ _____ is _____ _____, right?

24 Dr. Sci: _____ _____ we find one, there are many things _____ _____ before actually _____ _____ _____.

25 A wormhole _____ _____ very _____. If a spaceship _____ _____ one, it might _____ _____ or _____ _____ _____.

26 Sci Teen: Ouch! That's not _____ _____ _____. So, are we _____?

27 Is traveling in space _____ a wormhole _____ an idea _____ only _____ in theory?

28 Dr. Sci: I _____ _____ so. The debate about wormholes _____ still _____, but _____ _____ _____ and _____, I believe we will eventually find _____ and _____ _____ _____ _____ _____ it.

29 _____ _____ _____ our history. We've achieved _____ _____ _____ _____ _____ _____ at first.

30 Who _____? Maybe you can be the one _____ _____ _____!

본문 Test **37**

16 '그는 시공간이 실제로 구부러질 수 있다고 생각했습니다. 그것이 구부러질 때 서로 멀리 떨어져 있는 부분들이 갑자기 더 가까워질 수 있습니다.

17 이것을 이해하기 위해서, 종이를 한 장 갖고 와서 그 종이의 윗부분에 작은 점을 찍고 또 다른 점을 그 종이의 아랫부분에 찍어 보세요.

18 펼쳐 놓은 종이에서 그 점들은 서로 멀리 떨어져 있습니다.

19 이제 그 종이를 들고 점들이 맞춰지도록 그것을 접으세요. 종이에 구멍을 뚫으면 그 점들이 즉시 연결될 것입니다.

20 이와 마찬가지로 우주의 웜홀은 두 개의 입과 그 둘을 연결하는 목구멍을 지니고 있을 겁니다.

21 Sci Teen: 사과에 있는 벌레 구멍처럼요, 그렇죠? 그런 웜홀이 우주에 존재한다면 우리는 수십억 광년 떨어져 있는 곳에 빠르게 도달할 수 있을 텐데요!

22 Dr. Sci: 그렇죠, 하지만 축하하기에는 너무 이릅니다. 웜홀은 이론상에서만 존재합니다.

23 Sci Teen: 그러면 우리가 해야 할 것이라고는 그것을 찾는 거네요, 그렇죠?

24 Dr. Sci: 우리가 그것을 찾는다고 하더라도 실제로 그걸 통과하여 가기 전에 고려해야 할 것들이 많이 있습니다.

25 웜홀은 매우 불안정할 것입니다. 만약 우주선이 그 안으로 날아가게 되면, 그것은 부서지거나 산산조각이 날 수도 있습니다.

26 Sci Teen: 어이쿠! 그건 좋은 광경이 아니네요. 그럼 우리는 가망이 없는 건가요?

27 우주에서 웜홀을 통하여 여행을 하는 것은 단지 이론상으로만 존재하는 아이디어인가요?

28 Dr. Sci: 그렇게 말하지는 않겠어요. 웜홀에 대한 논쟁은 여전히 진행 중이긴 하지만, 끊임없는 탐구와 연구로 우리가 결국 하나를 찾아 그것을 통해 여행하는 법을 배울 수 있을 거라고 믿습니다.

29 우리의 역사를 돌아보세요. 우리는 처음에는 불가능해 보였던 아주 많은 것들을 달성해 왔습니다.

30 누가 알겠어요? 아마도 여러분이 그 답을 찾아내는 그 사람이 될 수 있을지도요!

※ 다음 문장을 우리말로 쓰시오.

1 Sci Teen: Hi, science fans. Today, we're going to talk about space travel.

➡ _____

2 As we all know, there is nothing faster than light in the universe.

➡ _____

3 So, if we travel at the speed of light, we should be able to get to another planet in the blink of an eye, right?

➡ _____

4 Dr. Sci: That would be nice, but space is so vast that it is not possible.

➡ _____

5 In the movie, *Passengers*, a spaceship headed to a different planet travels at one-half the speed of light.

➡ _____

6 So it should get to another planet very quickly, right?

➡ _____

7 But, the passengers sleep for 120 years because it is expected to take that much time to get to a different planet.

➡ _____

_____

8 Sci Teen: 120 years? Wow, that's a long time! Is there a faster way to travel through space?

➡ _____

9 Dr. Sci: Well, in order to answer that question, I'd like you to think about this apple for a second.

➡ _____

10 Imagine a worm is on this apple. It detects something sweet at the bottom and wants to move from the top to the bottom.

➡ _____

_____

11 For the worm, the apple's surface is as vast as our universe.

➡ _____

12 Now the worm can either move around the outer layer or down a wormhole.

➡ _____

13 Which do you think it will choose? Well, it would choose the wormhole because it is a shortcut.

➡ _____

_____

14 Sci Teen: Is there such a shortcut in the universe?

➡ _____

15 Dr. Sci: According to some researchers, yes. Einstein figured out that space and time are connected, and he called it space-time.

➡ _____

_____

16 He thought that space-time could actually be bent. When it is bent, parts that are far away from each other are suddenly closer.

➡ _____

17 To understand this, take a sheet of paper and make a small dot at the top of the paper and another at the bottom of the paper.

➡ _____

18 On a flat sheet of paper, the dots are far away from one another.

➡ _____

19 Now, take the paper and fold it with the dots matched up. Punch a hole in the paper and the dots will be instantly connected.

➡ _____

20 Like this, wormholes in space may contain two mouths, with a throat connecting the two.

➡ _____

21 Sci Teen: Just like a wormhole in the apple, right? If such wormholes existed in space, we could get to places billions of light-years away quickly!

➡ _____

22 Dr. Sci: Yes, but it's too early to celebrate. Wormholes exist in theory only.

➡ _____

23 Sci Teen: So all we need to do is find one, right?

➡ _____

24 Dr. Sci: Even if we find one, there are many things to consider before actually going through one

➡ _____

25 A wormhole would be very unstable. If a spaceship flew into one, it might be crushed or broken into pieces.

➡ _____

26 Sci Teen: Ouch! That's not a pretty picture. So, are we hopeless?

➡ _____

27 Is traveling in space through a wormhole simply an idea that only exists in theory?

➡ _____

28 Dr. Sci: I wouldn't say so. The debate about wormholes is still ongoing, but with persistent exploration and research, I believe we will eventually find one and learn how to travel through it.

➡ _____

29 Look back at our history. We've achieved so many things that seemed impossible at first.

➡ _____

30 Who knows? Maybe you can be the one to find the answer!

➡ _____

※ 다음 괄호 안의 단어들을 우리말에 맞도록 바르게 배열하시오.

1 (Sci Teen: / science / hi, / fans. // we're / today / to / going / about / talk / travel. / space)
➡ _____

2 (we / as / know, / all / is / there / faster / nothing / light / than / the / in / universe.)
➡ _____

3 (if / so, / travel / we / the / at / speed / light, / of / should / we / able / be / get / to / another / to / in / planet / blink / the / an / of / eye, / right?)
➡ _____

4 (Dr. Sci: / would / that / nice, / be / space / but / so / is / that / vast / is / it / possible. / not)
➡ _____

5 (the / in *Passengers*, / movie / spaceship / a / headed / a / to / planet / different / travels / at / the / one-half / of / speed / light.)
➡ _____

6 (it / so / get / should / another / to / planet / quickly, / very / right?)
➡ _____

7 (the / but, / sleep / passengers / for / years / 120 / because / is / it / to / expected / that / take / time / much / get / to / a / to / planet. / different)
➡ _____

8 (Sci Teen: / years? / 120 // that's / wow, / long / a / time! // there / is / faster / a / way / travel / to / space? / through)
➡ _____

9 (Dr. Sci: / in / well, / to / order / that / answer / question, / like / I'd / to / you / think / this / about / for / apple / second. / a)
➡ _____

10 (a / imagine / worm / on / is / apple. / this // detects / it / sweet / something / at / bottom / the / and / to / wants / from / move / top / the / the / to / bottom.)
➡ _____

11 (the / for / worm, / apple's / the / is / surface / vast / as / our / as / universe.)
➡ _____

12 (the / now / worm / can / move / either / the / around / outer / or / layer / a / down / wormhole.)
➡ _____

13 (do / which / think / you / will / it / choose? // it / well, / choose / would / wormhole / the / it / because / is / shortcut. / a)
➡ _____

14 (Sci Teen: / there / is / a / such / in / shortcut / universe? / the)
➡ _____

15 (Dr. Sci: / to / according / researchers, / some / yes. // figured / Einstein / out / that / and / space / time / connected, / are / he / and / called / space-time. / it)
➡ _____

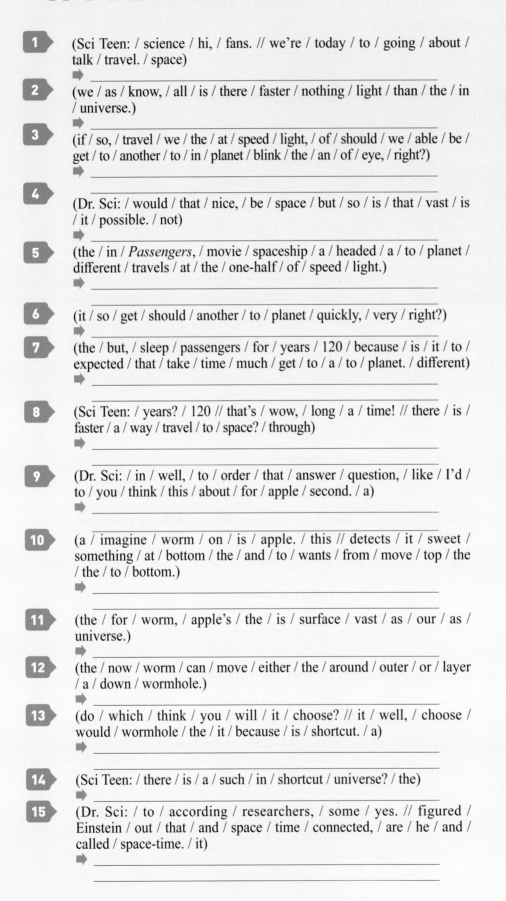

1 Sci Teen: 안녕하세요, 과학 팬 여러분. 오늘 우리는 우주여행에 대해 이야기할 것입니다.

2 우리가 모두 알다시피, 우주에서 빛보다 더 빠른 것은 없습니다.

3 그래서 만약 우리가 빛의 속도로 여행을 한다면, 우리는 다른 행성에 눈 깜박할 사이에 도달할 수 있어야 해요, 그렇죠?

4 Dr. Sci: 그렇다면 좋겠지만, 우주는 너무 광활해서 그건 불가능하답니다.

5 영화 〈Passengers〉에서 다른 행성으로 향하는 우주선이 빛의 속도의 절반으로 이동합니다.

6 그러면 그들은 다른 행성에 매우 빨리 도달해야겠지요, 그렇죠?

7 하지만 승객들은 120년 동안 잠을 자게 되는데, 왜냐하면 다른 행성에 도달하는 데 그만큼 많은 시간이 걸릴 것으로 예상되기 때문입니다.

8 Sci Teen: 120년이요? 우아, 그건 정말 긴 시간이네요! 우주를 여행하는 더 빠른 방법이 있나요?

9 Dr. Sci: 글쎄요, 그 질문에 답하기 위해서 여러분들이 이 사과에 대해 잠깐 생각해 보기 바랍니다.

10 한 마리 벌레가 이 사과 위에 있다고 상상해 보세요. 그것은 맨 아래에 있는 달콤한 무언가를 감지하고 맨 위에서 아래로 이동하기를 원합니다.

11 그 벌레에게 사과의 표면은 우리의 우주만큼이나 광대합니다.

12 이제 그 벌레는 바깥 표면의 껍질을 돌아서 이동하거나 벌레 구멍 아래로 이동할 수 있습니다.

13 그것이 어떤 것을 선택할 거라고 생각하십니까? 음, 그것은 벌레 구멍을 선택할 것인데 왜냐하면 그것이 지름길이기 때문입니다.

14 Sci Teen: 우주에 그런 지름길이 있나요?

15 Dr. Sci: 몇몇 연구자들에 따르면, 그렇습니다. 아인슈타인은 공간과 시간이 연결되어 있다는 것을 생각해 냈고, 그것을 시공간이라고 불렀습니다.

16 (thought / he / space-time / that / actually / could / bent. / be // it / when / bent, / is / that / parts / far / are / from / away / other / each / suddenly / are / closer.)

➡ _____

17 (understand / to / this, / a / take / of / sheet / paper / and / a / make / dot / small / at / top / the / the / of / paper / another / and / the / at / bottom / the / of / paper.)

➡ _____

18 (a / on / sheet / flat / paper, / of / dots / the / far / are / from / away / another. / one)

➡ _____

19 (now, / the / take / and / paper / fold / with / it / dots / the / up. / matched // a / punch / hole / the / in / paper / and / dots / the / be / will / connected. / instantly)

➡ _____

20 (this, like / in / wormholes / space / contain / may / mouths, / two / a / with / throat / the / connecting / two.)

➡ _____

21 (Sci Teen: / like / just / wormhole / a / the / in / right? / apple, // such / if / existed / wormholes / space, / in / could / we / to / get / places / of / billions / away / light-years / quickly!)

➡ _____

22 (Dr. Sci: / but / yes, / too / it's / to / early / celebrate. // exist / wormholes / theory / in / only.)

➡ _____

23 (Sci Teen: / all / so / need / we / do / to / find / is / right? / one,)

➡ _____

24 (Dr. Sci: / if / even / find / we / one, / are / there / things / many / consider / to / actually / before / through / going / one.)

➡ _____

25 (wormhole / a / be / would / unstable. / very // a / if / flew / spaceship / one, / into / might / it / be / or / crushed / into / broken / pieces.)

➡ _____

26 (Sci Teen: / ouch! // not / that's / pretty / a / picture. // are / so / hopeless? / we)

➡ _____

27 (traveling / is / space / in / a / through / simply / wormhole / idea / an / only / that / in / theory? / exists)

➡ _____

28 (Dr. Sci: / wouldn't / I / so. / say // debate / the / wormholes / about / is / ongoing, / still / with / but / exploration / persistent / and / I / research, / we / will / believe / eventually / one / find / and / how / learn / travel / to / it. / through)

➡ _____

➡ _____

29 (back / look / our / at / history. // achieved / we've / many / so / that / things / seemed / at / impossible / first.)

➡ _____

30 (knows? / who // you / maybe / be / can / one / the / find / to / answer! / the)

➡ _____

16 '그는 시공간이 실제로 구부러질 수 있다고 생각했습니다. 그것이 구부러질 때 서로 멀리 떨어져 있는 부분들이 갑자기 더 가까워질 수 있습니다.

17 이것을 이해하기 위해서, 종이를 한 장 갖고 와서 그 종이의 윗부분에 작은 점을 찍고 또 다른 점을 그 종이의 아랫부분에 찍어 보세요.

18 펼쳐 놓은 종이에서 그 점들은 서로 멀리 떨어져 있습니다.

19 이제 그 종이를 들고 점들이 맞춰지도록 그것을 접으세요. 종이에 구멍을 뚫으면 그 점들이 즉시 연결될 것입니다.

20 이와 마찬가지로 우주의 웜홀은 두 개의 입과 그 둘을 연결하는 목구멍을 지니고 있을 겁니다.

21 Sci Teen: 사과에 있는 벌레 구멍처럼요, 그렇죠? 그런 웜홀이 우주에 존재한다면 우리는 수십억 광년 떨어져 있는 곳에 빠르게 도달할 수 있을 텐데요!

22 Dr. Sci: 그렇죠, 하지만 축하하기에는 너무 이릅니다. 웜홀은 이론상에서만 존재합니다.

23 Sci Teen: 그러면 우리가 해야 할 것이라고는 그것을 찾는 거네요, 그렇죠?

24 Dr. Sci: 우리가 그것을 찾는다고 하더라도 실제로 걸 통과하여 가기 전에 고려해야 할 것들이 많이 있습니다.

25 웜홀은 매우 불안정할 것입니다. 만약 우주선이 그 안으로 날아가게 되면, 그것은 부서지거나 산산조각이 날 수도 있습니다.

26 Sci Teen: 어이쿠! 그건 좋은 광경이 아니네요. 그럼 우리는 가망이 없는 건가요?

27 우주에서 웜홀을 통하여 여행을 하는 것은 단지 이론상으로만 존재하는 아이디어인가요?

28 Dr. Sci: 그렇게 말하지는 않겠어요. 웜홀에 대한 논쟁은 여전히 진행 중이긴 하지만, 끊임없는 탐구와 연구로 우리가 결국 하나를 찾아 그것을 통해 여행하는 법을 배울 수 있을 거라고 믿습니다.

29 우리의 역사를 돌아보세요. 우리는 처음에는 불가능해 보였던 아주 많은 것들을 달성해 왔습니다.

30 누가 알겠어요? 아마도 여러분이 그 답을 찾아내는 그 사람이 될 수 있을지도요!

※ 다음 우리말을 영어로 쓰시오.

1 Sci Teen: 안녕하세요, 과학 팬 여러분. 오늘 우리는 우주여행에 대해 이야기할 것입니다.
➡ _____

2 우리가 모두 알다시피, 우주에서 빛보다 더 빠른 것은 없습니다.
➡ _____

3 그래서 만약 우리가 빛의 속도로 여행을 한다면, 우리는 다른 행성에 눈 깜박할 사이에 도달할 수 있어야 해요, 그렇죠?
➡ _____

4 Dr. Sci: 그렇다면 좋겠지만, 우주는 너무 광활해서 그건 불가능하답니다.
➡ _____

5 영화 〈Passengers〉에서 다른 행성으로 향하는 우주선이 빛의 속도의 절반으로 이동합니다.
➡ _____

6 그러면 그들은 다른 행성에 매우 빨리 도달해야겠지요, 그렇죠?
➡ _____

7 하지만 승객들은 120년 동안 잠을 자게 되는데, 왜냐하면 다른 행성에 도달하는 데 그만큼 많은 시간이 걸릴 것으로 예상되기 때문입니다.
➡ _____
_____

8 Sci Teen: 120년이요? 우아, 그건 정말 긴 시간이네요! 우주를 여행하는 더 빠른 방법이 있나요?
➡ _____

9 Dr. Sci: 글쎄요, 그 질문에 답하기 위해서 여러분들이 이 사과에 대해 잠깐 생각해 보기 바랍니다.
➡ _____

10 한 마리 벌레가 이 사과 위에 있다고 상상해 보세요. 그것은 맨 아래에 있는 달콤한 무언가를 감지하고 맨 위에서 아래로 이동하기를 원합니다.
➡ _____
_____

11 그 벌레에게 사과의 표면은 우리의 우주만큼이나 광대합니다.
➡ _____

12 이제 그 벌레는 바깥 표면의 껍질을 돌아서 이동하거나 벌레 구멍 아래로 이동할 수 있습니다.
➡ _____

13 그것이 어떤 것을 선택할 거라고 생각하십니까? 음, 그것은 벌레 구멍을 선택할 것인데 왜냐하면 그것이 지름길이기 때문입니다.
➡ _____

14 Sci Teen: 우주에 그런 지름길이 있나요?
➡ _____

15 Dr. Sci: 몇몇 연구자들에 따르면, 그렇습니다. 아인슈타인은 공간과 시간이 연결되어 있다는 것을 생각해 냈고, 그것을 시공간이라고 불렀습니다.
➡ _____
_____

16 그는 시공간이 실제로 구부러질 수 있다고 생각했습니다. 그것이 구부러질 때 서로 멀리 떨어져 있는 부분들이 갑자기 더 가까워질 수 있습니다.

➡ _____

17 이것을 이해하기 위해서, 종이를 한 장 갖고 와서 그 종이의 윗부분에 작은 점을 찍고 또 다른 점을 그 종이의 아랫부분에 찍어 보세요.

➡ _____

18 펼쳐 놓은 종이에서 그 점들은 서로 멀리 떨어져 있습니다.

➡ _____

19 이제 그 종이를 들고 점들이 맞춰지도록 그것을 접으세요. 종이에 구멍을 뚫으면 그 점들이 즉시 연결될 것입니다.

➡ _____

20 이와 마찬가지로 우주의 웜홀은 두 개의 입과 그 둘을 연결하는 목구멍을 지니고 있을 겁니다.

➡ _____

21 Sci Teen: 사과에 있는 벌레 구멍처럼요, 그렇죠? 그런 웜홀이 우주에 존재한다면 우리는 수십억 광년 떨어져 있는 곳에 빠르게 도달할 수 있을 텐데요!

➡ _____

22 Dr. Sci: 그렇죠, 하지만 축하하기에는 너무 이릅니다. 웜홀은 이론상에서만 존재합니다.

➡ _____

23 Sci Teen: 그러면 우리가 해야 할 것이라고는 그것을 찾는 거네요, 그렇죠?

➡ _____

24 Dr. Sci: 우리가 그것을 찾는다고 하더라도 실제로 그걸 통과하여 가기 전에 고려해야 할 것들이 많이 있습니다.

➡ _____

25 웜홀은 매우 불안정할 것입니다. 만약 우주선이 그 안으로 날아가게 되면, 그것은 부서지거나 산산조각이 날 수도 있습니다.

➡ _____

26 Sci Teen: 어이쿠! 그건 좋은 광경이 아니네요. 그럼 우리는 가망이 없는 건가요?

➡ _____

27 우주에서 웜홀을 통하여 여행을 하는 것은 단지 이론상으로만 존재하는 아이디어인가요?

➡ _____

28 Dr. Sci: 그렇게 말하지는 않겠어요. 웜홀에 대한 논쟁은 여전히 진행 중이긴 하지만, 끊임없는 탐구와 연구로 우리가 결국 하나를 찾아 그것을 통해 여행하는 법을 배울 수 있을 거라고 믿습니다.

➡ _____

29 우리의 역사를 돌아보세요. 우리는 처음에는 불가능해 보였던 아주 많은 것들을 달성해 왔습니다.

➡ _____

30 누가 알겠어요? 아마도 여러분이 그 답을 찾아내는 그 사람이 될 수 있을지도요!

➡ _____

※ 다음 우리말과 일치하도록 빈칸에 알맞은 말을 쓰시오.

After You Read A

1. _____ through space

2. ① _____ _____ an apple

3. A wormhole is a shortcut _____ _____ _____ _____ from _____ _____ to _____ _____.

4. ② Wormholes _____ _____

5. Einstein thought _____ and _____ _____ _____ and _____ _____ _____ _____.

6. When it is bent, _____ _____ _____ _____ each other can _____ _____.

7. Do wormholes _____ _____?

8. ③ _____ _____, wormholes _____.

9. Wormholes _____ _____ _____. A spaceship could _____ _____ or _____ _____ _____.

10. _____ I believe _____ _____ _____ and _____ we will find a wormhole!

1. 우주로 여행을 떠나는 더 빠른 방법
2. ① 사과에서 얻은 아이디어
3. 벌레 구멍은 벌레가 맨 위에서 아래로 이동하는 지름길이다.
4. ② 우주에서의 웜홀
5. 아인슈타인은 공간과 시간은 연결되어 있고 시공간은 구부러질 수 있다고 생각했다.
6. 그것이 구부러질 때, 서로 멀리 떨어져 있는 부분들이 더 가까워질 수 있다.
7. 웜홀이 실제로 존재할까?
8. ③ 이론상, 웜홀은 존재한다.
9. 웜홀은 불안정할 것이다. 우주선이 부서지거나 산산조각이 날 수도 있다.
10. 하지만 난 끊임없는 탐구와 연구로 우리가 결국 웜홀을 찾아낼 거라고 믿는다!

Language in Use

1. Is the universe _____ _____ _____?

2. _____, the driver is _____ _____ _____ _____ _____ after the accident.

1. 우주는 유한할까 아니면 무한할까?
2. 운 좋게도, 그 운전자는 사고 이후에 안정적인 상태이다.

Think & Write C

1. If I could make a planet _____ _____ _____ _____ _____ in the future, I _____ _____ _____ _____ _____ a planet _____ Atlas.

2. It would be a _____ _____ _____.

3. Its size would be _____ _____ _____ _____, but _____ _____ Earth.

4. _____ _____ of it _____ _____ _____ 30°C.

5. It would _____ _____ _____.

6. _____, if people _____ _____ it, they could _____ _____ animals _____ _____ _____.

1. 만약 제가 미래에 우리가 살 행성을 만든다면, 나는 아틀라스라고 불리는 행성을 만들고 싶습니다.
2. 그것은 아름다운 푸른 행성일 것입니다.
3. 그것의 크기는 달보다 더 크지만 지구보다 더 작을 것입니다.
4. 그것의 온도는 약 섭씨 30도일 것입니다.
5. 그것은 아름다운 자연을 가지고 있을 것입니다.
6. 흥미롭게도, 만약 사람들이 그곳으로 간다면, 그들은 이 행성에서 동물들과 의사소통할 수 있을 것입니다.

※ 다음 우리말을 영어로 쓰시오.

After You Read A

1. 우주로 여행을 떠나는 더 빠른 방법
➡ _____

2. ① 사과에서 얻은 아이디어
➡ _____

3. 벌레 구멍은 벌레가 맨 위에서 아래로 이동하는 지름길이다.
➡ _____

4. ② 우주에서의 웜홀
➡ _____

5. 아인슈타인은 공간과 시간은 연결되어 있고 시공간은 구부러질 수 있다고 생각했다.
➡ _____

6. 그것이 구부러질 때, 서로 멀리 떨어져 있는 부분들이 더 가까워질 수 있다.
➡ _____

7. 웜홀이 실제로 존재할까?
➡ _____

8. ③ 이론상, 웜홀은 존재한다.
➡ _____

9. 웜홀은 불안정할 것이다. 우주선이 부서지거나 산산조각이 날 수도 있다.
➡ _____

10. 하지만 난 끊임없는 탐구와 연구로 우리가 결국 웜홀을 찾아낼 거라고 믿는다!
➡ _____

Language in Use

1. 우주는 유한할까 아니면 무한할까?
➡ _____

2. 운 좋게도, 그 운전자는 사고 이후에 안정적인 상태이다.
➡ _____

Think & Write C

1. 만약 제가 미래에 우리가 살 행성을 만든다면, 나는 아틀라스라고 불리는 행성을 만들고 싶습니다.
➡ _____

2. 그것은 아름다운 푸른 행성일 것입니다.
➡ _____

3. 그것의 크기는 달보다 더 크지만 지구보다 더 작을 것입니다.
➡ _____

4. 그것의 온도는 약 섭씨 30도일 것입니다.
➡ _____

5. 그것은 아름다운 자연을 가지고 있을 것입니다.
➡ _____

6. 흥미롭게도, 만약 사람들이 그곳으로 간다면, 그들은 이 행성에서 동물들과 의사소통할 수 있을 것입니다.
➡ _____

MEMO

영어 기출 문제집

적중100

2학기

정답 및 해설

비상 | 김진완

중 3

영어 기출 문제집

적중100

2학기

정답 및 해설

비상 | 김진완

중 3

적중100

Lesson 7

Spend Wisely

시험대비 실력평가   p.08

| 01 ② | 02 ① | 03 When it comes to |
| 04 ⑤ | 05 ④ | 06 ④ | 07 ③ |

01 ②에서 en은 '안에'라는 'in'의 의미이다. en(= in)+close(닫다). 안에 넣고 닫다 → 둘러싸다, 동봉하다 ① en-+large → enlarge: 확대하다, 확장하다 ③ en-+able → enable: 가능케 하다 ④ en-+force → enforce: 집행하다, 강요하다 ⑤ en-+rich → enrich: 풍부하게 하다

02 replace: 바꾸다, 교체하다 / 우리는 이 양탄자를 곧 바꿔야 한다. ② 수리하다 ③ 제거하다 ④ 영향을 주다, 충격을 주다 ⑤ 지키다, 보호하다

03 when it comes to: ~에 관해서, ~에 대해 말하자면

04 consume: 소비하다, 소모하다 / 연료, 에너지, 혹은 시간을 특히 많은 양으로 쓰다, 또는 특히 어떤 것을 많이 먹고 마시다 ① 포함하다 ② 요구하다 ③ 유지하다 ④ 추정하다

05 <보기>는 동의어 관계이다. quality: 질, 품질, 특성, 자질 characteristic: 특질, 특징 ⓐ tight: 꽉 조이는 loose: 헐거운 ⓑ endanger: 위험에 빠뜨리다 save: 구하다 ⓒ effect: 결과, 효과 result: 결과, 성과 ⓓ replace: 바꾸다, 교체하다 substitute: 대신하다 ⓔ encourage: 부추기다, 조장하다 discourage: 낙담시키다

06 ① 그의 말은 위로하는 효과를 가지고 있었다. ② 아름다움의 개념을 정의하기는 어렵다. ③ 너의 의견은 많은 사람에게 영향을 줄 것이다. ④ allowance: 용돈 / 나는 부모님에게서 용돈을 받는다. ⑤ 그녀가 버스에 탔을 때, 그 버스는 거의 비어 있었다.

07 furthermore: 그뿐만 아니라, 더욱이 / 그 셔츠는 예쁠 뿐만 아니라 싸다. ① 따라서, 그러므로 ② 그럼에도 불구하고 ④ 그러므로 ⑤ 똑같이, 비슷하게

서술형 시험대비   p.09

01 com
02 (1) spending   (2) next time   (3) even though
    (4) go window shopping
03 on
04 (1) with   (2) In   (3) for   (4) at   (5) As
05 (1) mention   (2) compare   (3) combine
    (4) endangered

01 특정 어근 앞에 com-을 붙이면 '함께'라는 의미를 더한다. com-+parison → comparison: 비교 com-+promise → compromise: 타협(하다) com-+pose → compose: 구성하다

02 (1) record: 기록하다 spending: 지출, 소비 (2) the next time+주어+동사: 다음번에 ~할 때에 (3) even though: 비록 ~이지만 (4) go window shopping: 진열된 상품을 구경하고 다니다

03 on display: 진열된, 전시된 / 그림은 현재 뉴욕에 전시 중이다. on sale: 판매 중인 / 표는 매표소에서 판매하고 있다.

04 (1) go well with: ~와 잘 어울리다 / 나는 이 블라우스가 네가 입고 있는 치마와 잘 어울린다고 생각한다. (2) in comparison: 비교해 보면 / 그녀의 문제와 비교해 보면, 내 문제들은 사소해 보인다. (3) for a moment: 잠깐 / 너는 잠시 동안 숨을 참아야 한다. (4) at a glance: 한눈에, 즉시 / 나는 무슨 일이 일어났는지 한눈에 알아챘다. (5) as such: 그렇게, 이와 같이 / 이와 같이 그는 인내력이 있는 인물이었다.

05 (1) mention: 언급하다, 말하다 / 내가 다음 달에 캐나다로 이사 간다고 말했니? (2) compare: 비교하다 / 너는 물건을 사기 전에 가격을 비교해야 한다. (3) combine: 결합하다 / 그는 일과 즐거움을 결합하고 싶어 한다. (4) endanger: 위험에 빠뜨리다 / 불은 숲 속에 있는 동물들을 위험에 빠뜨렸다.

교과서 Conversation

핵심 Check   p.10~11

1 ②   2 I should have gotten up earlier.

교과서 대화문 익히기

Check(√) True or False   p.12

1 T   2 F   3 F   4 F

Check(√) True or False   p.13

5 T   6 F   7 F   8 T

Listen & Talk 1 A

1. help / try on / How do you like / but, suits, have / one

2. to / I'm looking for / popular among, How do you like / green one is lighter than, one

Listen & Talk 1 B

bought, ago / looks, How do you like / convenient, anywhere, quality / How long, last / doesn't last / too bad / pretty happy

Listen & Talk 2 A

1. too uncomfortable / What's wrong with it / tight / you try it on before buying / so, should have tried, on

2. are going to watch / I've spent, allowance / get it / should have kept track of my spending

Listen & Talk 2 B

on sale / on sale, has just been released / is having / at full price / at, discount / should have checked the sales before

Communication Step A

heard that you bought / not happy, it / Why, What's / gets overheated, have read / for / won't give me back, I've used / calling, explaining / do

Wrap Up

1. I'd like to / How do you like this red one / that, one / striped, Its / take

2. online used store / let me see / is a little broken, said that / before / I just trusted, should have checked a bit more / should call, ask for a refund

---

01 ②   02 ⑤   03 ①

01 여자가 별들이 그려진 모자를 써 볼 수 있는지 질문하자 남자가 된다고 대답한다. 그리고 이어진 질문에 여자가 써 본 모자와 색깔에 대해서 말하고 있으므로, 상대방의 의견 혹은 만족 여부를 물을 때 사용하는 'How do you like ~?'을 이용한 ②번이 적절하다.

02 (C) 코트가 불편하다는 말에 (D) 상대방은 이유를 물어본다. (B) 너무 꽉 껴서 불편하다고 대답하다. (A) 사기 전에 입어 보지 않았냐고 질문하고 자신의 사이즈여서 그냥 사버렸다는 얘기를 하면서, 미리 입어 보지 않은 것에 후회를 나타낸다.

03 'should have p.p. ~.'는 어떤 일을 했어야 했다고, 또는 하지 말았어야 했다고 후회할 때 사용한다. try on: (옷 등을 시험 삼아) 입어 보다

---

01 ②, ④, ⑤   02 (A) ⓔ   (B) ⓑ

03 I should have tried it on.   04 ③   05 ⑤

06 ④   07 ④   08 ③   09 ②

01 'I love them. They are very comfortable.'은 '좋아요, 매우 편안해요.'의 의미로 빈칸에 어울리는 질문은 them에 해당하는 것에 대한 상대방의 만족이나 불만족을 물어보는 질문이 어울린다. 'How do you like ~?'는 '~는 어때?'의 의미이며, 'Are you satisfied[happy] with ~?', 'How is ~?', 'Are you enjoying ~?' 등으로 바꿔 쓸 수 있다.

02 (A) 코트가 불편하다는 말에, 여자가 왜 그런지 질문을 하는 말에 이어, 'What's wrong with it?(무슨 문제가 있니?)'이라고 했을 때 옷이 꽉 낀다고 말하는 것이 어울린다. (B) 'No. It was my size, so I just bought it.(아니. 내 사이즈여서 그냥 사 버렸어.)'이라고 대답하는 것으로 볼 때 옷을 살 때 안 입어봤는지 질문하는 것이 적절하다.

03 'should have p.p. ~.'는 어떤 일을 했어야 했다고, 후회할 때 사용한다. 'try it on'의 어순에 주의한다. try on: (옷 등을 시험 삼아) 입어 보다

04 온라인에서 산 아이스티가 만족스럽지 않다는 말에, 이유를 물어보니 너무 설탕이 많이 들어 있다고 대답한다. 빈칸에는 영양 분석을 확인했어야 했다고 말하는 것이 어울린다. nutrition fact: 영양 분석

05 일요일에 본 영화에 대해 만족을 묻는 말인 'How did you like it?'에 Yes나 No로 대답할 수 없다.

06 주어진 문장 'That's too bad.'는 '그것 참 안됐다.'라는 뜻으로 상대방의 실망에 대해 위로하는 표현이다. 정가를 주고 샀다는 남자아이의 말에 여자아이가 위로하는 것이 어울리므로 ④가 적절하다.

07 (A) release: 출시하다, 발매하다, it이 가리키는 것은 a new phone을 의미하는 것이므로 수동태가 들어가야 한다. just는 '방금'이라는 뜻으로 'have p.p.'인 현재완료 중에서 '완료'의 의미로 사용하였다. (B) 'should have p.p. ~'는 '~했어야 했는데 (사실은 하지 않았다)'라는 뜻으로 과거 사실에 대한 유감을 나타내는 표현이다. 내용상 할인 판매를 확인했어야 했다는 내용이 들어가야 하므로 'should have p.p. ~'가 어울린다.

08 'How do you like ~?'는 '~는 어때?'라는 의미로 상대방에게 어떤 것에 대한 만족 또는 불만족을 묻는 표현이다.

09 Luke가 무엇을 위해 새 스피커를 사용할 것인지는 대화를 통해 알 수 없다. ① 새 스피커의 음질은 어떠한가? The sound quality is good. ③ Luke는 언제 새 스피커를 샀는가? He bought it a few weeks ago. ④ Luke는 새 스피커에 만족하는

3

가? He is pretty happy with it. ⑤ 배터리는 얼마나 지속되는
가? About 2 hours.

01 should have worn a warm jacket
02 How do you like it?
03 explaining
04 I should have read more reviews.
05 (A) on   (B) at
06 I should have checked the sales before buying
   mine.

01 'should have p.p. ~'는 '~했어야 했는데 (사실은 하지 않았
   다)'라는 뜻으로 과거 사실에 대한 유감을 나타내는 표현이다.

02 'Oh, I'm not happy with it.(아, 나는 별로 마음에 들지 않
   아.)'은 여자가 온라인으로 산 노트북에 대해 불만족을 표현하는
   말이다. 그러므로 빈칸에는 어떤 것에 만족하거나 불만이 있는
   지 묻는 'How do you like it?'이 어울린다.

03 'How about ~?'은 '~하는 게 어때?'라는 뜻으로 상대방에게
   권유할 때 사용하는 표현이고, about은 전치사이기 때문에 뒤에
   명사나 동명사가 올 수 있다. explaining은 calling과 접속사
   and로 연결되어 있다.

04 과거 사실에 대해 후회나 유감을 나타낼 때 '~했어야 했다'라는
   의미로 'should have p.p. ~'를 쓴다. review: 후기

05 (A) on sale: 할인 중인 (B) at full price: 정가에, 제값에

06 대화의 흐름상 '사기 전에 할인 판매를 확인했어야 했다'라는 내
   용이 어울리므로, 'should have p.p. ~'를 이용해서 문장을 완
   성한다. 여기서 before는 전치사이므로 뒤에 동명사형이 온다.

1 ④
2 (1) is (2) are (3) are

01 ④   02 ③   03 ①   04 ②
05 I love you as time goes by.

01 ④는 보어절을 이끄는 접속사 that이 적절하다.

02 부분을 나타내는 말은 뒤에 오는 명사의 수에 따라 그 수가 결정
   되는데, Half of 다음에 the money라고 단수 명사가 나오므로
   ③번이 적절하다.

03 '~함에 따라'로 해석되는 '비례, 추이'를 나타내는 as가 적절하
   다.

04 ②번에는 부사절과 주절의 내용이 서로 상반되므로 양보의 접
   속사 Though[Although]가 적절하다. 나머지는 모두 as가 들
   어갈 수 있다. 각각 ① '시간' ③ '방식, 양태' ④ '비례, 추이' ⑤
   '이유'를 나타낸다.

05 '비례, 추이(~함에 따라서, ~에 비례하여)'를 나타내는 as를 이
   용하여 영작한다.

01 ⑤   02 ②   03 ③   04 ⑤
05 ④   06 likes → like 07 ②   08 ①
09 ④   10 ③   11 ①   12 ⑤
13 ④   14 ②   15 ①
16 Strange as it may seem

01 ⑤는 '~으로, ~로서'라는 뜻으로 전치사로 쓰였다. 나머지는 모
   두 접속사 as로 사용되었다.

02 ②는 '~하기 때문에'라는 뜻이다. 나머지는 모두 '~함에 따라, ~
   할수록'이라는 비례의 의미를 나타낸다.

03 문맥상 '~하듯이, ~하는 것처럼'이라는 뜻의 접속사 As를 쓰는
   것이 가장 적절하다.

04 '부분을 나타내는 명사+of 다음에 명사가 올 때 동사의 수를 명
   사의 수에 일치시킨다. 모두 복수 명사가 이어지고 있으므로 복
   수 동사 were가 적절하다.

05 부분을 나타내는 말은 뒤에 오는 명사의 수에 따라 그 수가 결정
   되는데, 'About one third of' 다음에 all the students라고 복
   수 명사가 나오므로 wear가 적절하다.

06 '부분을 나타내는 말+단수 명사: 단수 동사', '부분을 나타내는 말
   +복수 명사: 복수 동사' the students로 복수 명사가 이어지고 있
   으므로 복수 동사 like가 적절하다.

07 (1) '비례, 추이'를 나타내는 접속사 (2) '이유'를 나타내는 접속사
   (3) '~으로, ~처럼'의 뜻으로 쓰인 전치사

08 '비례, 추이(~함에 따라서, ~에 비례하여)'를 나타내는 접속사
   as를 이용하는 것이 가장 적절하다.

09 'a number of+복수 명사+복수 동사' (많은= many), 'the
   number of+복수 명사+단수 동사' (~의 수). a great deal of
   = much

10 ① being 이하가 분사구문으로 쓰여서 as를 접속사로도 전치사로도 쓸 수 없다.(As → 삭제) ② as가 아니라 명사절을 이끄는 접속사가 필요하다.(as → that) ④ 내용상 know의 목적어 역할을 할 수 있는 '의문사+to부정사'가 적절하다. (as → what) ⑤ '부사구(In addition)'이 앞에 나온 완전한 절이므로, as는 접속사로도 전치사로도 쓸 수 없다.(as → 삭제)

11 부분을 나타내는 말이 있는 어구가 주어로 쓰일 때 뒤에 단수 명사가 나오면 단수 동사를 쓰고, 복수 명사가 나오면 복수 동사를 쓴다. ①은 is[was], 나머지는 모두 are[were]이다.

12 주어진 문장과 ⑤의 as는 '~함에 따라, ~할수록'이라는 뜻으로서 '비례, 추이'를 나타낸다. 나머지는 각각 ① 비록 ~할지라도, ~이지만(양보) ② ~ 때문에(이유) ③ ~하는 것처럼, ~하는 대로 (방식, 양태) ④ ~할 때(시간) 등이다.

13 서울에서 한국 음식을 먹어 봤고, 삼겹살을 먹어 봤으므로 '먹어 본 것 중의 하나'가 삼겹살이라고 쓸 수 있다. 'one of+복수 명사'가 주어일 경우 핵심이 되는 주어가 one이므로 동사는 단수로 쓴다.

14 ②는 '금반지를 껴도 원숭이는 원숭이다.'라는 뜻이다. 의미상 as를 양보의 접속사 though나 although 등으로 바꾸는 것이 적절하다.

15 주절의 동사가 과거시제인 경우 종속절의 시제는 과거나 과거완료가 나오지만 종속절이 불변의 진리, 격언, 현재의 습관, 과학적 사실 등을 나타내면 현재시제를 쓴다. 남편이 매일 아침 커피를 마시는 것은 '현재의 습관'이므로 현재시제로 나타낸다.

16 접속사 as가 '양보'의 의미로 쓰일 때는 '형용사/부사/무관사 명사'를 as 앞에 둔다.

서술형 시험대비 p.28~29

01 (1) Do as the Romans do when you are in Rome.
(2) As the song became more popular, he was known to more people.
(3) About half of the water is used to raise animals in the U.S.
(4) About 14 percent of all people don't know how to read due to lack of education.

02 (1) I caught him just as he was leaving the building.
(2) Brave as he was, he could not help weeping at the sight.
(3) Each blind student was paired with a sighted student.
(4) Jeff buys soccer shoes because more than half of the boys on his team wear them.

(5) Most of the allowance is spent on clothes and one fourth of the allowance is spent on snacks.

03 (1) As you give more love, you will receive more love.
(2) As you exercise harder, you become healthier.

04 is sitting

05 As you eat more

06 (1) like (2) are (3) knows (4) goes (5) decreases
(6) ended

07 (1) About two thirds of the books Sophie wrote were read by Steve.
(2) Some of the food that Mom made was thrown away by Mike.
(3) One of Dominic's hobbies is basketball.

---

01 (1) ~하듯이, ~하는 대로(방식)의 접속사 as를 이용한다. (2) ~함에 따라서, ~에 비례하여(비례, 추이)의 접속사 as를 이용한다. (3), (4) 부분을 나타내는 말이 있는 어구가 주어로 쓰일 때 뒤에 단수 명사가 나오면 단수 동사를 쓰고, 복수 명사가 나오면 복수 동사를 쓴다.

02 (1) just though → just as (2) 문맥상 양보의 의미가 적절하므로 '형용사+as+주어+동사 ~'의 어순이 적절하다. (3) each 다음에는 단수 명사와 단수 동사가 이어진다. (4) 'half of' 다음에 'the boys on his team'라는 복수 명사가 나오므로 복수 동사 wear가 적절하다. (5) 'Most of'와 'one fourth of' 다음에 'the allowance'라는 단수 명사가 나오므로 단수 동사 is가 적절하다.

03 'the 비교급 …, the 비교급 ~' 구문을 '비례, 추이'를 나타내는 as를 이용하여 바꿔 쓸 수 있다.

04 'one of+복수 명사'가 주어일 경우 핵심이 되는 주어가 one이므로 동사는 단수로 쓴다.

05 '비례, 추이(~함에 따라서, ~에 비례하여)'의 부사절을 이끄는 as를 이용한다.

06 (1), (2) 부분을 나타내는 말 뒤에 오는 명사가 단수이면 단수 동사를 쓰고 복수이면 복수 동사를 쓴다. (3) 'none of+명사+동사'에서 명사가 단수일 경우, 동사의 수는 명사에 일치시켜 단수 동사로 쓴다. 명사가 복수일 경우에는 복수 동사나 단수 동사를 모두 쓸 수 있다. (4) 주절의 시제가 과거일지라도 종속절이 불변의 진리, 격언, 현재의 습관, 과학적 사실 등을 나타내면 현재시제를 쓴다. (5) the number of+단수[복수] 명사+단수 동사 (6) 역사적인 사실은 주절의 시제와 상관없이 과거시제를 쓴다.

07 부분을 나타내는 말은 뒤에 오는 명사의 수에 따라 그 수가 결정된다. (1) 'two thirds of the books'에서 'the books'로 복수이므로 were를 써야 한다. (2) 'Some of the food'에서 'the food'로 단수이므로 was를 써야 한다. (3) 'one of' 다음에는 복수 명사가 나오며 핵심 주어가 one이므로 단수 동사로 받는다.

Reading

확인문제   p.30

1 T   2 F

확인문제   p.31

1 F   2 T   3 F

교과서 확인학습 A   p.32~33

01 why you've bought things that
02 what affects us, buying
03 what my friends bought
04 goes, sees a pair of, on display
05 recognizes, because, half of the boys, wear
06 Although, many pairs of, ends up buying
07 bandwagon effect, to explain
08 that encourages, to jump aboard
09 more and more people, others are, likely to get on
10 to buy, just because, have bought it
11 buy a pair of, after, have bought
12 that, realizes that, match
13 that go, with
14 that none of her bags match
15 buys, Most of her money is, on, to complete
16 made, search for, after buying
17 explain it, received, as
18 after receiving, noticed that, furniture, go well, replacing most of it
19 therefore, that purchasing a new item, leads to, unplanned
20 they are on sale
21 goes window shopping, sees
22 checks, finds out that, that, too expensive
23 approaches him, discount on
24 Even though, is still, low, to buy
25 described above, anchoring effect
26 mentioned, affects, opinion of prices
27 For example, seem cheap in comparison
28 Furthermore, becomes bigger, be more powerful
29 As such, mentioned first, anchor, fixes our thoughts
30 Just like, to buy, considering why we are buying
31 As, have shown, influence
32 The next time, think, about why you are buying

교과서 확인학습 B   p.34~35

1 Have you ever wondered why you've bought things that you don't even want or need?
2 Let's consider what affects us when it comes to buying things.
3 Why do I want to buy what my friends bought?
4 Jeff goes to the shopping center and sees a pair of soccer shoes on display.
5 He recognizes the shoes at a glance because more than half of the boys on his soccer team wear them.
6 Although he already has many pairs of soccer shoes, he ends up buying another new pair.
7 We can use the "bandwagon effect" to explain Jeff's behavior.
8 A bandwagon is a wagon in a parade that encourages people to jump aboard and enjoy the music.
9 As more and more people get on the bandwagon, others are more likely to get on or follow it.
10 In this way, people tend to buy something just because other people have bought it.
11 Why do I buy a pair of pants and a bag after I have bought a new coat?
12 Lisa buys a coat that she really loves. Immediately, she realizes that her pants do not match her new coat.
13 So, she buys new pants that go perfectly with her new coat.
14 But she sees that none of her bags match her new clothes.
15 So, she buys a new bag. Most of her money is spent on buying the new items to complete her new look.
16 What made Lisa search for new items immediately after buying a new coat?
17 The "Diderot effect" may explain it. Denis Diderot, a French writer, received a new gown as a gift.
18 Soon after receiving the gift, he noticed that all of his furniture did not go well with his new gown.

So, he ended up replacing most of it.

19 The Diderot effect, therefore, is the concept that purchasing a new item often leads to more unplanned purchases.

20 Why do I buy things just because they are on sale?

21 Nathan goes window shopping and sees a pair of headphones.

22 He checks the price and finds out that they are $200. He thinks that the headphones are too expensive.

23 The sales person approaches him and says, "You can get a 20 percent discount on those headphones."

24 Even though the discounted price is still not very low, Nathan decides to buy the headphones.

25 The situation described above is an example of the "anchoring effect."

26 "The price mentioned first affects our opinion of prices mentioned afterwards.

27 For example, if we start with $200, then $160 will seem cheap in comparison.

28 Furthermore, as the difference of the two prices becomes bigger, the effect will be more powerful.

29 As such, the price mentioned first acts as an "anchor" that fixes our thoughts about the price of an item.

30 Just like Jeff and his friends, we tend to buy things without seriously considering why we are buying them.

31 As these effects have shown, many things influence our purchases.

32 The next time you decide to buy something, think for a moment about why you are buying it.

시험대비 실력평가

p.36~39

01 ②   02 He goes to the shopping center.

03 behavior   04 ③   05 ④

06 ①, ④   07 ⑤

08 She bought a new bag.   09 ④   10 ③

11 ②   12 It is 200 dollars.

13 He says that Nathan can get a 20 percent discount on those headphones.

14 ③   15 ②

16 He sees a pair of soccer shoes on display.

17 ④

18 We can use the "bandwagon effect."

19 after I have bought a new coat

20 ⑤   21 his furniture   22 ③

23 ③   24 ②

25 They have shown that many things influence our purchases.

01 글의 내용은 다른 사람들이 어떤 것을 샀다는 이유로 그것을 구매하는 경향에 관한 것이므로 ②번이 가장 적절하다.

03 사람이나 동물이 하는 것은 '행동(behavior)'이다.

04 Jeff는 진열되어 있는 축구화 한 켤레를 보고 결국 사 버리고 말았다.

05 주어진 문장의 it은 Lisa로 하여금 새 코트를 산 후 즉시 새로운 물품을 찾게 하는 것을 가리킨다. 따라서 ④번에 들어가는 것이 가장 자연스럽다.

06 Lisa는 새 코트를 산 후 잇따라 바지와 가방을 샀다.

07 Lisa는 그녀의 새로운 모습을 완성하기 위하여 새로운 물품을 사는 데 돈의 대부분을 썼다고 하였다.

08 새로운 옷들을 산 후 Lisa는 새 가방을 샀다.

09 앵커링 효과는 처음에 언급된 가격이 이후에 언급되는 가격에 대한 우리의 의견에 영향을 미친다는 것이다. 처음에 언급된 가격이 물건의 가격에 대한 우리의 생각을 고정하는 닻으로서 작동하기 때문이다. 따라서 afterwards라고 쓰는 것이 적절하다.

10 예시를 들어 앞선 진술을 명확히 설명하고 있으므로 ③번이 가장 적절하다.

11 위 글은 "앵커링 효과"에 관한 글로, 단지 할인 중이라는 이유로 물건을 구입하는 이유에 관하여 설명하고 있다. 따라서 ②번이 가장 적절하다.

12 헤드폰의 가격에 대해 Nathan이 갖는 생각을 고정시키는 '닻' 역할을 하는 가격은 200달러이다.

13 점원은 Nathan에게 다가와 헤드폰에 20퍼센트 할인을 받을 수 있다고 말한다.

14 (C) Jeff는 쇼핑센터에서 축구팀에 있는 소년들의 반 이상이 신고 있는 축구화가 진열된 것을 봄 (A) 그에게 이미 축구화가 많이 있지만 결국 그것을 삼 (D) Jeff의 행동은 : '밴드왜건 효과'로 설명할 수 있는데, 밴드왜건에 사람들이 올라타서 음악을 즐기게 부추김 (B) 더 많은 사람들이 밴드왜건에 올라탈수록 다른 사람들도 그것을 따르려 함

15 when it comes to Ving: V에 대해서 말하자면

16 쇼핑센터에 간 Jeff는 진열되어 있는 축구화 한 켤레를 보게 된다고 하였다.

17 위 글은 원하거나 필요하지 않는 것들을 사는 이유에 대해 설명하는 글이다. 따라서 ④번 '우리가 돈을 쓰도록 만드는 것은 무엇인가?'가 가장 적절하다.

7

18 Jeff의 행동은 "밴드왜건 효과"로 설명할 수 있다.

19 위 글은 새 코트를 산 후 연이어 바지와 가방을 산 사례와 그 이유를 설명하는 내용이다.

20 빈칸 (B)에는 전치사 on이 들어간다. ① break down: 고장나다 ② stand for: 상징하다 ③ bring up: ~을 양육하다 ④ put off: ~을 미루다 ⑤ live on: ~을 먹고 살다

21 Diderot는 선물로 받은 새 가운과 자신의 모든 가구가 어울리지 않는 것을 알아채고 결국 대부분의 가구를 바꾸었다.

22 밑줄 친 (D)는 완전한 절을 이끄는 명사절 접속사이다. ③번은 불완전한 절을 이끄는 관계대명사이다.

23 approach는 타동사이므로 전치사 없이 목적어를 취한다. 따라서 'approaches him'이라고 쓰는 것이 적절하다.

24 글의 내용은 우리가 왜 물건들을 사는지 진지하게 고려하지 않고 구매한다는 것이다. 따라서 다음에 어떤 것을 구매하려고 결정할 때 자신이 그것을 왜 사려는지 잠시 동안 생각해 보라는 말이 들어가는 것이 적절하다.

25 이러한 효과들은 많은 것들이 우리의 구매에 영향을 미친다는 것을 보여주고 있다.

서술형 시험대비 p.40~41

01 what affects us when it comes to buying things

02 wear

03 a bandwagon

04 As more and more people get on the bandwagon, others are more likely to get on or follow it.

05 It's because other people have bought it.

06 She buys a coat (that she really loves).

07 She realizes (that) her pants do not match her new coat.

08 It was because he noticed that all of his furniture did not go well with his new gown.

09 planned → unplanned

10 He sees a pair of headphones.

11 He finds out that the headphones are 200 dollars.

12 anchor

13 The writer suggests that we should think for a moment about why we are buying it.

---

01 동사 consider의 목적어로 간접의문문을 쓰는 것에 유의한다.
when it comes to Ving: V에 관하여

02 'half of+명사'는 명사에 수의 일치를 한다. 따라서 the boys에 맞추어 복수동사 wear를 쓴다.

03 퍼레이드에 있는 사륜마차인 밴드왜건을 가리키는 말이다.

---

04 더 많은 사람들이 밴드왜건에 올라탈수록 다른 사람들이 더욱 그것에 올라타거나 그것을 따라가려 한다.

05 '밴드왜건 효과'는 단지 다른 사람들이 어떤 것을 샀다는 이유로 그것을 구매하는 현상을 의미한다.

06 Lisa가 처음에 산 것은 코트이다.

07 새 코트를 산 후 Lisa는 그녀의 바지가 새 코트와 어울리지 않는다는 것을 즉시 알아차린다.

08 새 가운을 선물로 받은 Diderot는 그의 모든 가구가 새로운 가운과 어울리지 않는다는 것을 알아채고는 결국 대부분의 가구를 바꾸고야 말았다.

09 디드로 효과는 새로운 물품을 구입하는 것이 흔히 계획에 없던 더 많은 구매로 이어지는 개념이라고 하였다.

10 Nathan은 진열된 상품을 구경하러 가서 헤드폰을 하나 본다고 하였다.

11 헤드폰의 가격을 확인했을 때, Nathan은 가격이 200달러라는 것을 알게 된다.

12 배가 움직이지 않도록 물 속에 떨어뜨리는 것은 '닻(anchor)'이다.

13 글쓴이는 다음번에 우리가 어떤 것을 구매하려고 결정할 때, 자신이 그것을 왜 사려는지 잠시 동안 생각해 보라고 하였다.

영역별 핵심문제 p.43~47

01 ⑤   **02** ①   **03** encourages

04 More   **05** ④

06 I should have kept track of my spending.

07 ⑤   **08** ④   **09** ④   **10** like

11 (1) How do you like them?

(2) Are you satisfied with them?   **12** ②

13 ③   **14** ②, ⑤   **15** ⑤   **16** ④

17 ①

18 (1) One third of the students are here.

(2) Much of the house was ruined by the heavy rain.

(3) Ten percent of the girls want to learn Spanish.

(4) None of the furniture in our house is made of wood.

(5) Last night she said that she takes a shower every day.

19 (1) as → though[although]

(2) as → unless

(3) like → as

20 enjoys → enjoy
21 ⑤
22 ④번 → enjoy
23 no other → other
24 ②
25 ③
26 She buys (a pair of) new pants and a new bag.
27 He ended up replacing most of it.
28 ④
29 ⑤
30 Most of the allowance is spent on clothes.

01 affect: ~에 영향을 주다 influence: ~에 영향을 주다 / 어린 사람들은 그들의 동료 그룹에 의해 크게 영향을 받는 경향이 있다. ① 발명하다 ② 조절하다 ③ 향상시키다 ④ 발생하다 *tend to: ~하는 경향이 있다 *peer: 동료

02 저 재킷은 너의 치마와 완벽하게 어울린다. ① 어울리다 ② 소비하다 ③ 오래가다, (기능이) 지속되다 ④ 교체하다 ⑤ 맞추다, 조정하다

03 courage: 용기 encourage: 부추기다, 조장하다 / 새 선생님은 학생들이 창의적인 생각을 하도록 부추긴다.

04 more and more: 점점 더 많은 / 점점 더 많은 사람들이 인터넷을 이용하고 있다. more than half: 반 이상의 / 길은 30분 이상 동안 폐쇄되었다.

05 주어진 문장에서 it은 용돈을 의미한다. 용돈을 어떻게 다 써버렸는지에 대한 대답으로 'I'm not sure.(잘 모르겠어.)'가 어울리므로 ④가 적절하다.

06 과거 사실에 대해 후회나 유감을 나타낼 때 '~했어야 했다'는 의미로 'should have p.p. ~'를 쓴다. keep track of: ~을 기록하다 spending: 지출

07 (A) 'I heard that ~.'은 '~에 대해 들었다'의 뜻으로 알고 있거나 들은 것에 대해 말할 때 쓰는 표현이다. 접속사 that 뒤에는 절이 오며 'I've heard that ~'으로 바꿔 쓸 수 있다. (B) 'What's wrong?'은 상대방이 뭔가에 불만족하거나 실망하고 있는 것을 보고 그 원인을 물을 때 사용하는 표현이므로 빈칸에는 not happy가 어울린다. (C) 'should have p.p. ~.'는 어떤 일을 했어야 했다고 후회할 때 사용한다

08 'How do you like ~?'는 '~는 어떠니?'라는 뜻으로 어떤 것에 대한 의견을 물을 때 쓰인다. 바꿔 쓸 수 있는 표현으로 'Are you satisfied[happy] with ~?', 'How is ~?', 'Are you enjoying ~?', 'Do you like ~?' 등이 있다.

09 캐릭터 티셔츠를 추천한 직원에게 여동생이 만화 캐릭터를 안 좋아한다고 얘기하면서 'Can I see the blue one?(파란 티셔츠 좀 볼 수 있을까요?)'이라고 물어본다.

10 (A) 'How do you like ~?'는 '~는 어떠니?'라는 뜻으로 어떤 것에 대한 의견을 물을 때 쓰인다. (B) like: 좋아하다

11 'How do you like ~?'는 상대방의 의견 혹은 만족 여부를 물

을 때 사용한다. 비슷한 표현인 'Are you satisfied[happy] with ~?'로 직접적으로 만족이나 불만족 여부를 물을 수 있다.

12 ⓐ 초록색 가방과 파란색 가방 중 무엇을 샀는가? (초록색 가방을 샀다.) ⓑ 초록색 가방과 파란색 가방 중 무엇이 더 가벼운가? (초록색 가방이 더 가볍다.) ⓒ 무슨 용도로 가방을 쓸 것인가? (하이킹할 때 사용할 것이다.) ⓓ 어떤 가방이 더 인기 있는가? (알 수 없다.)

13 각각 ①, ② '비례' ④ '시간' ⑤ '이유'이다. ③ as는 가정법의 if 대신 사용할 수 없다.

14 ① One of the highlights was seeing the Taj Mahal. ③ The number of employees was reduced from 40 to 25. ④ The rest of the money is used to run other government programs.

15 'Jane은 그가 건물을 나설 때 만났다.'는 내용으로서 so as는 어법상 어색하다. 'so as'를 'just as'로 바꾸는 것이 적절하다.

16 'a few of+복수 명사' 주어는 복수 동사로 받는다. Last weekend로 시제가 과거로 표시되어야 함에 주의한다.

17 주어진 문장과 ①의 접속사 As는 '~함에 따라'(비례)를 나타낸다. ② ~하는 동안(시간) ③ ~하는 대로(방식) ④ ~만큼(비교) ⑤ ~해서, ~ 때문에(이유)

18 (1), (3) 부분을 나타내는 말의 뒤에 단수 명사가 나오면 단수 동사를 쓰고 복수 명사가 나오면 복수 동사를 쓴다. (2) 'much of+단수 명사' 주어는 단수 동사로 받는다. (4) 'none of +명사+동사'에서는 명사가 단수일 경우 단수 동사를 쓰고 명사가 복수일 경우 복수 동사나 단수 동사를 모두 쓸 수 있다. (5) 주절의 시제가 과거일지라도 종속절이 불변의 진리, 격언, 현재의 습관, 과학적 사실 등을 나타내면 현재시제를 쓴다.

19 (1) 앞과 뒤의 절의 내용이 상반되므로 as가 아니라 though[although]가 적절하다. (2) 내용상 '정말로 춥지 않다면 창문을 열어 놓고 잔다.'고 하는 것이 자연스럽다. as를 unless로 고치는 것이 적절하다. (3) like는 전치사로 '~ 같은'이라는 뜻이고 as는 전치사로 '~로서'라는 뜻이다. 또한 'regard A as B'는 'A를 B로 여기다'라는 뜻이다.

20 부분을 나타내는 말은 뒤에 오는 명사의 수에 따라 그 수가 결정되는데, percent of 다음에 students라고 복수 명사가 나오므로 enjoy가 적절하다.

21 글의 내용은 '밴드왜건 효과'에 관한 것이므로 Jeff는 축구팀에 있는 소년들이 신는 축구화라는 이유로 결국 그 축구화를 사버리고 만다는 내용이 적절하다.

22 밴드왜건은 사람들이 올라타서 음악을 즐기게끔 부추기는 퍼레이드에 있는 사륜마차라는 의미이다. 따라서 to jump에 병렬 연결되도록 enjoy라고 쓰는 것이 적절하다.

23 다른 사람들이 어떤 것을 샀다는 이유로 그것을 구매하는 경향

이므로 부정어 no가 없어야 한다.

24 진열되어 있는 축구화 한 켤레를 본 Jeff는 그 신발을 한눈에 알아챘다고 하였다.

25 디드로 효과가 무엇인지를 설명한 후 한 문장으로 정리하여 진술하고 있으므로 결과를 이끄는 therefore가 적절하다.

26 Lisa는 새 코트를 산 후 새 바지와 새 가방을 샀다.

27 Diderot는 결국 대부분의 가구를 바꾸었다.

28 Lisa는 원래 마음에 드는 코트를 사려고 했지만 자신의 새로운 모습을 완성하기 위하여 계획에 없던 물건을 사고 있다.

29 이어지는 글의 내용으로 보아 용돈을 얼마나 자주 받는지 물어봤음을 알 수 있다.

30 대부분의 용돈은 옷에 쓰인다고 하였다.

단원별 예상문제

01 (1) (p)urchase (2) (t)ight 02 difference
03 ③
04 (a)ffect (c)ombine (c)oncept
　(1) concept (2) affects (3) combine
05 (D) → (B) → (C) → (A)
06 (A) ⓓ　(B) ⓑ　(C) ⓔ
07 suit　　　　08 ②　　　　09 for
10 ②
11 call the online shop and explain my problem
12 ①　　　13 ④　　　14 was → were
15 As people eat more junk food, they may gain
　　more weight.
16 ②
17 As you run more, you become stronger.
18 ③　　　19 anchor, lower　　　20 ⑤
21 The price mentioned first affects our opinion of
　　prices mentioned afterwards.
22 ⑤
23 They think (that) they should get a higher
　　allowance.　　　24 ②

01 (1) 두 단어의 관계는 동의어 관계이다. immediately: 즉시, 바로 at once: 즉시 buy: 사다 purchase: 사다, 구입하다 (2) 두 단어의 관계는 반의어 관계이다. waste: 낭비하다, 소모하다 save: 낭비를 막다, 절약하다 loose: 헐거운, 느슨한 tight: 꽉 조이는, 딱 붙는

02 differ: 다르다 difference: 차이, 차이점 / 이 두 컴퓨터의 차이점이 무엇인가요?

03 (A) spend A on 동사ing: A를 ~하는 데 쓰다 / 우리는 예전보다 음식에 더 많은 돈을 쓰고 있는 중이다. (B) keep track of: ~을 기록하다 / 우리는 비용을 기록하는 시스템이 필요하다.

(C) lead to: ~로 이어지다 / 스트레스가 신체적인 병으로 이어질 수 있다는 것에는 의심의 여지가 없다.

04 (1) concept: 개념. 어떤 원리나 생각 / 우리는 지금 새로운 개념을 생각해 내야 할 필요가 있다. (2) affect: ~에 영향을 주다. 어떤 사람이나 사물에 영향을 미치다, 혹은 어떤 사람이나 사물에 변화를 야기하다 / 네가 하는 모든 선택은 너의 삶에 영향을 준다. (3) combine: 결합하다. 하나 하나의 혹은 집단으로 만들기 위해 합치다 / 그는 일과 즐거움을 결합하고 싶어 한다.

05 새로운 스피커인지 물어보는 질문에 (D) 맞다고 대답하면서 몇 주 전에 샀다고 말한다. (B) 새로운 스피커에 대한 의견을 물어본다. (C) 편리하고, 어디든지 가져가서 음악을 들을 수 있고, 음질도 좋다고 말한다. (A) 배터리는 얼마나 오래가는지 질문하자 2시간 정도라고 대답한다.

06 (A) '무엇을 도와드릴까요?'라고 묻는 질문에 별들이 그려진 모자를 써 볼 수 있는지 묻는 것이 어울린다. (B) 별들이 그려진 모자에 대해 의견을 물어보고, 디자인은 좋은데 색깔은 어울리지 않는다고 대답하는 것이 어울린다. (C) 같은 모양의 검은색이 있는지 질문을 하고 안쪽에서 가져다 드리겠다고 말하는 것이 어울린다.

07 suit: 어울리다 / 어떤 특정한 사람이나 상황, 경우에 알맞다

08 노트북이 마음에 들지 않는다는 여자의 말에 무슨 문제가 있는지 물어보고, 그 말에 소음이 심하고 과열이 된다고 대답을 해 주는 것이 어울린다.

09 ask for: 요청하다

10 일주일 동안 사용했기 때문에 온라인 가게는 환불을 해 주지 않을 거라고 말하는 것이 어울리므로 이유의 접속사 because가 알맞다.

11 온라인 가게에 전화해 문제를 설명하라고 충고하는 말에 '그렇게 해야 할 것 같다'라고 말하고 있으므로 'do that'은 '온라인 가게에 전화해 문제를 설명하는 것'을 가리킨다.

12 버스를 또 놓쳤다고 말하고 있으므로 빈칸에는 일찍 일어나지 않았던 것에 대해 유감을 표현하는 말이 들어가는 것이 적절하다. 'should have p.p. ~'는 '~했어야 했는데 (사실은 하지 않았다)'의 뜻으로 과거 사실에 대한 유감을 나타내는 표현이다.

13 ④번의 as는 전치사이고, 나머지는 모두 접속사이다.

14 부분을 나타내는 말은 뒤에 오는 명사의 수에 따라 그 수가 결정되는데, part of 다음에 the expenses라고 복수 명사가 나오므로 were가 적절하다.

15 '~함에 따라, ~할수록'이라는 비례의 의미를 갖는 접속사 as를 이용한다.

16 ②에는 부분을 나타내는 말(Some of)의 뒤에 단수 명사(the pie)가 나왔으므로 단수 동사 is가 적절하다. 나머지는 모두 are가 적절하다.

17 'the 비교급 …, the 비교급 ~' 구문을 '비례, 추이'를 나타내는 as를 이용하여 바꿔 쓸 수 있다.

18 (A) on sale: 할인 중인, for sale: 판매를 위한 (B) 종속절이 주절의 이유라기보다는 양보절을 이끄는 것이 더 적절하다. (C) "닻"은 우리의 생각을 고정하는 역할을 한다.

19 처음에 언급된 가격이 '닻'으로서 작용한다. 만약 나중에 언급된 가격이 처음의 가격보다 더 낮으면 당신은 그 상품이 싸다고 생각할 것이다.

20 Nathan은 헤드폰이 여전히 별로 저렴하지 않다고 생각했지만 "앵커링 효과"에 영향을 받아 결국 헤드폰을 산다.

21 처음에 언급된 가격이 이후에 언급되는 가격에 대한 우리의 의견에 영향을 미친다고 하였다.

22 '~인지 아닌지'를 물어보았다는 표현이 적절하므로 that이 아니라 if나 whether를 써야 한다. 명사절 접속사 that은 확정적인 내용의 절을, if나 whether는 확정적이지 않은 내용의 절을 이끈다.

23 설문 조사에 참여한 10명의 학생 중 90퍼센트에 해당하는 9명의 학생들은 자신이 용돈을 더 많이 받아야 한다고 생각한다.

24 설문 조사를 받은 학생의 수는 10명이다.

서술형 실전문제　　　　　　　　p.52~53

01 should have brought an umbrella

02 (1) Are you enjoying this dress?

　(2) Are you satisfied with this dress?

　(3) Are you happy with this dress?

03 I should have tried it on.

04 (1) was spent　(2) is　(3) died　(4) has

05 (1) Jason came up to me as I was speaking.

　(2) Young as he was, he was very wise.

　(3) As these effects have shown, many things influence our purchases.

　(4) One third of the world's food is wasted.

06 Because more than half of the boys on his soccer team wear them.

07 It is a wagon in a parade that encourages people to jump aboard and enjoy the music.

08 Because she wants to complete her new look.

09 The "Diderot effect" may explain it.

10 It is the concept that purchasing a new item often leads to more unplanned purchases.

01 'should have p.p. ~'는 '~했어야 했는데 (사실은 하지 않았다)'의 뜻으로 과거 사실에 대한 유감을 나타내는 표현이다.

02 어떤 것에 만족하거나 불만이 있는지 물어보는 표현으로 'How do you like ~?', 'Are you satisfied[happy] with ~?', 'Are you enjoying ~?' 등을 쓸 수 있다.

03 사기 전에 입어 보지 않았느냐는 질문에, 자신의 사이즈여서 그냥 사 버렸다고 말하고 있으므로 빈칸에는 입어 보지 않은 것에 대해 후회를 하는 말이 어울린다. try on: (옷 등을 시험 삼아) 입어 보다

04 (1) 부분을 나타내는 말 뒤에 오는 명사가 단수이면 단수 동사를 쓰고 복수이면 복수 동사를 쓴다. the money가 주어이므로 수동태로 써야 함에 주의한다. (2) 학문 이름은 단수 취급한다. (3) 역사적인 사실은 주절의 시제와 상관없이 과거시제를 쓴다. (4) the number of+단수(복수) 명사+단수 동사

05 (1) as가 '시간'을 나타내는 부사절을 이끌도록 쓴다. (2) 접속사 as가 '양보'의 의미로 쓰일 때는 '형용사/부사/무관사 명사를 as 앞에 둔다. (3) as가 '방식'을 나타내는 부사절을 이끌도록 쓴다. (4) 부분을 나타내는 말 뒤에 오는 명사가 단수이면 단수 동사를 쓰고 복수이면 복수 동사를 쓴다.

06 위 글의 내용에 따르면, Jeff가 축구화를 산 이유는 그의 축구팀에 있는 소년들의 반 이상이 그 축구화를 신기 때문에 그는 그 축구화를 산다.

07 밴드왜건(악대차)은 사람들이 올라타서 음악을 즐기게끔 부추기는 퍼레이드에 있는 사륜마차라고 하였다.

08 Lisa는 그녀의 새로운 모습을 완성하기 위하여 대부분의 돈을 쓴다고 하였다.

09 Lisa의 소비는 '디드로 효과'가 설명해 줄지도 모른다고 하였다.

10 디드로 효과는 새로운 물품을 구입하는 것이 흔히 계획에 없던 더 많은 구매로 이어진다는 개념이다

창의사고력 서술형 문제　　　　　　　p.54

|모범답안|

01 should have stayed at home / should have not gone to school

02 (1) I respected her more

　(2) I was so hungry

　(3) I need more money

　(4) he becomes more curious about the world

03 how often they get an allowance, Twenty, every week, seventy percent of the students get an allowance every month, spent on clothes, one fourth of the allowance, whether[if] they think that they should get a higher allowance, Ninety percent of the students think that they should get a higher allowance

01 어제 아픈데도 불구하고 학교 간 것에 대해 후회를 하는 말이 어울리므로, 학교를 가지 않았어야 했는데 간 것에 대해 후회하는 표현이 어울린다.

단원별 모의고사   p.55~58

01 go
02 (1) are likely to be   (2) comfortable
    (3) (s)oon, (a)fter   (4) at a glance
03 (1) When   (2) because   (3) Although
04 comparison   05 ③
06 How do you like this red one[T-shirt]?
07 I regret not checking the sales before buying mine.
   I wish I had checked the sales before buying mine.
08 ③
09 (A) should   (B) should   (C) won't   (D) should
10 ⑤
11 (A) used   (B) see   (C) broken   12 ④
13 ③
14 As we cut more trees to make land, more forests disappear on Earth.
15 One third of the power (that[which]) your body consumes comes from the food (that[which]) you eat.
16 ①, ②, ⑤   17 It is $160.
18 It is the price mentioned first.
19 ④   20 ③   21
22 (B)-(A)-(C) 23 ②

01 go well with: ~와 잘 어울리다 / 어떤 신발이 이 옷에 가장 잘 어울리니? go window shopping: 진열된 상품을 구경하고 다니다 / 나는 다음 주말에 친구와 진열된 상품을 구경하고 다닐 것이다.

02 (1) be likely to: ~할 가능성이 있다, ~하기 쉽다 (2) comfortable: 편안한 tight: 꽉 조이는, 딱 붙는 (3) soon after: 직후 (4) at a glance: 한눈에, 즉시

03 (1) when it comes to: ~에 관해서, ~에 대해 말하자면 / 요리에 관해서라면, 그가 나보다 낫다. (2) just because: 단지 ~라는 이유로 / 단지 내가 불평을 안 하니까 사람들은 내가 만족해하는 줄 안다. (3) although: 비록 ~이지만 / 비록 해가 비치고 있긴 했지만, 날이 별로 따뜻하지는 않았다.

04 compare: 비교하다 in comparison: 비교해 보면 / 이에 비해

서 부유하고 호화롭게 사는 사람들이 있다.

05 여자가 파란 줄무늬 티셔츠를 선택한 것으로 보아, 여동생이 만화 캐릭터를 별로 좋아하지 않는다는 것을 유추할 수 있다.

06 'How do you like ~?'는 상대방의 의견 혹은 만족 여부를 물을 때 사용한다.

07 과거 사실에 대해 후회나 유감을 나타낼 때 '~했어야 했다'라는 의미로 'should have p.p. ~'를 쓴다. 이때 조동사 should 뒤에는 과거의 일을 의미하므로 동사원형 대신 'have+p.p.'를 써야 한다. 이외에도 'I regret -ing.', 'I wish I had p.p. ~' 등으로 쓸 수 있다.

08 남자는 할인 판매를 확인하지 않았던 것에 대해 후회하고 있다.

09 (A) 과거 사실에 대해 후회나 유감을 나타낼 때 '~했어야 했다'는 의미로 'should have p.p. ~'를 쓴다. (B), (D) should: ~해야 한다 (C) '일주일 동안 사용해서 환불을 해 주지 않을 것이다'라는 내용으로 will not의 줄임말인 won't가 어울린다.

10 Riley는 일주일 동안 노트북을 사용해서 환불을 해주지 않을 것이라고 말한다.

11 (A) used: 중고의 (B) let은 '~에게 …하게 하다'라는 의미를 가지는 사역동사로, 목적격보어로 동사원형을 쓴다. (C) 바깥 부분이 부서진 것이므로 수동태인 'be broken'을 사용한다.

12 ⓓ must → should, 'should have p.p. ~.'는 어떤 일을 했어야 했다고 후회할 때 사용한다.

13 각 부분은, '~할수록', '~하는 대로', '~로서' 등으로 접속사와 전치사로 모두 쓸 수 있는 것은 as이다.

14 '~함에 따라, ~할수록'이라는 '비례'의 의미를 갖는 as를 이용하여 영작한다.

15 '부분을 나타내는 명사+of' 다음에 명사가 올 때 동사의 수를 명사의 수에 일치시킨다.

16 글의 내용으로 미루어 보아 Nathan은 헤드폰의 가격이 비싸다고 생각했음을 유추할 수 있다. *bargain: 헐값의

17 할인된 헤드폰의 가격은 160달러라고 하였다.

18 물건의 가격에 대한 우리의 생각을 고정하는 '닻'으로서 작용하는 것은 먼저 언급된 가격이다.

19 "앵커링 효과"는 나중에 언급된 가격이 먼저 언급된 가격을 더 비싸 보이게 만든다.

20 밴드왜건에 올라타 함께 음악을 즐긴다고 하였으므로 '그것에 올라타거나 그것을 따라가려고 한다'는 것이 가장 적절하다.

21 밴드왜건 효과는 다른 사람들이 어떤 것을 샀다는 이유로 그것을 구매하는 경향이므로, 친구들이 노트북을 샀기 때문에 자신도 노트북을 샀다고 말한 Ethan이 밴드왜건 효과의 영향을 받

았다고 말할 수 있다.

22 (B)의 it이 주어진 문장의 'Lisa가 새 코트를 산 후 즉시 새로운 물품을 찾은 것'을 가리킴 (A) the gift는 (B)에서 나온 새 가운임 (C) 새 가운이 자신의 모든 가구와 어울리지 않는다는 사실을 알아챈 결과로 대부분의 가구를 교체함.

23 해석: 디드로 효과에 따르면, 하나의 새로운 물건 때문에 예상치 못한 지출이 있을 수 있다.

Wonders of Space Travel

01 ④   02 ⑤   03 ③   04 ③

05 ⑤

01 ④의 접두사 in은 '안에'의 의미를 가지며 나머지 보기들은 '부정'을 나타낸다. ① infinite: 무한한 ② incorrect: 부정확한, 사실이 아닌 ③ insecure: 안전하지 못한 ④ insight: 통찰력 ⑤ inexpensive: 비싸지 않은, 저렴한

02 주어진 단어의 관계는 동의어 관계이다. vast: 거대한, 광대한, huge: 막대한, 거대한 ⓐ achieve: 달성하다, 성취하다, accomplish: 이루다, 성취하다 ⓑ persistent: 끈질긴, 집요한, 지속적인, occasional: 이따금씩, 가끔씩 ⓒ tough: 힘든, 어려운, easy: 쉬운, 수월한 ⓓ bottom: 맨 아랫부분, 바닥, top: 꼭대기, 정상 ⓔ attach: 붙이다, stick: 붙이다

03 ③ stick: 찌르다 ① 웜홀은 두 개의 다른 우주를 연결할 수 있다. ② 왜 공룡이 멸종되었는지에 관한 많은 이론들이 있다. ③ 그들은 물 주머니에 튜브를 찌르고 마신다. ④ 모든 승객은 안전벨트를 매야 한다. ⑤ 지구는 태양에서 3번째로 가까운 행성이다.

04 (A) different from: ~와 다른 / 우주에서의 생활이 지구에서의 생활과 어떻게 다른가? (B) in theory: 이론상으로는, 원칙상으로는 / 이론상으로는 웜홀이 존재한다. (C) figure out: ~을 알아내다, 생각해 내다 / 아인슈타인은 우주와 시간에 대해 무엇을 생각해 내었는가?

05 ① detect: 감지하다, 발견하다 / 딱정벌레는 그들의 길을 별로 발견한다. ② connect: 연결되다, 이어지다 / SNS의 요점은 다른 사람들과 연결하는 것이다. ③ bend: 굽히다, 구부리다 / 너의 근육을 늘리기 위해 등을 굽혀야 한다. ④ punch: 구멍을 뚫다 / 이 벨트가 너무 커서 나는 여분의 구멍을 뚫을 것이다. ⑤ contain: ~이 들어 있다, 포함하다 / 즉석 면류는 많은 소금을 포함하고 있다.

01 able

02 (1) surface (2) layer (3) bottom (4) dots

03 (1) According to (2) (f)ar (a)way (f)rom

(3) float around (4) in the blink of an eye

(5) look back on   04 if

05 (1) eatable (2) incorrect (3) impossible

(4) changeable

01 동사 뒤에 –able을 붙이면 '~할 수 있는'이라는 의미의 형용사가 된다. eatable: 먹을 수 있는 / 그 음식은 먹을 수 있지만 좋지는 않다. changeable: 바뀔 수 있는, 변덕스러운 / 그 규칙들은 아주 바뀔 수 있다.

02 (1) surface: 표면 / 너는 태양의 표면에서 작은 검은 점을 볼 수 있다. (2) layer: 층 / 엄마는 양파의 바깥쪽 층을 제거했다. (3) bottom: 맨 아랫부분, 바닥 / 그들의 부리 덕분에, 돌고래들은 바다의 맨 아랫부분에서 물고기를 사냥할 수 있다. (4) dot: 점 / 나의 새로운 치마는 파란색에 하얀 점들이 있다.

03 (1) according to ~: ~에 따르면 (2) far away from: ~에서 멀리 떨어져 (3) float around: 떠다니다 (4) in the blink of an eye: 눈 깜박할 사이에 (5) look back on: ~을 되돌아보다

04 even if는 '~이지만, 비록 ~일지라도'라는 뜻이며, 상반된 내용의 두 문장을 연결하는 접속사로 양보의 부사절을 이끈다. 단순 조건절에서 접속사 if는 '만일 ~라면'의 의미로 조건절을 이끈다. • 훈민정음이 많은 책에 언급되어 있을지라도, 어느 누구도 그것이 정말 어디에 있는지 알지 못했다. • 그가 돌아오기 전에 그 음식을 먹으면, 그는 화가 날 거야.

05 (1) eatable: 먹을 수 있는 / 그 음식점의 음식은 먹을 수가 없다. (2) incorrect: 부정확한, 사실이 아닌 / 이렇게 많은 부정확한 대답들로는 테스트에 통과할 수 없다. (3) impossible: 불가능한 / 물 없이 사는 것은 불가능하다. (4) changeable: 바뀔 수 있는, 변덕스러운 / 런던의 날씨는 매우 변덕스럽다.

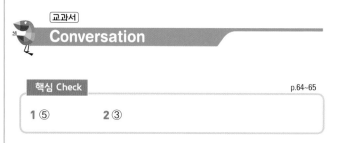

1 ⑤   2 ③

1 T   2 F   3 T   4 T

probable[likely] ~?'로 바꿔 쓸 수 있다. 하지만 that 다음에는 주어와 동사인 절의 형태가 나와야 한다.

03 빈칸에는 우주에서는 하루에 일출을 여러 번 보는 게 가능한지 묻는 질문에 대답을 해야 하므로 'Yes. It's possible because we moved around Earth every 90 minutes in the station.(네, 가능해요. 왜냐하면 우주 정거장이 지구 주위를 90분마다 돌았거든요.)'이 어울린다.

Check(√) True or False
p.67

5 F   6 T   7 T   8 T

교과서 확인학습
p.69~71

Listen & Talk 1 A

1. to, What, being / could see, times a day / Is it possible to see, a day / possible because / amazing
2. the best food you ate / grew, ate, fresh and tasty / is it possible to grow / Since, had to, helped the roots to

Listen & Talk 1 B

Have you heard that, send / into space / I've heard that, will be used to print out / possible to print out / in less than / what it would taste like

Listen & Talk 2 A

1. I wish I could see, from, with my own eyes / do that / that, in space
2. seems, different / it's because, no gravity / I wish I could, astronaut / looks uncomfortable

Listen & Talk 2 B

lived in / must have been tough / while in space / possible / it's because, gravity / I wish I could live in, become taller / I'm sure there, ways to become taller

Communication Step A

to talk about, that we wish were real / start with / I wish I could have / somewhere that / Is it actually possible to fly / have applied

Wrap Up

1. enjoy, the best experience, what was the best part, by myself, Is it possible to fly, by yourself, attached myself
2. heard that, How / zero gravity / real astronauts / adventure / astronaut, explore Mars

---

시험대비 실력평가
p.73~74

01 ③   02 ①, ③   03 ④
04 Is it possible to wash their body in space
05 from   06 ⑤   07 ①   08 ④
09 ②   10 saw
11 Is it possible to fly in space by yourself?

01 국립 청소년 우주 센터에서 가상 현실 안경을 써 봄으로써 실제로 우주에 있는 것 같은 기분이 들게 할 수 있다고 말하고 있으므로 빈칸에는 지구를 우주에서 직접 자신의 눈으로 보는 것을 바라는 말이 들어가는 것이 적절하다.

02 ① 남자는 국립 청소년 우주 센터에 가본 적이 있는가? ② 여자는 무엇을 하기를 원하는가? (지구를 우주에서 직접 자신의 눈으로 보기를 원한다.) ③ 그들은 언제 국립 청소년 우주 센터에 갈 것인가? ④ 그들은 무엇을 보고 있는 중인가? (우주 사진들을 보고 있다.) ⑤ 어디서 여자는 우주에 있는 것 같은 기분을 느낄 수 있는가? (국립 청소년 우주 센터)

03 많은 돈을 벌면 무엇을 하기를 원하는지 소망을 물어보는 말에 돈을 버는 것이 가능하지 않다고 말하는 것은 어색하다.

04 어떤 일이 실제로 가능한지 묻는 표현으로 'Is it possible to ~?'를 쓸 수 있다.

05 different from: ~와 다른

06 우주 비행사처럼 떠다니는 것에 대해 소망을 표현하는 남자의 말에 여자는 그렇지 않다고 말한 것과 떠다니는 모습이 편안해 보인다는 말은 어울리지 않는다.

07 'must have+과거분사'는 과거 사실에 대한 강한 추측을 나타내는 표현으로 '~이었음에 틀림이 없다'라는 의미를 가진다.

08 '키가 더 커지기 위해 우주에 가기를 바라는 남자에게 우주에 가는 것 말고 키가 더 커지는 방법들이 있다고 말하는 것이 어울린다.

09 남자가 얼마나 더 키가 크고 싶어하는지에 대해서는 언급되어 있지 않다.

10 flew와 saw는 문장의 동사로 접속사 and로 연결되어 있다.

11 'Is it possible to+동사원형 ~?'은 '~하는 것이 가능한가요?'라

시험대비 기본평가
p.72

01 ②   02 ③   03 ⑤

01 어떤 일이 이루어지기를 바라는 같은 표현으로 '~ would be a dream come true.', 'How I wish I could ~!', 'It would be great if I could ~.' 등이 있다.

02 'Is it possible to 동사원형 ~?'은 '~하는 것이 가능할까?'라는 뜻으로 상대방에게 가능성을 물을 때 사용한다. 'Is it

는 의미로 가능 여부를 물을 때 사용하는 표현이다. by oneself: 혼자서

01 what was the best food you ate in the space station

02 (p)ossible

03 grow / to grow

04 vegetables

05 I wish I could see Earth from space with my own eyes.

06 to print

07 Is it possible to print out food using a 3D printer?

01 the best food와 you ate 사이에 목적격 관계대명사 which나 that이 생략되어 있으므로, you ate in the space station이 the best food를 수식하고 있다.

02 'Is it possible to 동사원형 ~?'은 '~하는 것이 가능한가요?'의 의미로 상대방에게 가능성을 묻는 표현이다.

03 'help+목적어+목적격보어'는 '…에게 ~하도록 도움을 주다'이며, 목적격보어에는 동사원형이나 to부정사가 올 수 있다.

04 우주 정거장에서 채소를 키우는 것이 가능한지 묻는 질문에, 중력이 없기 때문에 그것을 특수한 봉지 안에서 키워야 한다고 말하고 있으므로 them은 vegetables(채소)를 의미한다.

05 'I wish I could ~.'는 '내가 ~할 수 있으면 좋겠다.'의 뜻으로 현재 사실과 반대되거나 현재 이룰 수 없는 소망을 말할 때 사용한다.

06 be used to 동사원형: ~하기 위해 사용되다

07 어떤 일이 실제로 가능한지 묻는 표현으로 'Is it possible to ~?'을 쓸 수 있다. print out: (프린터로) 출력하다

교과서
Grammar

핵심 Check
p.76~77

1 If I were you, I would start looking for another job.

2 (1) turned   (2) crying

01 (1) has → had   (2) can → could
   (3) know → knew   (4) will → would

02 ③   03 ④

04 (1) with her legs crossed.
   (2) with the cool wind blowing

01 문제에서 모든 문장이 가정법 문장이라고 했으며, 모든 문장의 구조는 '가정법 과거' 형태이므로, 부사절의 동사를 과거로, 주절의 조동사도 과거형으로 고치는 것이 적절하다.

02 with+명사(구)+분사: ~이 …한 채로, ~이 …하면서

03 주절에 조동사의 과거형이 나왔으므로, 가정법 문장이다. 문장의 구성상 be동사의 과거형이 필요한데, 일반적으로 가정법 과거에서 be동사의 과거형은 were를 쓴다.

04 'with+명사(구)+분사'는 '~이 …한 채로, ~이 …하면서'라는 뜻으로 동시 동작이나 부가적인 상황을 생생하게 표현할 때 사용한다. 이때 명사와 분사가 능동 관계이면 현재 분사를, 수동 관계이면 과거 분사를 쓴다. (1) 다리가 교차시키는 것이 아니라 교차되는 것이므로 수동의 과거분사가 적절하다. (2) 바람이 부는 것이므로 능동의 현재분사가 적절하다.

01 ④   02 ②   03 ①   04 ⑤

05 ③

06 (1) won   (2) had   (3) finished   (4) flying   07 ③

08 ②   09 ①   10 ④   11 ②

12 ⑤   13 ④   14 ③

15 (1) with her umbrella folded
   (2) with a book in her hand
   (3) with her hair blowing

16 (1) If I could travel into the past, I would bring back all the latest technology.
   (2) If your coach were here, he would be proud of you.
   (3) Andy slept with the door closed.

01 가정법 문장이라면 will을 would로, 직설법 문장이라면 studied를 studies로 쓰는 것이 적절하다.

02 'with+명사+분사'에서 명사와의 관계가 능동이면 현재분사를, 수동이면 과거분사를 쓴다.

03 주절에 조동사의 과거형인 might가 나와 있고 내용상 가정법으로 보아야 하므로 fly를 flew로 고치는 것이 적절하다.

04 'with+명사+분사'에서 명사와의 관계가 수동이므로 turning이 아니라 turned가 나와야 한다.

05 ①번과 ④번은 직설법 전환이 잘못된 이상한 문장이며, ②번은 가정법 과거가 아닌 가정법 과거완료를 전환한 것이고, ⑤번은 가정법 전환이 잘못된 이상한 문장이다.

06 (1), (2) 주절에 조동사의 과거형이 나왔으므로, 가정법 문장이다. (3) 명사와의 관계가 수동이므로 finished가 나와야 한다. (4) 명사와의 관계가 능동이므로 flying이 나와야 한다.

07 가정법 과거 시제의 문장으로 쓴다. 'If Sam didn't wake up early'로 종속절을 쓰고, 주절에 조동사의 과거형 could not을 쓰는 것에 유의한다.

08 'with+명사+분사'의 어순으로 셔츠가 밖으로 드러난 것으로 능동이므로 현재분사가 적절하다.

09 'with+명사+분사'에서 명사와의 관계가 능동이면 현재분사를, 수동이면 과거분사를 쓴다.

10 가정법 과거의 문장들이다. If절에는 동사의 과거형을, 주절에는 조동사의 과거형을 쓰는 것이 적절하다. Were it not for computers = If there were no computers = Without computers = But for computers

11 옳은 문장은 ⓒ, ⓔ 2개이다. ⓐ am → were[was], ⓑ can → could, ⓓ have → had ⓕ closing → closed ⓖ folding → folded ⓔ는 분사 자리에 형용사가 온 경우이다.

12 가정법 과거 문장은 현재시제의 직설법으로 바꿔 쓸 수 있다. 가정법은 반대로 가정하는 것이므로 부정하는 것이 서로 바뀌는 것에 주의한다.

13 'with+명사(구)' 다음에는 분사, 형용사, 부사, 전치사구' 등이 올 수 있으며, 분사의 경우 명사와의 관계가 능동이면 현재분사를, 수동이면 과거분사를 쓴다. 'with the alarm ringing'이 적절하다.

14 '~가 없다면'이라는 가정법 표현은 'If there were no ~'로 나타낸다. If there were no corn = If it were not for corn = Were it not for corn = Without corn = But for corn

15 'with+명사(구)' 다음에는 분사, 형용사, 부사, 전치사구' 등이 올 수 있으며, 분사의 경우 명사와의 관계가 능동이면 현재분사를, 수동이면 과거분사를 쓴다.

16 가정법 과거는 'If+주어+were/동사의 과거형 ~, 주어+조동사의 과거형(would/should/could/might)+동사원형 …'의 형태이므로 (1)에서는 can을 could로 고치는 것이 적절하고 (2)에서는 will을 would로 고치는 것이 적절하다. (3) 'with+명사(구)+분사'에서 명사와의 관계가 능동이면 현재분사를, 수동이면 과거분사를 쓰므로 'closing'을 'closed'로 고치는 것이 적절하다.

01 If I went to space, I would take a selfie.
02 Chris looked at the stars through a telescope with one eye closed.
03 (1) If it were not for   (2) Were it not for
   (3) If there were not   (4) But for   (5) As there is
04 in his hand
05 came
06 turned on
07 could live, would live
08 (1) If we lived on the moon, we would weigh less.
   (2) If we had more time, we could help you.
   (3) Lower your head to the ground with your arms stretched.
   (4) Alice was standing with tears running down her cheeks.
09 can → could, will → would, calling → called
10 (1) If I were an architect, I could build my own house.
   (2) If Mom had an apple, she would make me apple pie.
   (3) If it rained, we would not go on a picnic.
   (4) If she had had enough time, she could have spent time with us.
11 (1) is → were[was]   (2) can → could
   (3) with her closed eyes → with her eyes closed
   (4) played → playing

01 가정법 과거 시제의 문장으로 쓴다. 'If I went to space'로 종속절을 쓰고 주절에 조동사의 과거형 would를 쓰는 것에 유의한다.

02 'with+명사(구)+분사'에서 명사와의 관계가 능동이면 현재분사를, 수동이면 과거분사를 쓴다. 눈이 감기는 것이므로 수동의 과거분사가 적절하다.

03 '게으르지만 않다면, 그는 좋은 사람일 텐데.'라는 뜻이다. 가정법 과거의 경우, 'Without = If it were not for = Were it not for = If there were no(not) = But for'이다.

04 'with+명사(구)' 다음에는 분사, 형용사, 부사, 전치사구' 등이 올 수 있으며, 여기서는 전치사구 'in his hand'가 적절하다.

05 주절에 '주어+could'가 나오므로 가정법 과거의 문장이며, 'If+주어+동사의 과거형/were ~, 주어+조동사의 과거형(would/should/could/might)+동사원형 …'의 형태이다.

06 'with+명사(구)+분사'에서 2 단어로 써야 하고, 명사와의 관계가 수동이므로 'turned on'이 적절하다.

07 가정법 과거는 현재 사실과 반대되는 가정을 나타낼 때 사용하므

17

로 직설법 문장을 가정법으로 나타낼 수 있다.

08 (1), (2) '가정법 과거를 이용한다. (3), (4) 'with+명사(구)+분사'에서 명사와의 관계가 능동이면 현재분사를, 수동이면 과거분사를 쓴다.

09 가정법 과거는 'If절에 동사의 과거형이나 were, 주절에 조동사의 과거형+동사원형 …'의 형태로 나타내며, Zetopia로 불리는 것이므로 과거분사 called가 되어야 한다.

10 직설법 현재 문장을 가정법 과거 문장으로 바꿀 때, 종속절에는 동사의 과거형을, 주절에는 '조동사의 과거형+동사원형'을 쓰는 것에 유의한다. (4)번은 가정법 과거완료로 과거의 사실을 반대로 가정하거나 실현 가능성이 없는 일에 대해서 가정할 때 쓰며, 'If+주어+had+p.p. ~, 주어+조동사의 과거형(would/should/could/might)+have+p.p. ~'의 형태로 쓴다.

11 (1) 주절에 would가 있는 가정법 과거 문장이다. is를 was나 were로 고치는 것이 적절하다. (2) 가정법 과거 문장이므로 can을 could로 고치는 것이 적절하다. (3) 감긴 눈으로 냄새를 맡는 것이 아니므로 'with+명사(구)+분사'의 어순으로 쓴다. (4) 'with+명사(구)+분사'에서 명사와의 관계가 능동이므로 현재분사를 쓴다.

Reading

교과서

확인문제 p.84

1 T 2 F 3 F

확인문제 p.85

1 T 2 F 3 F 4 T

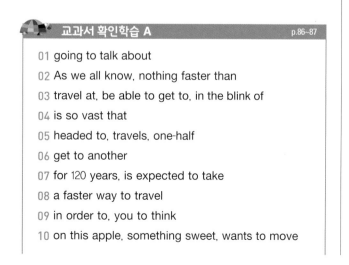

교과서 확인학습 A p.86~87

01 going to talk about
02 As we all know, nothing faster than
03 travel at, be able to get to, in the blink of
04 is so vast that
05 headed to, travels, one-half
06 get to another
07 for 120 years, is expected to take
08 a faster way to travel
09 in order to, you to think
10 on this apple, something sweet, wants to move

11 as vast as
12 either move around, or down
13 Which do you think, because it is a shortcut
14 such a shortcut
15 figured out, are connected, space-time
16 space-time could actually be bent, that are far away, are
17 To understand, take, make, at the top of, another, bottom
18 On a flat sheet, far away
19 fold, with, matched up, Punch, the dots, be, connected
20 contain two mouths, connecting
21 Just like, existed, get to places, away
22 too early to celebrate, exist
23 all, to do, find one
24 Even if, to consider, going through one.
25 would be, unstable, flew into, be crushed, broken
26 a pretty picture, hopeless
27 through, that, exists
28 wouldn't say, is, ongoing, with persistent exploration, research, one, learn how to travel
29 Look back at, so many things that
30 knows, to find the answer

교과서 확인학습 B p.88~89

1 Sci Teen: Hi, science fans. Today, we're going to talk about space travel.
2 As we all know, there is nothing faster than light in the universe.
3 So, if we travel at the speed of light, we should be able to get to another planet in the blink of an eye, right?
4 Dr. Sci: That would be nice, but space is so vast that it is not possible.
5 In the movie, *Passengers*, a spaceship headed to a different planet travels at one-half the speed of light.
6 So it should get to another planet very quickly, right?
7 But, the passengers sleep for 120 years because it is expected to take that much time to get to a different planet.
8 Sci Teen: 120 years? Wow, that's a long time! Is there a faster way to travel through space?
9 Dr. Sci: Well, in order to answer that question, I'd like you to think about this apple for a second.

10 Imagine a worm is on this apple. It detects something sweet at the bottom and wants to move from the top to the bottom.

11 For the worm, the apple's surface is as vast as our universe.

12 Now the worm can either move around the outer layer or down a wormhole.

13 Which do you think it will choose? Well, it would choose the wormhole because it is a shortcut.

14 Sci Teen: Is there such a shortcut in the universe?

15 Dr. Sci: According to some researchers, yes. Einstein figured out that space and time are connected, and he called it space-time.

16 He thought that space-time could actually be bent. When it is bent, parts that are far away from each other are suddenly closer.

17 To understand this, take a sheet of paper and make a small dot at the top of the paper and another at the bottom of the paper.

18 On a flat sheet of paper, the dots are far away from one another.

19 Now, take the paper and fold it with the dots matched up. Punch a hole in the paper and the dots will be instantly connected.

20 Like this, wormholes in space may contain two mouths, with a throat connecting the two.

21 Sci Teen: Just like a wormhole in the apple, right? If such wormholes existed in space, we could get to places billions of light-years away quickly!

22 Dr. Sci: Yes, but it's too early to celebrate. Wormholes exist in theory only.

23 Sci Teen: So all we need to do is find one, right?

24 Dr. Sci: Even if we find one, there are many things to consider before actually going through one

25 A wormhole would be very unstable. If a spaceship flew into one, it might be crushed or broken into pieces.

26 Sci Teen: Ouch! That's not a pretty picture. So, are we hopeless?

27 Is traveling in space through a wormhole simply an idea that only exists in theory?

28 Dr. Sci: I wouldn't say so. The debate about wormholes is still ongoing, but with persistent exploration and research, I believe we will eventually find one and learn how to travel through it.

29 Look back at our history. We've achieved so many things that seemed impossible at first.

30 Who knows? Maybe you can be the one to find the answer!

---

01 ③   02 ②

03 They're going to talk about space travel.

04 ⑤   05 ④

06 It is as vast as our universe.   07 ③

08 ⑤   09 a wormhole

10 We've achieved so many things that seemed impossible at first.

11 if we travel at the speed of light   12 ②

13 (C)-(B)-(A)   14 ④

15 On the apple, it detects something sweet at the bottom.

16 ③   17 ⑤

18 The dots on the paper will be instantly connected.

19 ②   20 ⑤   21 impossible

01 영화 <Passengers>에서 다른 행성으로 향하는 우주선이 빛의 속도 절반으로 이동함에도 120년이나 걸릴 것으로 예상한다고 하였다. 따라서 우주가 매우 광활하다고 할 수 있다.

02 앞 문장에서 말한 '눈 깜박할 사이에 다른 행성에 도달할 수 있어야 한다'는 것을 가리키는 말이다.

03 오늘 우주여행에 대해 이야기할 것이라고 하였다

04 이어지는 글의 내용으로 보아 우주를 여행하는 더 빠른 방법이 있는지를 묻는 말이 가장 적절하다.

05 모두 벌레를 가리키는 말이지만 ④는 벌레구멍을 가리키는 말이다.

06 벌레에게 사과의 표면은 우리의 우주만큼이나 광대하다고 하였다.

07 주어진 문장의 this가 가리키는 것은 시공간이 구부러질 때 서로 멀리 떨어져 있는 부분들이 갑자기 더 가까워질 수 있다는 것이다. 따라서 ③번에 들어가는 것이 적절하다.

08 아인슈타인은 시간과 공간이 연결되어 있다는 것을 생각해 냈다고 하였다.

09 '웜홀'을 가리키는 말이다.

10 역사를 돌아보면 우리는 처음에는 불가능해 보였던 아주 많은 것들을 달성해 왔다고 하였다.

11 '빛의 속도'는 'the speed of light'이다. If는 조건절을 이끄는 부사절 접속사로 '~라면'이라고 해석된다.

12 과학 팬들에게 인사를 하며 대화를 시작하고 있다. 따라서 ②번이 이 글의 내용과 일치한다..

13 (C) 영화 <Passengers>에서 다른 행성으로 향하는 우주선이 빛의 속도의 절반으로 이동함 (B) 그렇게 이동하면 다른 행성에

매우 빨리 도달해야겠지만 (A) 다른 행성에 도달하는 데 120년
이 걸릴 것으로 예상되어 승객들이 120년 동안 잠을 잠.

14 밑줄 친 (A)는 to부정사의 형용사적 용법으로 쓰였다. ① 명사
적 용법 중 진주어 ② 부사적 용법 중 목적 ③ 부사적 용법 중
감정의 원인 ④ 형용사적 용법 ⑤ 명사적 용법 중 목적격 보어

15 사과 위에서 벌레는 맨 아래에 있는 달콤한 무언가를 감지한다
고 하였다.

16 위 글은 우주에 지름길로서 존재하는 웜홀에 대한 설명이므로
③번이 가장 적절하다.

17 펼쳐 놓은 종이에서 그 점들은 서로 멀리 떨어져 있지만 그 종이
를 들고 점들이 맞춰지도록 접고, 종이에 구멍을 뚫으면 그 점들
이 즉시 연결된다는 의미이다. 따라서 hold가 아닌 fold라고 쓰
는 것이 자연스럽다.

18 종이에 구멍을 뚫으면 그 점들이 즉시 연결될 것이라고 하였다.

19 unstable, insecure: 불안정한, exclusive: 배타적인

20 핵심 주어는 The debate이므로 단수 취급하여 is라고 쓰는 것이
적절하다.

21 역사를 되돌아보면 처음에는 불가능해 보였던 아주 많은 것들을
달성해 왔다고 하였다.

🦉 서술형 시험대비   p.94~95

01 It travels at one-half the speed of light.
02 Because it is expected to take that much time to get
to a different planet.
03 get to another planet in the blink of an eye
04 wormhole
05 I'd like you to think about this apple for a second.
06 시공간이 구부러질 때 서로 멀리 떨어져 있는 부분들이
갑자기 더 가까워질 수 있는 것
07 We need to take the paper and fold it with the dots
matched up.
08 Wormholes, connected, bent, bent, closer
09 It is because wormholes exist in theory only.
10 We will learn how to travel through it.
11 It might be crushed or broken into pieces.
12 No, it's still ongoing.

01 영화 <Passengers>에 나오는 우주선은 빛의 속도의 절반으로
이동한다고 하였다.

02 영화 <Passengers>에서 승객들이 120년 동안 잠을 자게 되는
이유는 다른 행성에 도달하는 데 그만큼 많은 시간이 걸릴 것으
로 예상되기 때문이다.

---

03 해석: 우주는 너무 광활해서 우리가 빛의 속도로 여행을 한다 해
도 다른 행성에 눈 깜빡할 사이에 도달할 수 없다.

04 지름길이라고 하였으므로. 바깥 표면의 껍질을 돌아서 이동하는
것이 아닌 구멍 아래로 이동하는 것이 적절하다.

05 would like는 to부정사를 목적격 보어로 취하여 'would
like+목적어+to부정사' 형태로 쓰인다.

06 앞 문장 'When it is bent, parts that are far away from
each other are suddenly closer.'를 가리키는 말이다.

07 종이에 점들을 찍은 후 종이를 들고 점들이 맞춰지도록 그것을
접어야 한다.

08 아인슈타인은 시간과 공간이 연결되어 있고 시공간이 구부러질
수 있다고 생각했다. 이것이 구부러질 때 서로 멀리 떨어져 있는
부분들이 갑자기 더 가까워지는데, 이렇게 두 개의 입과 그 둘을
연결하는 목구멍을 지니고 있을 것이라고 추정하는 것이 우주의
웜홀이다.

09 웜홀은 이론상에서만 존재하기 때문에 축하하기에는 너무 이르
다고 말한 것이다.

10 우리가 결국 웜홀 하나를 찾으면 그것을 통해 여행하는 법을 배
울 수 있을 것이라고 믿는다고 하였다.

11 만약 우주선이 웜홀 안으로 날아가게 되면, 우주선이 부서지거
나 산산조각이 날 수도 있다고 하였다.

12 웜홀에 대한 논쟁은 여전히 진행 중이라고 하였다.

🐾 영역별 핵심문제   p.97~101

01 ④   02 movable   03 exploration
04 ④   05 (A) from (B) from
06 ③   07 ②   08 gravity
09 I wish I could float around like an astronaut!
10 impossible 11 ②   12 ③   13 ③
14 ④   15 ②
16 with a throat connecting
17 didn't lie, would not be
18 (1) crossed   (2) blowing   (3) closed   (4) following
    (5) closed
19 became, could enjoy   20 ④   21 ①
22 ②   23 ④
24 Light is the fastest thing in the universe.
25 Sci Teen thinks if we travel at the speed of light,
we should be able to get to another planet in the
blink of an eye.
26 ③   27 ③   28 ③   29 ②
30 ⑤
31 They could communicate with animals on the
planet 'Atlas'.

01 correct의 반의어는 incorrect이다.

02 동사 뒤에 –able을 붙이면 '~할 수 있는'이라는 의미의 형용사가 된다. movable: 움직일 수 있는

03 explore: 탐험하다, exploration: 탐사, 탐구 / 우주 탐사는 나에게 흥미로워 보인다.

04 (A) too ~ to+동사원형: 너무 ~해서 …할 수 없다 / 이 퍼즐은 너무 복잡해서 조립할 수 없다. (B) such+(부정관사)+형용사+명사: 그렇게 ~한 / 나는 그렇게 신나는 게임을 본 적이 없다.

05 (A) different from: ~와 다른 / 그들은 여러 면에서 서로 아주 다르다. (B) far away from: ~에서 멀리 떨어져 / 우리 집은 여기서 멀리 떨어져 있지 않다.

06 (B) 우주 정거장에서 보낸 시간 중 최고의 기억이 무엇인지 물어보는 질문에 (C) 하루에 16번 일출을 볼 수 있었다고 대답한다. (D) 하루에 일출을 여러 번 보는 것이 가능한지 물어보는 질문에 (A) 그렇다고 대답하면서 우주 정거장이 지구 주위를 90분마다 돌기 때문이라고 이유를 설명하고 있다.

07 주어진 문장은 '모든 것이 너무 달라 보인다.'라는 뜻으로, 이어지는 말로 'Yes, it's because there's no gravity in space. (응, 왜냐하면 우주에는 중력이 없기 때문이지.)'가 어울리므로 ②가 적절하다.

08 gravity: 중력 / 물체를 서로 당기는 힘으로, 특히 사물을 땅으로 떨어지게 하는 힘

09 어떤 일이 이루어지기를 바라는 표현으로 'I wish I could ~.'를 쓸 수 있다. 이는 가능성이 낮거나 이루어지기 힘든 일에 대해 '할 수 있으면 좋겠다'라는 바람의 의미로 쓰인다. float around: 떠다니다 astronaut: 우주 비행사

10 스케이트보드를 타고 날아다니는 것이 실제로 가능하다고 말하고 있으므로 전혀 불가능한 일이 아니라고 말하는 것이 어울린다. impossible: 불가능한

11 apply: 적용하다, 응용하다

12 남자가 아니라 여자가 날아다니는 스케이트보드를 가지기를 원한다.

13 ③번의 if는 간접의문문에 쓰였지만 나머지는 모두 가정법의 조건절을 이끌고 있다.

14 'with+명사(구)+분사'에서 명사와의 관계가 수동이므로 과거분사를 써야 한다. crossing을 crossed로 고쳐야 한다.

15 가정법 과거는 'If+주어+were/동사의 과거형 ~, 주어+조동사의 과거형+동사원형 …'의 형태로 나타낸다.

16 'with+명사(구)+분사'에서 명사와의 관계가 능동이면 현재분사를, 수동이면 과거분사를 쓴다.

17 가정법 과거에는 조건절에 동사의 과거형이 나오고 주절에는 '조동사의 과거형(would/should/could/might)+동사원형'이 나온다.

18 'with+명사(구)+분사'에서 명사와의 관계가 능동이면 현재분사를, 수동이면 과거분사를 쓴다. (1), (3), (5) 명사와의 관계가 수동이므로 각각 과거분사 crossed, closed, closed를 써야 한다. (2), (4) 명사와의 관계가 능동이므로 각각 현재분사 blowing, following을 써야 한다.

19 가정법 과거는 'If+주어+were/동사의 과거형 ~, 주어+조동사의 과거형(would/should/could/might)+동사원형 …'의 형태이다.

20 'with+명사(구)+분사'는 부대상황을 나타내며, 목적어와 능동의 관계일 경우 현재분사를 쓴다.

21 ① Jean and Tom are listening to music with their eyes closed.

22 지름길이기 때문에 웜홀을 선택한다는 의미이다. 따라서 ②번이 적절하다.

23 영작하면 'Which do you think it will choose?'이므로 think이다. 생각동사 think는 간접의문문의 의문사를 문두에 배치하는 것에 유의한다.

24 우주에서 가장 빠른 것은 빛이다.

25 Sci Teen은 우리가 빛의 속도로 여행을 한다면, 우리는 다른 행성에 눈 깜박할 사이에 도달할 수 있다고 생각한다.

26 영화에서 승객들은 다른 행성에 도달하는 120년 동안 잠을 잔다고 하였다.

27 'ongoing'은 진행 중이라는 의미이다. 따라서 ③번이 가장 적절하다. ① 다가오는 ② 유망한 ⑤ 근원적인

28 Dr. Sci는 끊임없는 탐구와 연구로 결국 웜홀 하나를 찾아 그것을 통해 여행하는 법을 배울 수 있을 것이라고 믿는다고 말하며, 여러분이 그 답을 찾아내는 사람이 될 수 있을지도 모른다고 말하고 있다. encouraging: 격려하는, 용기를 북돋아주는

29 행성 위에서 사는 것이므로 'a planet to live on'이라고 쓰는 것이 어법상 적절하다. ① to부정사의 의미상 주어로 'for+목적격'을 쓴다.

30 행성의 위치와 그곳에 갈 방법은 위 글에 나와 있지 않다.

31 사람들은 행성 '아틀라스'에서 동물들과 의사소통을 할 수 있을 것이라고 하였다.

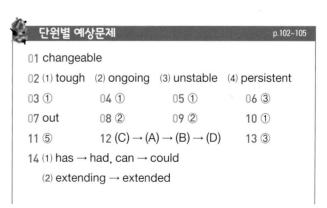

단원별 예상문제
p.102~105

01 changeable

02 (1) tough   (2) ongoing   (3) unstable   (4) persistent

03 ①   04 ①   05 ①   06 ③

07 out   08 ②   09 ②   10 ①

11 ⑤   12 (C) → (A) → (B) → (D)   13 ③

14 (1) has → had, can → could

　(2) extending → extended

15 (1) If Carrie passed the exam, she would be a lawyer. / As Carrie doesn't pass the exam, she won't be a lawyer.

(2) If we traveled at the speed of light, we could go to Mars in 13 minutes. / Since we don't travel at the speed of light, we can't go to Mars in 13 minutes.

(3) Take the paper and fold it with the dots matched up.

16 ④ **17** ⑤ **18** (B)-(A)-(C) **19** ④

20 theory **21** ③ **22** ②

23 It is Atlas.

---

01 unstable: 불안정한, changeable: 변덕스러운 / 정치 상황이 여전히 매우 불안정하다.

02 (1) tough: 힘든, 어려운 / 부산으로 이사 가는 것은 어려운 결정이었다. (2) ongoing: 계속 진행 중인 / 계속 진행 중인 이 이슈에 대해 어떻게 생각하니? (3) unstable: 불안정한 / 나는 저 의자가 불안정해 보인다. (4) persistent: 끈질긴, 집요한, 지속적인 / 나는 지속적인 두통과 목 통증이 있다.

03 achieve: 달성하다, 성취하다 / 특히 많은 작업이나 노력 후에 일을 끝내거나 목적을 달성하는 데 성공하다

04 apply: 적용하다, 응용하다 / 그 규칙은 아이들에게는 적용되지 않는다.

05 우주에 중력이 없기 때문에 채소를 특수한 봉지 안에서 키워야 한다고 하고 있으므로 이유의 접속사 since가 들어가는 것이 적절하다.

06 어떤 일이 실제로 가능한지 묻는 표현으로 'Is it possible to ~?'를 쓸 수 있다. 같은 표현으로 'Are we able to ~?', 'Can we actually ~?', 'Is there a possibility that 주어+동사 ~?', 'Would it be possible ~?' 등이 있다. ③의 should는 '~해야 한다'의 의미이므로 어울리지 않는다.

07 print out: (프린터로) 출력하다

08 어떤 일이 실제로 가능한지 묻는 표현으로 'Is it possible to ~?'를 쓸 수 있다.

09 ⓐ that, 'Have you heard that 주어+동사 ~?'는 '~를 들어 본 적 있니?'의 의미로 알고 있는지 묻는 표현이다. ⓑ into, send A into B: A를 B로 보내다 ⓒ to print, be used to 동사원형: ~하기 위해 사용되다 ⓓ possible, 신선한 피자를 5분도 안 돼서 출력해 낼 수 있다고 말하고 있으므로 3D프린터를 이용해 음식을 만드는 것은 가능하다. ⓔ what

10 'Actually, you can do that at the National Youth Space

Center.'에서 do that이 'see Earth from space with your own eyes'를 의미하므로 ①이 적절하다.

11 직접 자신의 눈으로 우주에서 지구를 볼 수 있기를 희망하는 여자에게 국립 청소년 우주 센터에서 가상 현실 안경을 쓰면 실제로 우주에 있는 것 같은 기분이 든다고 얘기하고 있다.

12 무엇을 보고 있는지 물어보는 질문에 (C) 우주에서의 삶에 관한 다큐멘터리를 보고 있다고 대답하면서 모든 것이 달라 보인다고 말한다. (A) 우주에 중력이 없기 때문에 달라 보인다고 얘기해 준다. (B) 자신도 우주 비행사처럼 떠다니는 것을 바란다고 말하자 (D) 상대방은 자신은 아니라고 대답하면서 불편해 보인다고 말한다.

13 ① If I were the principal of my school, I would let students have PE class every day. ② If there were no cold air and warm air, a wind could not be made. ④ Were it not for water, no living things could survive. ⑤ But for your advice, I would ruin my reputation.

14 (1) 가정법 과거에서 종속절에는 동사의 과거형을 쓴다. (2) 'with+명사(구)+분사'에서 명사와의 관계가 능동이면 현재분사를, 수동이면 과거분사를 쓴다. 다리가 무엇을 뻗도록 하는 것이 아니라 뻗게 되는 것이므로 수동의 과거분사가 적절하다.

15 (1), (2) 가정법 과거 문장은 현재시제의 직설법으로 바꿔 쓸 수 있다. (3) 'with+명사(구)+분사'는 부대상황을 나타내며, 목적어와 수동의 관계일 경우 과거분사를 쓴다.

16 If there were no ~ = If it were not for ~ = Were it not for ~ = But for ~ = Without ~

17 이어지는 설명으로 보아 우주에 지름길이 존재하는지 묻는 말이 들어가는 것이 자연스럽다.

18 (B)의 this는 '시공간이 구부러질 때 서로 멀리 떨어져 있는 부분들이 갑자기 더 가까워질 수 있다'는 앞 문장을 받음 (A) the dots는 (B)에서 찍은 점들을 가리킴 (C) 멀리 있던 점들이 구멍을 뚫으면 즉시 연결됨

19 밑줄 친 ⓐ는 완전한 절을 이끄는 명사절 접속사이다. ④번은 불완전한 절을 이끄는 관계대명사 that이다.

20 어떠한 학문의 바탕이 되는 규칙을 정식으로 진술하는 것은 '이론(theory)'이다.

21 웜홀이 다른 행성으로 안전하게 이동하는 것을 가능하게 한다는 말은 나와 있지 않다.

22 행성 위에서 사는 것이므로 'on'이 가장 적절하다.

23 글쓴이가 만들기를 원하는 행성의 이름은 아틀라스이다.

01 (1) I wish I could take a space trip.
   (2) Taking a space trip would be a dream come true.
   (3) It would be great if I could take a space trip.

02 (1) I wish I could open my (own) restaurant.
   (2) I also wish (that) I could appear on a cooking show.

03 Is it possible to lie down / their sleeping bag to

04 (1) As Mary doesn't hear the news, she isn't happy.
   (2) My father doesn't know the fact, so he lets me go there.
   (3) If the man could speak English, I would employ him.
   (4) Were the weather fine, Jini would go on a picnic.
   (5) Without television, half the pleasure of our daily lives could be lost.

05 (1) Mr. Jones is sitting on a chair with his legs crossed.
   (2) Bella laughed out loud with her finger pointing at me.
   (3) It was a beautiful morning, with little wind blowing.

06 matched

07 He figured out that space and time are connected.

08 A throat connects them.

09 light

10 (B) headed   (C) travels   (D) expected

01 어떤 일이 이루어지기를 바라는 표현으로 'I wish I could ~.'를 쓸 수 있다. 이는 가능성이 낮거나 이루어지기 힘든 일에 대해 '할 수 있으면 좋겠다'라는 바람의 의미로 쓰인다. 같은 표현으로 '~ would be a dream come true.', 'How I wish I could ~!', 'It would be great if I could ~.' 등이 있다.

02 어떤 일이 이루어지기를 바라는 표현으로 'I wish I could ~.'를 쓸 수 있다. 이는 가능성이 낮거나 이루어지기 힘든 일에 대해 '할 수 있으면 좋겠다'라는 바람의 의미로 쓰인다. appear: 나타나다, 등장하다

03 어떤 일이 실제로 가능한지 묻는 표현으로 'Is it possible to ~?'를 쓸 수 있다. lie down: 눕다, 누워 있다

04 (1)~(3) 가정법 과거 문장은 현재시제의 직설법으로 바꿔 쓸 수 있다. (4) 가정법으로 고친 후, if를 생략하고 were를 문두에 쓰고 도치시킨다. (5) if there were no = if it were not for =

were it not for = without = but for

05 'with+명사(구)+분사'는 부대상황을 나타내며, 목적어와 능동의 관계일 경우 현재분사를, 목적어와 수동의 관계일 경우 과거분사를 쓴다. (1) 다리가 교차되는 것이므로 과거분사crossed를 쓴다. (2) 손가락이 나를 가리키는 것이므로 현재분사 pointing을 쓴다. (3) 바람이 부는 것이므로 현재분사 blowing을 쓴다.

06 'with+명사+분사' 형태로 부대 상황을 나타낸다. 분사의 의미상 주어인 the dots가 분사와 수동의 관계이므로 과거분사인 matched를 쓰는 것이 적절하다.

07 아인슈타인은 공간과 시간이 연결되어 있다는 것을 생각해 냈다고 하였다.

08 우주의 웜홀은 두 개의 입과 그 둘을 연결하는 목구멍을 지니고 있을 것이라고 하였다.

09 뒤에서 빛의 속도로 이동하면 다른 행성에 눈 깜박할 사이에 도달할 수 있다고 말하고 있으므로 '우주에서 빛보다 더 빠른 것은 없다'로 말하는 것이 적절하다.

10 (B) 다른 행성으로 향한다는 의미로 head는 타동사이므로 과거분사로 쓴다. (B) 주어가 a spaceship이며 빛의 속도의 절반으로 이동한다는 의미이므로 단수동사 travels를 쓴다. (D) 다른 행성에 도달하는 데 그만큼 많은 시간이 걸릴 것으로 예상된다는 의미이므로 수동태를 쓴다.

|모범답안|

01 (1) I wish I could sing better.
   (2) I wish I could play soccer better.
   (3) I wish I were a famous writer.

02 (1) If Earth had no air, the sky would always be black.
   (2) (a) If there were no gravity, the air would go away to space.
     (b) If it were not for gravity, the air would go away to space.
     (c) Were it not for gravity, the air would go away to space.
     (d) But for gravity, the air would go away to space.
     (e) Without gravity, the air would go away to space.

03 Minas / pink / bigger than the moon, but smaller than Earth / 20℃ / cotton candy mountains / feel time pass slowly on this planet

01 어떤 일이 이루어지기를 바라는 표현으로 'I wish I could[were] ~.'를 쓸 수 있다.

23

if there were no = if it were not for = were it not for = without = but for임을 숙지하는 것이 좋다.

단원별 모의고사
p.109~113

01 ②, ⑤   02 ③
03 (1) extend   (2) attach   (3) crushed   (4) exists
04 (1) billions of   (2) (c)elebrate   (3) (d)etect
   (4) (e)ventually
05 (A) comfortable   (B) impossible
06 distance   07 ⑤   08 ③
09 I wish I could live in space.   10 ④
11 I wish I could become an astronaut like them and
   explore Mars.
12 ⓐ, ⓒ, ⓓ 13 ③   14 ④   15 ②
16 (1) They jogged with their dog following them.
   (2) Drake walked for a long time with his eyes
      fixed upon the floor.
   (3) The prince entered the hall with the people
      cheering.
17 (1) If I were[was] an astronaut, I would walk in space.
   (2) If it stopped raining, we could play baseball.
   (3) I wish I could bring my mom back to life.
   (4) Balance on your arms with your knees resting on
      the upper arms.
   (5) My teacher worked all day with the door closed.
18 with a throat connecting the two
19 ③
20 The worm can either move around the outer layer
   or down a wormhole.   21 ⑤
22 ④   23 ②
24 We will do that with persistent exploration and
   research.
25 We could get to places billions of light-years
   away quickly.

01 ① in theory: 이론상으로는, 원칙상으로는 / 이론상 그 산을 오르는 데는 이틀 밖에 안 걸리지만 실제로는 그건 불가능하다. ② print out: (프린터로) 출력하다 / 너의 보고서를 출력해 줄래? ③ in the blink of an eye: 눈 깜짝할 사이에 / 그것은 눈 깜짝할 사이에 사라져 버렸다. ④ in order to 동사원형: ~하기 위하여 / 나는 내가 그 시험에 통과할 수 있도록 열심히 공부했다. ⑤ lie down: 눕다, 누워 있다 / 여기 누워서 좀 쉬어라.

02 ① im-+partial → impartial 공정한 ② im-+patient → impatient 안달하는 ③ un-+usual → unusual 보통이 아닌, 평소와 다른 ④ in-+credible → incredible 믿을 수 없는, 믿

기 힘든 ⑤ in-+sensitive → insensitive 둔감한, 몰이해한

03 (1) extend: (팔, 다리를) 뻗다 / 바닥에 누워서 다리를 뻗어라. (2) attach: 붙이다 / 너는 이 양식에 너의 사진을 붙여야 한다. (3) crush: 눌러 부수다, 찌부러뜨리다 / 이 차들은 그 사고에서 찌부러졌다. (4) exist: 존재하다 / 너는 생명체가 다른 행성들에 존재한다는 것을 믿니?

04 (1) billions: 수십억의 (2) celebrate: 축하하다 (3) detect: 감지하다, 발견하다 (4) eventually: 결국

05 (A) comfortable: 편안한, 우주에 중력을 만드는 것이 가능하다면, 우주 여행이 더 편해질 것이다. (B) impossible: 불가능한, 과학자들이 기술을 개발하고 있는 중이라고 말했으므로, 우주에 중력을 만드는 것이 전혀 불가능 일이 아니라고 하는 것이 적절하다.

06 distance: 거리 / 두 장소 사이의 공간의 총계

07 우주에 살면 키가 더 커질 수 있다는 말에 여자가 우주에 가는 것 말고 키가 더 커지는 다른 방법이 있을 거라고 확신하다고 말하는 것이 어울린다.

08 (A) while 뒤에 주어와 be동사가 생략되어 있다. while: ~하는 동안 (B) 'It's because'는 '~하기 때문이다'라는 의미로 이유를 말할 때 사용한다.

09 'I wish I could ~.'는 소망이나 바람을 나타낼 때 사용하는 표현으로 '내가 ~할 수 있다면 좋을 텐데.'라는 뜻이다.

10 주어진 문장은 직접 진짜 우주인을 만났는지 물어보는 질문으로 대답으로는 'Yes, and I heard about their adventure stories.(응, 그리고 나는 그들의 모험 이야기를 들었어.)'가 어울리므로 ④가 적절하다.

12 ⓐ Cindy는 국립 우주 센터에서 무엇을 했는가? (무중력 상태와 우주 비행사들의 우주 생활을 경험했다.) ⓑ Cindy가 우주 비행사가 되는 것은 가능한가? ⓒ Cindy가 언제 국립 우주 센터에 갔는가? (지난 주말에) ⓓ Cindy는 우주인을 만났는가? (만났다.)

13 ③ 내가 마법의 램프를 갖고 있기 때문에, 행복과 건강을 빌 수 있다. ①, ②, ④, ⑤ 내가 마법의 램프를 갖고 있다면, 행복과 건강을 빌 수 있을 텐데. (내가 마법의 램프를 갖고 있지 않기 때문에, 행복과 건강을 빌 수 없다.)

14 'with+명사(구)+분사'는 부대상황을 나타내며, 목적어와 능동의 관계일 경우 현재분사를, 목적어와 수동의 관계일 경우 과거분사를 쓴다.

15 ②번의 if는 간접의문으로 명사절을 이끄는 접속사이며, 나머지는 모두 가정법의 조건절을 이끄는 종속접속사이다.

16 'with+명사(구)+분사'는 부대상황을 나타내며, 목적어와 능동의 관계일 경우 현재분사를, 목적어와 수동의 관계일 경우 과거분사를 쓴다. (1) 개가 따라오는 것이므로 능동의 현재분사 following을 써야 한다. (2) 눈이 고정되는 것이므로 수동의 과거분사 fixed를 써야 한다. (3) 사람들이 갈채를 보내는 것이므로 능동의 현재분사 cheering을 써야 한다.

17 (1), (2) '만약 ~라면 …할 텐데'라는 뜻으로, 현재 사실을 반대로 가정하거나 실현 가능성이 없는 일에 대해서 가정할 때 사용하는 가정법과거로 'If+주어+were/동사의 과거형 ~, 주어+조동사의 과거형(would/should/could/might)+동사원형 …'의 형태로 쓴다. (3) 'I wish I could ~.'는 현재는 이룰 수 없는 어떤 소망에 대해 말할 때 사용된다. (4) 'with+명사(구)+분사'는 부대상황을 나타내며, 목적어와 능동의 관계이므로 현재분사를 써야 하는 것에 유의한다. (5) 'with+명사(구)+분사'는 부대상황을 나타내며, 목적어와 수동의 관계이므로 과거분사를 써야 하는 것에 유의한다.

18 두 점을 맞춰지도록 종이를 접고 종이에 구멍을 뚫으면 그 점들이 즉시 연결되듯, 웜홀 역시 두 개의 입과 그 둘을 연결하는 목구멍을 지니고 있다는 의미이다. 'with+목적어+분사'에서 목적어와 분사의 관계가 능동이므로 현재분사를 쓰는 것에 유의한다.

19 주어진 문장의 the dots는 종이 윗부분과 아랫부분에 찍은 각각의 점을 가리키는 말이다. 또한 펼쳐진 종이에서는 이 점들이 서로 멀리 떨어져 있지만 이것을 들어서 점들이 맞춰지도록 접고 종이에 구멍을 뚫으면 점들이 즉시 연결이 된다는 흐름이 자연스럽다.

20 벌레는 바깥 표면의 껍질을 돌아서 이동하거나 벌레 구멍 아래로 이동할 수 있다고 하였다.

21 아인슈타인이 시공간이 연결되어 있는 것을 어떻게 발견하게 되었는지는 위 글을 읽고 답할 수 없다.

22 웜홀은 매우 불안정할 것이므로 실제로 그것을 통과하여 가기 전에 고려해야 할 것들이 많이 있다고 하였다.

23 위 글은 웜홀을 통한 우주여행에 관한 글이므로 ②번이 가장 적절하다.

24 Dr. Sci는 끊임없는 탐구와 연구로 우리가 결국 웜홀을 찾아 그것을 통해 여행하는 법을 배울 수 있을 것이라고 믿는다고 하였다.

25 웜홀이 존재한다면 우리는 수십억 광년 떨어져 있는 곳에 빠르게 도달할 수 있을 것이라고 하였다.

교과서 파헤치기

Lesson **7**

단어 TEST Step 1   p.02

01 편리한, 간편한   02 오래가다, (기능이) 지속되다

03 어울리다   04 경쟁하다   05 용돈

06 구매하다, 구입하다   07 출시하다, 발매하다

08 ~에 영향을 주다   09 사라지다   10 행동, 행위

11 결합하다   12 바꾸다, 교체하다 13 언급하다, 말하다

14 ~에 탑승하고, ~에 타서   15 할인; 할인하다

16 부추기다, 조장하다   17 효과

18 비교하다   19 환불   20 지출

21 개념   22 위험에 빠뜨리다   23 완성하다

24 고정하다   25 줄무늬가 있는   26 차이, 차이점

27 즉시, 바로   28 꽉 조이는, 딱 붙는 29 ~에 영향을 주다

30 부족, 결핍   31 닻; 닻을 내리다   32 10억

33 지나치게 뜨거운, 과열된   34 소비하다, 소모하다

35 진열된, 전시된   36 비교해 보면   37 ~와 잘 어울리다

38 단지 ~라는 이유로   39 ~을 기록하다

40 ~에 관해서, ~에 대해 말하자면

41 ~할 가능성이 있다, ~하기 쉽다   42 반 이상의

43 한눈에, 즉시

단어 TEST Step 2   p.03

01 allowance   02 combine   03 immediately
04 effect   05 convenient   06 deal
07 billion   08 complete   09 affect
10 mention   11 consume   12 anchor
13 behavior   14 miss   15 difference
16 compare   17 encourage   18 compete
19 endanger   20 concept   21 striped
22 refund   23 release   24 influence
25 lack   26 disappear   27 discount
28 match   29 purchase   30 raise
31 replace   32 spending   33 tight
34 waste   35 on display   36 at a glance
37 in comparison   38 keep track of 39 as such
40 just because   41 go well with
42 when it comes to   43 be likely to

단어 TEST Step 3   p.04

1 immediately, 즉시, 바로   2 concept, 개념

3 disappear, 사라지다   4 purchase, 구입하다, 구매하다

5 release, 출시하다   6 suit, 어울리다

7 tight, 꽉 조이는, 딱 붙는   8 combine, 결합하다

9 waste, 낭비하다, 소모하다

10 convenient, 편리한, 간편한

11 encourage, 부추기다, 조장하다

12 allowance, 용돈   13 consume, 소비하다, 소모하다

14 endanger, 위험에 빠뜨리다   15 lack, 부족, 결핍

16 affect, ~에 영향을 주다

대화문 TEST Step 1   p.05~07

Listen & Talk 1 A

1 help, with / try on, with / How do you like / but, suits, have / one / take

2 Welcome to / I'm looking for / popular among, How do you like / green one is lighter than, one, lighter one / choice

Listen & Talk 1 B

bought, few weeks ago / looks, How do you like / convenient, anywhere, quality, too / How long, last / About, doesn't last / too bad / pretty happy, anyway

Listen & Talk 2 A

1 too uncomfortable / What's wrong with it / tight / you try it on before buying / so, bought, should have tried, on

2 are going to watch / to join / love to, I've spent, allowance / get it, ago / should have kept track of my spending

Listen & Talk 2 B

like mine / on sale / on sale, has just been released / is having, sale / at full price / selling, at, discount / should have checked the sales before

Communication Step A

heard that you bought, How, like / not happy, it / Why, What's / gets overheated, have read, reviews / ask for / won't give me back, I've used / calling, explaining / do

Wrap Up

1 I'd like to / How do you like this red one, among / that, one / striped, Its / take

2 package / bought, online used store, ago / let me see / is a little broken, said that / before / I just trusted, should have checked a bit more / should call, ask for a refund

p.08~10

Listen & Talk 1 A

1 M: Hi, can I help you with anything?

W: Yes, can I try on that cap with stars over there?

M: Sure. How do you like it?

W: The design is nice, but I don't think the color suits me. Do you have it in black?

M: Yes. I'll get one from the back. (*pause*) Here it is.

W: Great. I'll take it.

2 M: Good morning. Welcome to Kelly's Sporting Goods Store.

W: Hi, I'm looking for a backpack for hiking.

M: These two are popular among hikers. How do you like them?

W: The green one is lighter than the blue one. I'll take the lighter one.

M: Great choice.

Listen & Talk 1 B

W: Hi, Luke. Is that a new speaker?

M: Yes, I bought it a few weeks ago.

W: It looks cool. How do you like it?

M: It's convenient. I can take it anywhere and listen to music. The sound quality is good, too.

W: Great. How long does the battery last?

M: About 2 hours. The battery doesn't last long.

W: That's too bad.

M: Yeah, but I'm pretty happy with it, anyway

Listen & Talk 2 A

1 M: Oh, this coat is too uncomfortable.

W: Why? What's wrong with it?

M: It's too tight.

W: Didn't you try it on before buying it?

M: No. It was my size, so I just bought it. I should have tried it on.

2 W: Hey, Eric. Camilla and I are going to watch a movie. Do you want to join us?

M: I'd love to, but I can't. I've spent all of my allowance for this week.

W: Didn't you just get it a few days ago? How did you spend it all?

M: I'm not sure. I should have kept track of my spending.

Listen & Talk 2 B

M: Did you get a new phone, Jamie? It's just like mine.

W: Yeah, I got it last weekend on sale.

M: It was on sale? But it has just been released, hasn't it?

W: Right, but the store on Green Street is having a year-end sale.

M: Oh, I bought mine at full price!

W: Really? That's too bad. They're selling them at a 40 percent discount.

M: I should have checked the sales before buying mine.

Communication Step A

M: Hi, Riley. I heard that you bought a laptop online. How do you like it?

W: Oh, I'm not happy with it.

M: Why ? What's wrong?

W: It makes too much noise and gets overheated. I should have read more reviews.

M: Oh, then you should ask for your money back.

W: The online store won't give me back my money because I've used it for a week.

M: How about calling the online shop and explaining your problem?

W: Yeah, I think I should do that.

Wrap Up

1 M: Good morning. May I help you?

W: I'd like to buy a T-shirt for my sister. She's eleven years old.

M: How do you like this red one? This character is quite popular among children.

W: Well, she doesn't like animation characters that much. Can I see the blue one?

M: You mean this blue striped T-shirt? Its design is simple and cool.

W: Yes, I think my sister will like it. I'll take it.

2 W: Jake, here's a package for you.

M: It's my helmet. I bought it at an online used store a few days ago.

W: Oh, open it and let me see it.

M: Okay. (*pause*) Oh, this outer part is a little broken. The seller said that it's perfectly fine though.

W: Didn't you check the pictures of the helmet before you bought it?

M: No, I just trusted the seller. I should have checked a bit more.

W: You should call the seller and ask for a refund.

01 wondered why, bought, even
02 what affects, comes, buying
03 what my friends bought
04 goes, pair, on display
05 recognizes, because, half, wear
06 Although, ends up, another
07 effect, to explain, behavior
08 parade, encourages, jump aboard
09 others, likely get, follow
10 way, tend, just, bought
11 buy, pair, after, bought
12 that, Immediately, realizes, match
13 buys, go perfectly with
14 sees, none, match, clothes
15 Most, on, items, complete
16 made, search, after buying
17 explain, received, as, gift
18 noticed, furniture, go, replacing
19 therefore, purchasing, leads, unplanned
20 just because, on sale
21 goes window, sees, pair
22 checks, finds out, expensive
23 sales, approaches, discount on
24 though, discounted, still, low
25 described above, example, effect
26 mentioned, affects, opinion, prices
27 seem cheap in comparison
28 Furthermore, becomes bigger, powerful
29 As such, fixes, thoughts
30 like, things, considering, buying
31 As, shown, influence, purchases
32 time, think, about, buying

01 why you've bought things that
02 what affects us, comes to buying
03 what my friends bought
04 goes, sees a pair of, on display
05 recognizes, because, half of the boys, wear
06 Although, many pairs of, ends up buying another
07 bandwagon effect, to explain, behavior
08 that encourages, to jump aboard
09 more and more people, others are, likely to get on, follow
10 In, way, to buy, just because, have bought it

11 buy a pair of, after, have bought
12 that, Immediately, realizes that, match
13 that go, with
14 that none of her bags match, new clothes
15 buys, Most of her money is, on, to complete, new look
16 made, search for new items, after buying
17 effect, explain it, received, as, gift
18 after receiving, noticed that, furniture, go well, replacing most of it
19 therefore, that purchasing a new item, leads to, unplanned purchases
20 just because they are on sale
21 goes window shopping, sees, pair
22 checks, finds out that, that, too expensive
23 approaches him, discount on
24 Even though, is still, low, to buy
25 described above, example, anchoring effect
26 mentioned, affects, opinion of prices mentioned
27 For example, seem cheap in comparison
28 Furthermore, the difference, becomes bigger, be more powerful
29 As such, mentioned first, anchor, fixes our thoughts
30 Just like, to buy, without, considering why we are buying
31 As, have shown, influence our purchases
32 The next time, decide to buy, think, about why you are buying

1 여러분은 원하거나 필요로 하지도 않는 것들을 자신이 왜 구입했는지 궁금해 한 적이 있는가?
2 물건들을 구입하는 것에 관하여 무엇이 우리에게 영향을 주는지 생각해 보자.
3 나는 왜 친구들이 산 것을 사고 싶은 걸까?
4 Jeff는 쇼핑센터에 가서 진열되어 있는 축구화 한 켤레를 보게 된다.
5 그의 축구팀에 있는 소년들의 반 이상이 그 축구화를 신기 때문에 그는 그 신발을 한눈에 알아챈다.
6 이미 그에게는 축구화가 많이 있지만 결국 그는 또 다른 새 축구화를 사 버리고 만다.
7 우리는 Jeff의 행동을 설명하기 위해 '밴드왜건 효과'를 이용할 수 있다.
8 밴드왜건(악대차)은 사람들이 올라타서 음악을 즐기게끔 부추기는 퍼레이드에 있는 사륜마차이다.

9 더 많은 사람들이 밴드왜건에 올라탈수록 다른 사람들이 더욱 그것에 올라타거나 그것을 따르려 한다.

10 이런 식으로, 사람들은 단지 다른 사람들이 어떤 것을 샀다는 이유로 그것을 구매하는 경향이 있다.

11 나는 왜 새 코트를 구입한 후에 바지와 가방을 사는 걸까?

12 Lisa는 정말 마음에 드는 코트를 산다. 그녀는 그녀의 바지가 새 코트와 어울리지 않는다는 것을 즉시 알아차린다.

13 그래서 그녀는 새 코트와 완벽하게 어울리는 새 바지를 구입한다.

14 하지만 그녀는 자신의 가방 중 어느 것도 새로운 옷들과 어울리지 않는다는 것을 알게 된다.

15 그래서 그녀는 새 가방을 산다. 그녀의 돈 대부분이 그녀의 새로운 모습을 완성하기 위하여 새로운 물품을 사는 데 쓰인다.

16 무엇이 Lisa로 하여금 새 코트를 산 후 즉시 새로운 물품을 찾게 했을까?

17 '디드로 효과'가 그것을 설명해 줄지도 모른다. 프랑스 작가인 Denis Diderot는 선물로 새 가운을 받았다.

18 그 선물을 받은 후에 곧 그는 그의 모든 가구가 새로운 가운과 어울리지 않는다는 것을 알아챘다. 그래서 그는 결국 대부분의 가구를 바꾸고 말았다.

19 그러므로 디드로 효과는 새로운 물품을 구입하는 것이 흔히 계획에 없던 더 많은 구매로 이어진다는 개념이다.

20 나는 왜 단지 할인 중이라는 이유로 물건을 구입하는 걸까?

21 Nathan은 진열된 상품을 구경하러 가서 헤드폰을 하나 본다.

22 그는 가격을 확인하고 그것이 200달러임을 알게 된다. 그는 그 헤드폰이 너무 비싸다고 생각한다.

23 점원이 그에게 다가와 "이 헤드폰에 20퍼센트 할인을 받을 수 있어요."라고 말한다.

24 비록 할인된 가격이 여전히 별로 저렴하지는 않지만 Nathan 은 그 헤드폰을 사기로 결심한다.

25 위에 기술된 상황은 '앵커링 효과'의 한 예이다.

26 처음에 언급된 가격이 이후에 언급되는 가격에 대한 우리의 의견에 영향을 미친다.

27 예를 들어, 만약 우리가 200달러로 시작한다면, 비교해 볼 때 160달러는 저렴해 보일 것이다.

28 그뿐만 아니라, 두 가격의 차이가 커질수록 그 효과는 더욱 강력해질 것이다.

29 이와 같이 처음에 언급된 가격이 물건의 가격에 대한 우리의 생각을 고정하는 '닻'으로서 작동한다.

30 Jeff와 그의 친구들처럼, 우리는 우리가 왜 물건들을 사는지 진지하게 고려하지 않고 그것들을 구입하는 경향이 있다.

31 이러한 효과들이 보여 주듯이, 많은 것들이 우리의 구매에 영향을 미친다.

32 다음번에 여러분이 어떤 것을 구매하려고 결정할 때에는, 자신이 그것을 왜 사려는지 잠시 동안 생각해 보아라.

1 Have you ever wondered why you've bought things that you don't even want or need?

2 Let's consider what affects us when it comes to buying things.

3 Why do I want to buy what my friends bought?

4 Jeff goes to the shopping center and sees a pair of soccer shoes on display.

5 He recognizes the shoes at a glance because more than half of the boys on his soccer team wear them.

6 Although he already has many pairs of soccer shoes, he ends up buying another new pair.

7 We can use the "bandwagon effect" to explain Jeff's behavior.

8 A bandwagon is a wagon in a parade that encourages people to jump aboard and enjoy the music.

9 As more and more people get on the bandwagon, others are more likely to get on or follow it.

10 In this way, people tend to buy something just because other people have bought it.

11 Why do I buy a pair of pants and a bag after I have bought a new coat?

12 Lisa buys a coat that she really loves. Immediately, she realizes that her pants do not match her new coat.

13 So, she buys new pants that go perfectly with her new coat.

14 But she sees that none of her bags match her new clothes.

15 So, she buys a new bag. Most of her money is spent on buying the new items to complete her new look.

16 What made Lisa search for new items immediately after buying a new coat?

17 The "Diderot effect" may explain it. Denis Diderot, a French writer, received a new gown as a gift.

18 Soon after receiving the gift, he noticed that all of his furniture did not go well with his new gown. So, he ended up replacing most of it.

19 The Diderot effect, therefore, is the concept that purchasing a new item often leads to more unplanned purchases.

20 Why do I buy things just because they are on sale?

21 Nathan goes window shopping and sees a pair of headphones.

22 He checks the price and finds out that they are $200. He thinks that the headphones are too expensive.

23 The sales person approaches him and says, "You can get a 20 percent discount on those headphones."

24 Even though the discounted price is still not very low, Nathan decides to buy the headphones.

25 The situation described above is an example of the "anchoring effect."

26 The price mentioned first affects our opinion of prices mentioned afterwards.

27 For example, if we start with $200, then $160 will seem cheap in comparison.

28 Furthermore, as the difference of the two prices becomes bigger, the effect will be more powerful.

29 As such, the price mentioned first acts as an "anchor" that fixes our thoughts about the price of an item.

30 Just like Jeff and his friends, we tend to buy things without seriously considering why we are buying them.

31 As these effects have shown, many things influence our purchases.

32 The next time you decide to buy something, think for a moment about why you are buying it.

Language in Use

1. It is difficult to compare the results in detail.

2. We encourage children to think for themselves.

Grammar in Real Life B Look and Write

1. About half of the water is used to raise animals in the U.S.

2. One third of the world's food is wasted—1.3 billion tons every year.

3. In Somalia, only ten percent of the children go to school.

4. About fourteen percent of all people don't know how to read due to lack of education.

Think & Write C

1. I did a survey about allowance.

2. First, I asked 10 students how often they get an allowance.

3. Twenty percent of the students get an allowance every week and seventy percent of the students get an allowance every month.

4. Second, I asked them what they spend most of their allowance on.

5. Most of the allowance is spent on clothes and one fourth of the allowance is spent on snacks.

6. Lastly, I asked them whether they think that they should get a higher allowance.

7. Ninety percent of the students think that they should get a higher allowance.

Language in Use

1. It, to compare, in detail

2. encourage, to think for themselves

Grammar in Real Life B Look and Write

1. half of, is used to raise

2. One third of, is wasted, billion tons

3. only ten percent of, go to school

4. About, don't, how to read due to lack of

Think & Write C

1. did a survey, allowance

2. how often they get an allowance

3. get an allowance, seventy percent, get an allowance every month

4. what, spend most of their allowance on

5. Most of the allowance, one fourth, is spent on snacks

6. whether they think, should get a higher allowance

7. Ninety percent of the students think

8 ongoing, 계속 진행 중인   9 sunrise, 일출

10 astronaut, 우주 비행사   11 achieve, 달성하다, 성취하다

12 detect, 감지하다, 발견하다   13 gravity, 중력

14 celebrate, 축하하다   15 passenger, 승객, 탑승객

16 planet, 행성

단어 TEST Step 1   p.25

01 표면	02 굽히다, 구부리다	03 연결되다, 이어지다
04 일출	05 ~이 들어 있다, 포함하다	
06 지름길	07 눌러 부수다, 찌부러뜨리다	
08 거리	09 바뀔 수 있는, 변덕스러운	
10 붙이다	11 힘든, 어려운	12 먹을 수 있는
13 달성하다, 성취하다		14 결국
15 감지하다, 발견하다		16 (팔, 다리를) 뻗다
17 불안정한	18 맨 아랫부분, 바닥	19 층
20 거대한, 광대한	21 끈질긴, 집요한, 지속적인	
22 즉시	23 적용하다, 응용하다	
24 존재하다	25 중력	26 몸을 숙이다, 굽히다
27 구멍을 뚫다	28 무한한	29 낮추다
30 탐사, 탐구	31 측정하다	32 이론, 학설
33 계속 진행 중인	34 부정확한, 사실이 아닌	
35 되돌아보다	36 ~을 알아내다, 생각해 내다	
37 ~에 따르면	38 ~에서 멀리 떨어져	
39 눕다, 누워 있다	40 이론상으로는, 원칙상으로는	
41 ~의 아래에	42 ~와 다른	43 눈 깜박할 사이에

단어 TEST Step 2   p.26

01 researcher	02 shortcut	03 lean
04 ongoing	05 passenger	06 incorrect
07 crush	08 theory	09 lower
10 tough	11 infinite	12 apply
13 persistent	14 bottom	15 exist
16 unstable	17 vast	18 connect
19 achieve	20 detect	21 eatable
22 eventually	23 changeable	24 exploration
25 gravity	26 attach	27 contain
28 bend	29 instantly	30 layer
31 measure	32 physics	33 distance
34 celebrate	35 match up	36 lie down
37 at the speed of ~		38 float around
39 according to~	40 figure out	41 look back
42 far away from	43 at the bottom of ~	

단어 TEST Step 3   p.27

1 vast, 거대한, 광대한   2 connect, 연결되다, 이어지다

3 attach, 붙이다   4 distance, 거리   5 unstable, 불안정한

6 measure, 측정하다   7 chef, 요리사

대화문 TEST Step 1   p.28~30

Listen & Talk 1 A

1 back to, What, being / could see, sunrise, times a day / Is it possible to see, a day / possible because, moved around / amazing

2 the best food you ate / grew, ate, fresh and tasty / is it possible to grow / Since, no gravity, had to, helped the roots to grow

Listen & Talk 1 B

Have you heard that, send, into / going to send, into space / I've heard that, will be used to print out / possible to print out, using / print out, in less than / what it would taste like

Listen & Talk 2 A

1 colorful, universe / I wish I could see, from, with my own eyes / do that / that, feel like, actually in space

2 are, watching / seems, different / it's because, no gravity / I wish I could float around, astronaut / looks uncomfortable

Listen & Talk 2 B

lived in / must have been tough / while in space / possible / not sure, maybe it's because, gravity / I wish I could live in, become taller / I'm sure there, ways to become taller, going to space

Communication Step A

welcome to, to talk about, that we wish were real / start with / I wish I could have / somewhere that, entirely impossible / Is it actually possible to fly / have applied, to create

Wrap Up

1 enjoy / the best experience / what was the best part during / by myself / Is it possible to fly, by yourself / attached myself, so, safe

2 heard that, How / zero gravity, astronauts' space life / real astronauts / heard, adventure / astronaut, explore Mars

Listen & Talk 1 A

1 M: Welcome back to Earth, Irene. What was your favorite part about being in the space station?

W: I could see a beautiful sunrise 16 times a day. It was great.

M: Is it possible to see the sunrise several times a day in space?

W: Yes, it's possible because we moved around Earth every 90 minutes in the station.

M: Wow, that's amazing!

2 M: Irene, what was the best food you ate in the space station?

W: Hmm…. We grew some vegetables and ate them every day. They were pretty fresh and tasty!

M: Wow, is it possible to grow vegetables in the space station?

W: Yes. Since there's no gravity in space, we had to grow them in special bags. The bags helped the roots to grow.

M: How interesting!

Listen & Talk 1 B

M: Have you heard that NASA is going to send a 3D printer into space?

W: They're going to send a 3D printer into space? Why?

M: I've heard that the 3D printer will be used to print out food for astronauts.

W: Is it possible to print out food using a 3D printer?

M: Yes, it's possible. It can print out a fresh pizza in less than five minutes.

W: Really? I wonder what it would taste like.

Listen & Talk 2 A

1 M: Look at these colorful pictures of the universe.

W: Oh, they're beautiful. I wish I could see Earth from space with my own eyes.

M: Actually, you can do that at the National Youth Space Center.

W: Really?

M: Yeah, you can use the VR glasses. I heard that you feel like you are actually in space!

2 W: What are you watching?

M: It's a documentary about life in space. Everything seems so different.

W: Yes, it's because there's no gravity in space.

M: Right. I wish I could float around like an astronaut!

W: Really? I don't. It looks uncomfortable.

Listen & Talk 2 B

W: Look at this man, Jake. He lived in space for one year.

M: It must have been tough for him.

W: Right, but you know what's interesting? He grew 2 inches while in space.

M: Really? How is that possible?

W: I'm not sure, but maybe it's because there's no gravity in space.

M: That's so cool. I wish I could live in space. That way, I could become taller.

W: I'm sure there are other ways to become taller than going to space.

Communication Step A

W: Hello, everyone, welcome to *All about Movies*! Today, we're going to talk aboutthe top three things from movies that we wish were real.

M: Let's start with number three, the flying skateboard from *Back to the Future*.

W: It's a cool item. I wish I could have a flying skateboard.

M: Actually, I read somewhere that this is not entirely impossible.

W: Really? Is it actually possible to fly on a skateboard?

M: Yes. Some companies have applied physics to create flying skateboards.

Wrap Up

1 W: Mr. Scott, did you enjoy your trip to space?

M: Yes, it was the best experience of my life.

W: Can you tell us what was the best part during your trip?

M: I flew in space by myself and saw our blue planet, Earth.

W: Is it possible to fly inspace by yourself?

M: Yes, I attached myself to a special line, so it was safe.

W: Sounds fantastic!

2 M: Hey, Cindy. I heard that you went to the National Space Center last weekend. How was it?

W: It was great, Chris. I experienced zero gravity and astronauts' space life.

M: Sounds fun. Did you meet real astronauts in person?

W: Yes, and I heard about their adventure stories.

M: Oh, I wish I could become an astronaut like them and explore Mars.

01 fans, going, about, travel
02 As, nothing, light, universe
03 travel, able, get, blink
04 space, vast that, possible
05 headed, travels, one-half, light
06 get to another planet
07 for, expected, take, get
08 faster way, travel though
09 in order, like, think
10 something sweet, move, bottom
11 worm, surface, vast, universe
12 either, around, or down
13 think, choose, because, shortcut
14 there such a shortcut
15 figured out, connected, space-time
16 space-time, bent, far away
17 understand, top, another, bottom
18 flat sheet, far away
19 fold, matched, Punch, connected
20 contain, mouths, throat connecting
21 existed, get, places, away
22 early, celebrate, exist, theory
23 all, do, find one
24 Even, consider, actually, through
25 unstable, flew, crushed, broken
26 pretty picture, hopeless
27 traveling, simply, exists, theory
28 ongoing, persistent exploration, research
29 Look back, seemed impossible
30 Maybe, be, find, answer

01 going to talk about space travel
02 As we all know, nothing faster than light
03 travel at, be able to get to, in the blink of, right
04 is so vast that, not possible
05 headed to, travels, one-half
06 get to another planet
07 for 120 years, is expected to take, to get to
08 a faster way to travel through
09 in order to, you to think, for a second
10 on this apple, something sweet, wants to move from, to
11 as vast as
12 either move around, or down

13 Which do you think, because it is a shortcut
14 such a shortcut
15 According to, figured out, are connected, space-time
16 space-time could actually be bent, that are far away, are suddenly closer
17 To understand, take, make, at the top of, another, bottom
18 On a flat sheet, far away from
19 fold, with, matched up, Punch, the dots, be instantly connected
20 contain two mouths, throat connecting
21 Just like, existed, get to places, away
22 too early to celebrate, exist in theory
23 all, to do, find one
24 Even if, to consider, going through one
25 would be, unstable, flew into, be crushed, broken into pieces
26 a pretty picture, hopeless
27 through, simply, that, exists
28 wouldn't say, is, ongoing, with persistent exploration, research, one, learn how to travel through
29 Look back at, so many things that seemed impossible
30 knows, to find the answer

1 Sci Teen: 안녕하세요, 과학 팬 여러분. 오늘 우리는 우주여행에 대해 이야기할 것입니다.
2 우리가 모두 알다시피, 우주에서 빛보다 더 빠른 것은 없습니다.
3 그래서 만약 우리가 빛의 속도로 여행을 한다면, 우리는 다른 행성에 눈 깜박할 사이에 도달할 수 있어야 해요, 그렇죠?
4 Dr. Sci: 그렇다면 좋겠지만, 우주는 너무 광활해서 그건 불가능하답니다.
5 영화 〈Passengers〉에서 다른 행성으로 향하는 우주선이 빛의 속도의 절반으로 이동합니다.
6 그러면 그들은 다른 행성에 매우 빨리 도달해야겠지요, 그렇죠?
7 하지만 승객들은 120년 동안 잠을 자게 되는데, 왜냐하면 다른 행성에 도달하는 데 그만큼 많은 시간이 걸릴 것으로 예상되기 때문입니다.
8 Sci Teen: 120년이요? 우아, 그건 정말 긴 시간이네요! 우주를 여행하는 더 빠른 방법이 있나요?
9 Dr. Sci: 글쎄요, 그 질문에 답하기 위해서 여러분이 이 사과에 대해 잠깐 생각해 보기 바랍니다.
10 한 마리 벌레가 이 사과 위에 있다고 상상해 보세요. 그것은 맨

아래에 있는 달콤한 무언가를 감지하고 맨 위에서 아래로 이동하기를 원합니다.

11 그 벌레에게 사과의 표면은 우리의 우주만큼이나 광대합니다.

12 이제 그 벌레는 바깥 표면의 껍질을 돌아서 이동하거나 벌레 구멍 아래로 이동할 수 있습니다.

13 그것이 어떤 것을 선택할 거라고 생각하십니까? 음, 그것은 벌레 구멍을 선택할 것인데 왜냐하면 그것이 지름길이기 때문입니다.

14 Sci Teen: 우주에 그런 지름길이 있나요?

15 Dr. Sci: 몇몇 연구자들에 따르면, 그렇습니다. 아인슈타인은 공간과 시간이 연결되어 있다는 것을 생각해 냈고, 그것을 시공간이라고 불렀습니다.

16 '그는 시공간이 실제로 구부러질 수 있다고 생각했습니다. 그것이 구부러질 때 서로 멀리 떨어져 있는 부분들이 갑자기 더 가까워질 수 있습니다.

17 이것을 이해하기 위해서, 종이를 한 장 갖고 와서 그 종이의 윗부분에 작은 점을 찍고 또 다른 점을 그 종이의 아랫부분에 찍어 보세요.

18 펼쳐 놓은 종이에서 그 점들은 서로 멀리 떨어져 있습니다.

19 이제 그 종이를 들고 점들이 맞춰지도록 그것을 접으세요. 종이에 구멍을 뚫으면 그 점들이 즉시 연결될 것입니다.

20 이와 마찬가지로 우주의 웜홀은 두 개의 입과 그 둘을 연결하는 목구멍을 지니고 있을 겁니다.

21 Sci Teen: 사과에 있는 벌레 구멍처럼요, 그렇죠? 그런 웜홀이 우주에 존재한다면 우리는 수십억 광년 떨어져 있는 곳에 빠르게 도달할 수 있을 텐데요!

22 Dr. Sci: 그렇죠, 하지만 축하하기에는 너무 이릅니다. 웜홀은 이론상에서만 존재합니다.

23 Sci Teen: 그러면 우리가 해야 할 것이라고는 그것을 찾는 거네요, 그렇죠?

24 Dr. Sci: 우리가 그것을 찾는다고 하더라도 실제로 그걸 통과하여 가기 전에 고려해야 할 것들이 많이 있습니다.

25 웜홀은 매우 불안정할 것입니다. 만약 우주선이 그 안으로 날아가게 되면, 그것은 부서지거나 산산조각이 날 수도 있습니다.

26 Sci Teen: 어이쿠! 그건 좋은 광경이 아니네요. 그럼 우리는 가망이 없는 건가요?

27 우주에서 웜홀을 통하여 여행을 하는 것은 단지 이론상으로만 존재하는 아이디어인가요?

28 Dr. Sci: 그렇게 말하지는 않겠어요. 웜홀에 대한 논쟁은 여전히 진행 중이긴 하지만, 끊임없는 탐구와 연구로 우리가 결국 하나를 찾아 그것을 통해 여행하는 법을 배울 수 있을 거라고 믿습니다.

29 우리의 역사를 돌아보세요. 우리는 처음에는 불가능해 보였던 아주 많은 것들을 달성해 왔습니다.

30 누가 알겠어요? 아마도 여러분이 그 답을 찾아내는 그 사람이 될 수 있을지도요!

1 Sci Teen: Hi, science fans. Today, we're going to talk about space travel.

2 As we all know, there is nothing faster than light in the universe.

3 So, if we travel at the speed of light, we should be able to get to another planet in the blink of an eye, right?

4 Dr. Sci: That would be nice, but space is so vast that it is not possible.

5 In the movie, *Passengers*, a spaceship headed to a different planet travels at one-half the speed of light.

6 So it should get to another planet very quickly, right?

7 But, the passengers sleep for 120 years because it is expected to take that much time to get to a different planet.

8 Sci Teen: 120 years? Wow, that's a long time! Is there a faster way to travel through space?

9 Dr. Sci: Well, in order to answer that question, I'd like you to think about this apple for a second.

10 Imagine a worm is on this apple. It detects something sweet at the bottom and wants to move from the top to the bottom.

11 For the worm, the apple's surface is as vast as our universe.

12 Now the worm can either move around the outer layer or down a wormhole.

13 Which do you think it will choose? Well, it would choose the wormhole because it is a shortcut.

14 Sci Teen: Is there such a shortcut in the universe?

15 Dr. Sci: According to some researchers, yes. Einstein figured out that space and time are connected, and he called it space-time.

16 He thought that space-time could actually be bent. When it is bent, parts that are far away from each other are suddenly closer.

17 To understand this, take a sheet of paper and make a small dot at the top of the paper and another at the bottom of the paper.

18 On a flat sheet of paper, the dots are far away from one another.

19 Now, take the paper and fold it with the dots matched up. Punch a hole in the paper and the dots will be instantly connected.

20 Like this, wormholes in space may contain two mouths, with a throat connecting the two.

21 Sci Teen: Just like a wormhole in the apple, right? If such wormholes existed in space, we could get to places billions of light-years away quickly!

22 Dr. Sci: Yes, but it's too early to celebrate. Wormholes exist in theory only.

23 Sci Teen: So all we need to do is find one , right?

24 Dr. Sci: Even if we find one, there are many things to consider before actually going through one.

25 A wormhole would be very unstable . If a spaceship flew into one, it might be crushed or broken into pieces.

26 Sci Teen: Ouch! That's not a pretty picture. So, are we hopeless?

27 Is traveling in space through a wormhole simply an idea that only exists in theory?

28 Dr. Sci: I wouldn't say so. The debate about wormholes is still ongoing, but with persistent exploration and research, I believe we will eventually find one and learn how to travel through it.

29 Look back at our history. We've achieved so many things that seemed impossible at first.

30 Who knows? Maybe you can be the one to find the answer!

구석구석지문 TEST Step 1 p.44

After You Read A

1. A faster way to travel
2. Idea from
3. for a worm to move, the top, the bottom
4. in space
5. space, time are connected, space-time can be bent
6. parts far away from, become closer
7. really exist
8. In theory, exist
9. would be unstable, be crushed, broken into pieces
10. Still, with persistent exploration, research

Language in Use

1. finite or infinite
2. Luckily, is in a stable condition

Think & Write C

1. for us to live on, would like to make, called
2. beautiful green planet
3. bigger than the moon, smaller than
4. The temperature, would be about
5. have beautiful nature

6. Interestingly, moved to, communicate with, on this planet

구석구석지문 TEST Step 2 p.45

After You Read A

1. A faster way to travel through space
2. ① Idea from an apple
3. A wormhole is a shortcut for a worm to move from the top to the bottom.
4. ② Wormholes in space
5. Einstein thought space and time are connected and space-time can be bent.
6. When it is bent, parts far away from each other can become closer.
7. Do wormholes really exist?
8. ③ In theory, wormholes exist.
9. Wormholes would be unstable. A spaceship could be crushed or broken into pieces.
10. Still I believe with persistent exploration and research we will find a wormhole!

Language in Use

1. Is the universe finite or infinite?
2. Luckily, the driver is is in a stable condition after the accident.

Think & Write C

1. If I could make a planet for us to live on in the future, I would like to make a planet called Atlas.
2. It would be a beautiful green planet.
3. Its size would be bigger than the moon, but smaller than Earth.
4. The temperature of it would be about 30.
5. It would have beautiful nature.
6. Interestingly, if people moved to it, they could communicate with animals on this planet.

MEMO

적중100
영어 기출 문제집
정답 및 해설

비상 | 김진완